Happiness and the Christian Moral Life

Happiness and the Christian Moral Life

An Introduction to Christian Ethics

Paul J. Wadell

A SHEED & WARD BOOK

ROWMAN & LITTLEFIELD PUBLISHERS, INC.
Lanham • Boulder • New York • Toronto • Plymouth, UK

A SHEED & WARD BOOK

ROWMAN & LITTLEFIELD PUBLISHERS, INC.

Published in the United States of America
by Rowman & Littlefield Publishers, Inc.
A wholly owned subsidiary of The Rowman & Littlefield Publishing Group, Inc.
4501 Forbes Boulevard, Suite 200, Lanham, Maryland 20706
www.rowmanlittlefield.com

Estover Road
Plymouth PL6 7PY
United Kingdom

British Library Cataloguing in Publication Information Available

Library of Congress Cataloging-in-Publication Data

Wadell, Paul J.
An introduction to Christian ethics : happiness and the Christian moral life / Paul J. Wadell.
p. cm.
"A Sheed & Ward book."
Includes bibliographical references and index.
ISBN-13: 978-0-7425-5178-7 (cloth : alk. paper)
ISBN-10: 0-7425-5178-4 (cloth : alk. paper)
ISBN-13: 978-0-7425-5179-4 (pbk. : alk. paper)
ISBN-10: 0-7425-5179-2 (pbk. : alk. paper)
1. Christian ethics. 2. Christian life. 3. Happiness—Religious aspects—Christianity. I. Title.
BJ1251.W2155 2008
241—dc22 2007007161

Printed in the United States of America

♾™ The paper used in this publication meets the minimum requirements of American National Standard for Information Sciences—Permanence of Paper for Printed Library Materials, ANSI/NISO Z39.48-1992.

To

My Brothers- and Sisters-in-Law

John Tierney, Neal Augustus, Carl Duncan II, Jill Wadell

Patrick Docter, Steve Collard, Kristan Wadell, Gabrielle Wadell

~

Contents

Preface and Acknowledgments

Some ideas never quite leave us. Like old friends, they hang around for a long time, sometimes unnoticed, but exerting their influence all the same. This book grew out of an idea that never quite left me. Many years ago—longer than I care to remember—I was asked to consider graduate studies in Christian ethics. The prospect did not appeal to me because my one exposure to the academic study of ethics had been fairly miserable. In my junior year at college, I enrolled in a course on philosophical ethics. My interest decreased with each passing class. It was as if we were tourists on a cross-country trip to survey the landscape of philosophical ethics. On our way we visited shrines dedicated to deontology, teleology, utilitarianism, consequentialism, the natural law, and virtue theory, examining them all as interesting specimens of philosophical reflection, but not encouraged to settle down with any of them. We were tourists, casual observers, who would jot down a few notes, make a few comments, and then move on. The longer the trip continued (and a fifteen-week semester is a long time when you're bored), the more disengaged I became. My disillusionment had nothing to do with the expertise of our guide. The professor knew all the important details about each of the sites we visited along the way, but he gave us no reason to care about any of them, and certainly no reason to plan a return trip. The lessons learned from traveling can be sobering. Just as there are some countries we vow never to visit again, I knew one trip deep into the country of philosophical ethics was enough for me.

After such an unpromising beginning, why did I accept the invitation to pursue graduate study in Christian ethics? Because not too many years after my initial exposure to the field of ethics, I did a little exploring on my own. I read Aristotle's *Nicomachean Ethics* and the section of Thomas Aquinas's *Summa Theologiae* that focuses on morality, and I discovered that for both of them the moral life revolves around the question of happiness. In a way, it was so simple. Aristotle and Aquinas shape their accounts of the moral life on the claim that everyone wants to be happy. It is our most fundamental, indelible desire. The trajectory of our lives can be read as an endless pursuit for whatever we think will satisfy us, content us, and fulfill us. The choices and decisions we make, the careers we pursue, the relationships we develop, and the ambitions we espouse all reveal what we believe will bring us happiness and satisfaction. The trouble, however, is that we are often confused, and easily misled, about what will really fulfill us. Why is it that so many of the things we pursue leave us unsettled, disappointed, and even angry? Why, after investing so much of our time, energy, and attention in chasing after certain goods, do we feel that whatever we gained certainly didn't match our investment? Each day we encounter messages about happiness, suggestions about what to want and what to pursue in order to be fulfilled. How do we distinguish the wise suggestions from the foolish ones? How do we tell the difference between ways of life that will bring us excellence as human beings, and ways of life that are little more than moral and spiritual dead ends?

Aristotle and Aquinas hooked me because as soon as they talked about happiness they had my attention. How could anyone not be interested when somebody promises to teach you what happiness is about? But they also challenged me, because they argued that happiness might not be what I think it is. For both, happiness does not reside in having my wants and desires satisfied, unless I have learned to want and desire what is best. For both, happiness cannot be reduced to pleasure, unless I have learned to take pleasure in whatever constitutes the unique excellence of human beings. Aristotle and Aquinas taught that happiness is found in goodness, in what Aristotle called the life of virtue and Aquinas called a life of love and friendship with God. For Aristotle, the virtuous life constitutes happiness because it is through the virtues that men and women become good. For Aquinas, a Christian, happiness is found in friendship with God—and with all God loves—because it is in being conformed to the supreme goodness of God that we achieve our distinctive fulfillment as human beings. If Aristotle and Aquinas are right, happiness may indeed be a natural desire, but it is hardly a natural achievement. We have to learn what it means to be happy by being initiated into ways of life that form us into people who are good. Happiness is something we enter into as we are educated in the attitudes, habits, and practices constitutive of happiness and embody them over time. Aristotle's and Aquinas's accounts of the moral life are glaringly contrary to what we customarily think about happiness, first because we believe we naturally know what happiness involves, and second because we assume happiness is easily achieved and hardly something that would require deep changes in ourselves.

Like old friends who hang around for a long time, what Aristotle and Aquinas proposed about the moral life stayed with me because my belief that they are right never diminished. The heart of Christian ethics is not about laws and rules and principles and obligations, but about being initiated into a way of life capable of making one good and, therefore, happy. Laws, rules, principles, and obligations are important, and surely an essential part of the study of ethics. But they should never overshadow or displace what ought to be the principal concern of ethics: how to grow in a way of life designed to help us reach our grandest possibilities in goodness. Similarly, the chief business of ethics is not to help us make our way through a thicket of controversial moral issues, but to form us into people who love the good and who seek to extend it in everything they do. Again, this does not mean that addressing difficult moral questions or dilemmas is not an important aspect of Christian ethics, but it ought not to be its fundamental focus. After all, we will hardly know how to think rightly about any moral question unless we have first striven to become good people whose character and integrity enables them to think and to choose wisely.

If a book is more or less a matter of taking an idea and running with it, this book is an attempt to take the idea that Christian morality is most promisingly described as "training in happiness," and reenvisioning the basic elements of morality in light of that conviction. Moreover, it is intentionally a work of Christian theology. What I attempt here is a theological argument about the Christian moral life, an argument that builds on the claim that God wants our happiness and has shown us the way of happiness in Christ. The gospels may unmask many of our common assumptions about happiness—they may even unnerve us—but their core message is that in Jesus we encounter the answer to our hearts' deepest desires. In this respect, to be a Christian is to be initiated into a community's way of life, the whole purpose of which is to form us into people who can share in the joy of God by having been formed in the goodness of God.

Chapter 1 lays out the principal argument of the book. By focusing on Augustine's troubled search for happiness—a story he recounts in *The Confessions*—and on Aquinas's analysis of the nature of authentic happiness, I will suggest that happiness is best understood not as our own achievement, but as a gift. If the Christian moral life is training in happiness, it begins with God befriending us in grace, Christ, and the Spirit, and working with us to achieve our good. This gives a different slant to the Christian moral life because it suggests that the happiness we seek we already have. We do not create this happiness; rather, we receive it, are entrusted with it, and are called to grow more deeply into it. We learn what this might mean by following Christ, our teacher or "mentor" in the way of happiness, and by taking to heart Jesus' own counsel about happiness that he outlined in the Beatitudes and throughout the gospels.

One of the key arguments of the book is that happiness is a shared activity; it is something we do together. Thus, chapter 2 examines the role of friendships and communities in our pursuit of happiness. It looks first at Aristotle's classic account of the role of friendship in the life of virtue, but then focuses on Aquinas's claim that the greatest happiness for human beings is found in a life of friendship with God. Aquinas calls this the life of charity. What does such a life look like? What would it involve? And why might we resist it? As we shall see, there is nothing more challenging—and nothing riskier—than to live in friendship with God because it commits us to always expanding the circle of love, even to the point of loving our enemies.

If the moral life is a quest for happiness, we need to be equipped with certain skills and dispositions if we are not to be defeated along the way. That is what the virtues give us, and they are the focus of chapter 3. Any worthwhile quest is replete with challenges, obstacles, momentary setbacks, and periods of discouragement. This is especially true if the goal of the quest is happiness in fellowship with God. What do we need if we are not to fall short of the goodness and happiness to which we are called? What must we do if we are not to "lower our sights" and settle for something whose goodness could never content us? Thus, chapter 3 will examine what the virtues are and why we need them. But it will also look at particular virtues we must develop if we are to enjoy the happiness for which we are made.

We will never be happy unless we rightly understand who we are. Who, exactly, are we? It's a deceptively simple question and one Christian ethics must ask, for how we answer it makes all the difference not only for how we understand ourselves, but also for how we see others. What makes us persons? Is it our freedom? Is it our ability to reason? Is it our conscience and moral awareness? These questions are taken up in chapter 4 as we examine a Christian understanding of the person. In particular, the chapter will explore three fundamental claims Christian theology makes about human beings: We are creatures, we are made in the image and likeness of God, and we are called to do the work of God. The chapter concludes with some reflections on how these claims might shape how we approach, and understand, issues of medical ethics and bioethics.

Every study of ethics wrestles with the question of freedom; after all, without freedom we cannot be moral. But freedom, the subject of chapter 5, is a dangerous topic because if we misunderstand freedom we can do great harm. Mistakes about freedom cause all sorts of woe for ourselves and for others. Freedom is certainly at the heart of the Christian life, but what does it mean? How should Christians think about freedom? Are we naturally free or is freedom like a virtue, something we have to develop? These are some of the questions chapter 5 will investigate.

Mistakes about freedom often result in the wrongheaded behavior Christians call sin, the topic of chapter 6. Sin never makes sense, but that doesn't discourage us from embracing it. Sin is rooted in misunderstandings about where happiness will be found. This is what makes sin essentially self-destructive, and why its harvest is never peace or contentment, but sadness. And so chapter 6 begins with an analysis of sin, focusing on sin as a rejection of our true identity, and as a way of life that distances us from happiness. That is followed by an examination of the Christian teaching of original sin, what it reveals about ourselves and our world, and why it makes the Christian life a "rescue" operation. The chapter concludes with the suggestion that we will never understand happiness unless we claim our identity as "recovering" sinners.

Chapter 7 explores the importance of narrative, or story, for the Christian moral life. This is not only because every human life takes the form of a story, but also, and more importantly, because our happiness hinges on finding a story truly worthy of our lives. Christians believe they have found such a story in Jesus. If we take that story to heart, where will it take us? What will it make of us? Is it a story worth remembering and handing on? After some consideration of why the language of narrative has emerged as a fitting way to speak about the Christian moral life, the chapter concludes by reflecting on what it might practically mean to "put on" the story that comes to us in Jesus. If we make Jesus' story the one that illumines and guides our own, perhaps people will be able to say of us, "That person really lived!"

The final three chapters examine the topics of conscience, love, and justice. Chapter 8 looks at conscience and prudence, its primary virtue. If we need to be of "good conscience" in order to love and be committed to the good, we need prudence to help us express that commitment in actions that are right and good. Thus, chapter 8 explores the meaning and purpose of conscience, what it means to be responsible for one's conscience, and the various components of prudence, the virtue that enables us to do what is right and good with wisdom and insight. Chapter 9 looks at love, the central virtue of the Christian life and the quintessential attribute of God. If God is love, and we are happy insofar as we grow in likeness to God, then our happiness pivots on learning to love as God loves. Why is it that we are fulfilled in giving and receiving love? What exactly does it mean to love? And if Jesus calls us to love God, ourselves, and all of our neighbors, how do we best do that over the course of a lifetime? The book concludes with a study of the virtue of justice. Justice is indispensable to any account of the Christian moral life centered on happiness because if we are "all in this together," I can hardly secure my happiness and well-being by excluding or diminishing somebody else. For Christians, any one person's happiness is inherently connected to every other person's happiness. This is why happiness is impossible apart from justice, the virtue that teaches us how to live in right relationship not only with other human beings, but indeed with the whole of creation.

Every book reflects a legacy of indebtedness. Much in the following pages was inspired by the monumental achievements of Aristotle, Aquinas, and Augustine. But I am also keenly indebted to the work of more recent thinkers, particularly Josef Pieper, Alasdair MacIntyre, Iris Murdoch, Bernard Häring, Enda McDonagh, Stanley Hauerwas, Charles Pinches, Servais Pinckaers, Jean Porter, Herbert McCabe, Gilbert Meilaender, and Livio Melina. Each of them has been an indispensable conversation partner both prior to undertaking this project and while working my way through it. In addition to being trustworthy mentors from whom I have learned much, I am grateful to call Stanley Hauerwas and Charles Pinches friends. Their goodness, their joyfulness of spirit, and the abiding witness of their lives have inspired and enriched me. I also want to thank Ross Miller of Rowman & Littlefield. His questions helped me clarify what this book was really attempting to achieve, and his guidance and patience were a tremendous support to me. I am also grateful to Jeremy Langford. His enthusiasm and support convinced me that this was a worthy project. Thanks must also be given to the readers who took time to carefully review the book before its publication. Their comments, insights, and suggestions were immensely helpful.

I could not have undertaken this project without a sabbatical granted by St. Norbert College. I am grateful for the semester free of teaching duties, committee meetings, and other responsibilities, which gave me time to begin researching and writing this book. I also want to thank my colleagues in religious studies for their ongoing collegial support and for generously rearranging their teaching schedules so that I could enjoy the freedom of a sabbatical. I am especially grateful to Bridget Burke Ravizza, my colleague in Christian ethics. Being able to teach with her and learn from her has been a special blessing. And special thanks are owed to Howard Ebert, a colleague in religious studies, and to Darin Davis. While I was writing this book Howard was associate dean of Humanities and Fine Arts at St. Norbert College and Darin was a professor in philosophy. Both are wonderful friends and valued conversation partners to whom I am immeasurably indebted. Being able to talk, pray, and laugh with them while working on this book "lightened the load" considerably.

Lastly, I want to thank my mother and father, and my wife, Carmella. Whenever I would call my parents in Louisville they would unfailingly ask, "How's the book going?" I wasn't always sure how to answer that; but the one thing I did know for sure is that nobody has witnessed more profoundly and beautifully and faithfully for me what happiness and a good life truly are about. And Carmella? It is no surprise that writing about happiness offered me plenty of occasions to think about her. Though she never mentioned it, I know at least a little of Carmella's happiness was sacrificed (and much of her patience tested!) as I navigated the ups and downs of writing a book. That she adjusted so much of her life in order to make this possible for me taught me much about the happiness that can be found in faithful love.

CHAPTER ONE

~

Finding a Path for Life

The Quest for Goodness and Happiness

We are made for happiness, fashioned for bliss.

This is an odd way to begin a book on the moral life, because we do not customarily associate the study of morality with learning about happiness. If a friend told you she was about to begin a course in ethics, you would not be likely to respond, "Good! After so many years of searching, you'll finally discover where real happiness can be found!" Wouldn't we more likely assume that in the weeks ahead our friend would be introduced to the world of moral principles, rules, and laws; to the language of rights and obligations; and to an array of ethical traditions and theories? Wouldn't we conclude that such a class would teach our friend what to do when confronted with difficult matters of conscience or how to make a decision when no trouble-free choice seems possible? Or wouldn't a good course in ethics—a really practical course—address some of the confounding ethical dilemmas of our day so that by the end of the semester our friend could tell us how best to think about abortion, gay marriage, euthanasia, cloning, war, or capital punishment? Besides, given the ever-expanding list of seemingly insurmountable problems facing the world, doesn't focusing on happiness trivialize the real work of ethics? And wouldn't it encourage precisely the self-centeredness and indifference that enflame so much of the suffering and misery that diminish life throughout the world?

Not necessarily. It all depends on what we take happiness to be, and a book on the Christian moral life might answer this in surprising ways. After all, Christians believe that the martyrs, despite the gruesome terrors they suffered, were happy, because no tribulation could separate them from the God in whom they found joy. Even the threat of death did not rob them of happiness. On the contrary, confident that they had found the most exquisite happiness in loving God, they were empowered to face death with resilient hope, and even joy, rather than be conquered by sadness and despair. Generations of Christians have been schooled in stories of the saints precisely because they believe the lives of the saints display a wisdom about happiness, but one that often challenges what we ordinarily take happiness to be.[1]

Investigating the nature of authentic happiness is a fitting subject for ethics because happiness is the one thing everyone seeks. Everyone wants to be happy. Nobody wants to be unhappy, unless in some twisted way they have made misery their joy. Human beings are naturally seekers of happiness; it is our most powerful innate desire. A hunger for happiness propels everything we do. It explains the relationships we seek, the jobs we desire, the hobbies we pursue, the clothes we wear, and even the food we eat. We don't need a Declaration of Independence to tell us to pursue happiness. We do it naturally, albeit sometimes misguidedly. The story of our lives can be read as one unfolding search for happiness because we relentlessly pursue whatever we think will be good for us, whatever we suspect will fulfill us, delight us, bring us peace, and deepen the meaning of our lives. It is the intention behind every intention, the key to unlocking all motivation. When we look back over our lives, even the mistakes we made and the wrong choices we embraced often came from misunderstanding where true happiness would be found. The greedy person covets money because he believes wealth is the answer to happiness. The unfaithful lover betrays because she thinks the excitement of a new affair will be delightful. The ambitious professor manipulates because he believes contentment lies in promoting self-interest over the well-being of his colleagues. Much of the harm we bring to others, as well as ourselves, stems from costly fantasies about what constitutes real joy. But happiness is the pursuit of a lifetime. No matter how much sadness we reap by not knowing where real happiness can be found, we never relinquish the search, because finding joy abides as the most passionate desire of our hearts.

Years ago the French philosopher Etienne Gilson said that the purpose of Christian morality was to teach men and women how they must live if the story of their lives was to have a happy ending. How must we shape our lives, what must we learn to desire and to seek, Gilson asked, if we are to bring our humanity "to the very peak of achievement"?[2] What must we learn to love and to cherish if we are to reach the greatest excellence possible to us as human beings? Or, more briefly if not more simply, what would it mean to live a good life? What kind of life is truly worth living? Learning principles and rules, being conversant with a variety of traditions and theories, and being skilled in addressing controversial moral issues are all crucial elements of moral education. But they are not the heart and center of any exploration of the moral life, because they present a much too narrow and constricted view of the moral adventure. We need to go deeper. The scope of morality is much grander and more dramatic because its essential business is not the solving of problems but the transformation of persons in whatever goods will truly fulfill them. Helping us discover, and then achieve, the most promising possibilities for human beings is the primary business of ethics, because ultimately nothing less will content us. How must we plan our lives so they can be lived as well as possible?[3] This is the question that drives the study of ethics and makes it both challenging and practical. The philosopher and theologian Herbert McCabe put it well when he suggested that one studies ethics in order to learn "how to be good at being human."[4] And, as McCabe insisted, the business of ethics is not simply to teach people how "to *talk* about being good," but more importantly "to *make* people good as well."[5]

As any good novel shows, human life takes the form of a quest. Dealing with nettlesome moral dilemmas or debating complex moral questions may be episodes in this journey, and may even make the journey interesting; but they are not the heart of the adventure. What drives us on the quest is not a desire to master a theory, know a principle, or resolve a dilemma, but to discover the good for which we are made, the good or goods that can satisfy us, complete us, and still the turbulence of our restless hearts. There are days when we must wrestle with tough moral choices or suffer through anguished matters of conscience. But to reduce morality to these occasions, however momentous, does not do justice to the overall drama of our lives. What do we do on those multiple other days when there are no momentous decisions to be made and no dilemmas to resolve? We do what we always do: We search for a happiness that lasts, a happiness that endures despite adversity and hardship. We admire, are attracted to, and sometimes even envy people who are genuinely happy. We want to know what they know, we want to discover their secret. What brought them to happiness? What did they do to find joy? Did it come quickly or was it the work of a lifetime? We ask these questions because every human being shares one resounding ambition: we want a joy that abides.

Morality comes to life with the question of happiness because the real business of ethics is helping us discover in what happiness consists.[6] If the story of every human life can be read as a never-ending quest for happiness, a good morality guides us on that journey. It helps us understand how we must live and what we must learn to love if we are to find peace and satisfaction in our lives. If everything we do begins in an intention for happiness, then the critical first step in moral education is coming to understand what constitutes happiness for human beings. Indeed, the study of morality can best be understood as training in happiness, as an ongoing initiation into the desires, attitudes, habits, and practices that make for a happy and good life. For those accustomed to parsing morality through the grammar of laws, obligations, principles, and rules, this may seem mistaken. But there is a venerable tradition in Christian ethics that sees the heart of morality to be discovering, and entering into, a way of life that answers the deep human desire for happiness and goodness. We may have lost a rich sense of the good life, but a fundamental purpose of Christian ethics is to help us understand what such a life might be.

This was the approach of Augustine and Thomas Aquinas, two of the most influential theologians in the history of Christianity, and their account of happiness will be our focus in this opening chapter. They understood the substance of Christian morality not principally through the language of law and obligation, but as the ongoing quest to discover, share in, and ultimately be perfected by whatever brings the most perfect and enduring happiness to our lives. They found this in God because they believed only in God is there the truth, the beauty, and the goodness in which women and men are ultimately fulfilled. We will be happy, they argued, in the measure that we grow in, and are transformed by, the goodness of God. It may take us a lifetime to discover this, and that life might be speckled with countless costly detours and endless wrong turns, but ultimately it is this quest that alone is worthy of us and that alone can answer our most pressing need.

Augustine and Aquinas are worthy guides as we begin our exploration of the Christian moral life. But they may challenge our customary understandings of happiness. First, both Augustine and Aquinas maintain that happiness is inextricably connected to goodness and inseparable from goodness. Happiness and goodness are one; therefore, in order to be happy we must become good.[7] In this life we may never be perfectly happy, but we will advance in happiness to the degree that we advance in goodness. But not just any goodness. Christians believe happiness comes as we grow in the goodness of God. In more theological language, holiness brings happiness. This is a hard truth for us to swallow because we are more likely to connect holiness with squelching happiness than fulfilling it. Even more, we link happiness with the satisfaction of desires, not necessarily with goodness, including the goodness of God.

Second, through Augustine and Aquinas we will learn that we misunderstand happiness if we think of it primarily in terms of positive and uplifting feelings. Such feelings would be better described as pleasure than happiness. Pleasure and happiness may be connected, but they are not the same. Pleasures come and go in ways that happiness should not. Happiness is something deeper, something much more lasting and stable than pleasure, because happiness comes from excellence in goodness.[8] Happiness has to be something more substantial than the pleasure that comes on those wonderful days where everything seems to go well. What really matters is knowing how to sustain happiness on those unfortunate days when nothing goes well or during those painful periods of life when we experience more defeats than successes, more adversity than good. Can we be happy amid trials and tribulations? Does suffering necessarily extinguish happiness? Augustine and Aquinas believed that happiness is not so much an emotional state, but a discernible and distinctive way of life that brought joy because it made one good. Goodness is the cause of joy, and the greatest possible joy is found in possessing the greatest possible good. Thus, Christian morality is not a set of theories and ideas, but an initiation into a way of life that itself constitutes happiness because it unites us to the most perfect and perfecting good.

In this chapter we'll explore what Augustine and Aquinas took that way of life to be. Along the way we'll explore what happiness is and what makes it possible, but also why we sometimes fear it and flee from it. We'll consider how easy it is to be confused about happiness, and thus why we need a mentor or guide as we make our way in search of something to complete us and bring us joy.

Augustine

One of the most important, complex, and, admittedly, controversial figures in the history of western Christianity is Augustine (354–430). A man of tremendous intellect and talent, Augustine was an amazingly prolific writer whose theological works became the cornerstone of much of subsequent western Christian theology. Augustine's writings address virtually every dimension of Christian theology, but he is perhaps best known for *The Confessions*, a spiritual autobiography that recounts the first thirty-three years of Augustine's life prior to his conversion to Christianity. One reason Augustine wrote *The Confessions* is that he believed the story of his life, for all its drama and uniqueness, was everyone's story. Like Augustine, each of our lives can be read as an ongoing search to discover in what human happiness and peace consists. But also, like Augustine, we lose our way on that journey because despite our deep desire for love and peace and contentment, we stubbornly cling to things that can never bring us real joy. This is why in the narrative that is our life there may be more chapters of disillusionment and disappointment than fulfillment and delight.

Seekers Who Go Astray

No wonder the biblical figure with whom Augustine most compares himself in *The Confessions* is the prodigal son, the infamous figure whose story is told in the fifteenth chapter of the Gospel of Luke. Convinced that he knows best where the path to happiness lies, the son asks his father for his share of the inheritance, breaks free of family and home, and sets forth on his quest. With wealth and freedom as provisions for the journey, the son has no reason not to expect happiness and good fortune to be his; after all, he sets out on his quest beholden to no one, responsible for nothing, and free of all restraints. With an open road and seemingly limitless horizons of opportunity before him, why wouldn't he succeed? But the choices he makes lead not to bliss and fulfillment but to destitution and disillusionment. As Jesus tells the story, the prodigal son's attempt to find happiness bottoms out in desperation and despair because the path he felt surely would fulfill him led not to pleasure and success, but to barely surviving as a servant whose job is to watch over pigs (Luke 15:15).

Augustine sees himself, and all of us, in that story. He opens *The Confessions* with his famous prayer to God, a prayer written to tell us something important about ourselves: "Great are you, O Lord, and exceedingly worthy of praise. . . . And so we humans, who are a due part of your creation, long to praise you. . . . You arouse us so that praising you may bring us joy, because you have made us and drawn us to yourself, and our heart is unquiet until it rests in you."[9] Men and women, Augustine suggests, are made for God and will find happiness and peace only in God. Fashioned from God and for God, we are fulfilled in loving, praising, and worshiping God. God is our joy, God is our delight.

But, as Augustine's story poignantly reveals, we refuse to accept this truth. We reject the identity given to us by God and choose to find happiness on our own. The first thirty-three years of Augustine's life read as one long, and increasingly frustrating attempt, to find happiness apart from God. Augustine seeks happiness through sexual pleasure, through a series of love affairs, through fame and reputation as a teacher, through the wisdom of philosophy, through social status, and even by consulting astrologers about his horoscope. Early in *The Confessions*, Augustine says that as a young man what he wanted more than anything was "loving and being loved,"[10] but he had no idea what real love involved. He describes himself as "casting about for something to love,"[11] for something to which he could devote his life, but with every attempt ends up frustrated and confused. The longer he pursues happiness, the more miserable he becomes. Late in his adolescence, Augustine describes himself as an "unhappy beast,"[12] as "floundering in the mud,"[13] and despite the apparent freedom and pleasure of his life, as little more than "a runaway slave."[14]

One of the key scenes in *The Confessions*, and a pivotal moment in Augustine's quest for happiness, involves Augustine's unexpected encounter with a drunken beggar. Now thirty-one years old, Augustine has already distinguished himself both as a teacher and an accomplished speaker. According to the expectations of his society, Augustine ought to be happy because he has attained all the things that are said to count for happiness: material well-being, social status and reputation, connections to people of influence. On this day, Augustine and some of his friends are walking through the streets of Milan. The emperor has died and Augustine, in recognition of his skills as a speaker, has been invited to offer a eulogy in his honor. It is clear from what he writes that Augustine didn't think much of the emperor, but he knows giving the eulogy will embellish his reputation and advance him in the eyes of people who matter. An ambitious man, Augustine admits he was willing to lie about the virtues of the emperor if in doing so he can win favor with others. It does not matter that he really does not believe what he is about to say as long as the speech profits him. "I was preparing to deliver a eulogy upon the emperor in which I would tell plenty of lies," Augustine writes, "with the object of winning favor with the well-informed by my lying."[15]

But on his way to give the eulogy, Augustine and his friends stumble across a drunken beggar and make an unsettling discovery. What confounds Augustine is that this disheveled mess of a man who has failed all of society's criteria for success, with only a few coins and a bottle of wine is much happier and content than Augustine and his sophisticated friends. They had worked so hard and devoted so many years to securing success and reputation—indeed, they had plotted their entire lives to achieve them—but remained dissatisfied and discontent. By contrast, before them sits this beggar who may have been overlooked, scorned, and dismissed by society, but who nonetheless seems far more carefree than Augustine. Augustine may not want to change places with the beggar, but admits that the man had achieved a happiness and freedom that continue to elude him. It is a moment of unnerving recognition.

Despite so many years of experimenting with different possibilities for happiness, Augustine, with all his education and opportunity, remains burdened with anxieties and fears. His friends and he had devoted all of their talents and all of their time toward achieving happiness, but "it appeared that this beggar had already beaten us to the goal."[16] Moreover, even if the beggar's happiness was incomplete, he was at least doing some good in achieving it. As he begged for coins and drank his wine, he would "wish good-day to passers-by, while I was seeking a swollen reputation by lying."[17] The experience makes Augustine think about what he takes happiness to be. Are his ambitions worthy? Are the dreams he has been chasing truly promising? If he finally achieves everything he has been seeking, will he really be happy? And perhaps most unsettling, what has this beggar learned about happiness that Augustine still has not?

The Confessions resounds with the cry of the restless heart. Throughout his first thirty-three years, Augustine lives to find the answer to two questions: What will make me happy? What will bring me peace? His discontent grows not only because he makes wrong choices about happiness, but also, more strikingly, because he fears where his search may ultimately lead and what his discovery might ask of him. The older he grows, the more Augustine knows he is not happy. Still, the closer he comes to knowing real happiness the more he resists it. Augustine fears what he most claims to desire. He is *afraid of happiness* and therefore resists discovering it. He fears happiness because he knows embracing it will force him to change. He may be miserable, but his misery asks nothing of him. Happiness, however, will ask much of Augustine. It will ask him to change his heart and refashion his attachments. It will demand that he love new things, or at least love old things in new ways. Augustine senses it will be safer to stay with misery and discontent than risk happiness because happiness will require that he reorder his life.

And so every time Augustine comes near happiness, he retreats. Like a boy attempting his first dive off the high board, Augustine inches up to happiness then backs away. He wants the new life happiness will bring, but is afraid to relinquish his old life. He wants to be freed from his misery, but fears letting go of the very things that drag him down. He compares himself to the person who has been asleep for a long, long time and knows that "the hour for rising has come," but begs for a few more minutes of sleep: "'Just a minute,' 'One more minute,' 'Let me have a little longer.'"[18] The prospect of happiness makes Augustine anxious because he knows it will demand surrendering to a way of life that will ultimately re-create him. A man with a divided heart, both wanting and not wanting peace, paralyzed by indecision and enslaved by fear, Augustine describes himself as "turning and twisting in my chain."[19]

The climactic scene of *The Confessions* occurs in a garden. Exhausted by the tug-of-war taking place in his soul, Augustine sits alone in a garden and begins to weep. He speaks of the tears flowing from his eyes "like rivers"[20] and writes as if he is at the point of an emotional and psychological breakdown. He knows his life cannot continue as it is, but feels absolutely powerless to change it. Near despair, Augustine realizes he cannot give himself the peace and happiness he seeks. Then he hears the voice of a child "from a house nearby—perhaps a voice of some boy or girl, I do not know—singing over and over again, 'Pick it up and read, pick it up and read.'"

Taking the child's words as a sign from God, Augustine, who had been reading the New Testament, describes how he picked up the Bible, opened it, "and read in silence the passage on which my eyes first lighted."[21] It is from Paul's letter to the Romans, a passage in which Paul summons the reader to "put on the Lord Jesus Christ" (Rom. 13:14).

Happiness—More a Gift Than an Achievement?

Augustine's conversion occurs when he heeds the advice of a child. After thirty-three years of searching for happiness on his own, the bliss Augustine had been seeking comes not by his own efforts, but in a sudden, unexpected moment when he hears and responds to the counsel of a child. This suggests that the happiness we seek is more a gift than our own singular achievement, more the result of grace than the work of our own agency. In the Christian life, we are not the primary agents of our happiness, God is. We have to respond to and work with the grace of God in our lives, but a foundational truth of Christian morality is that the happiness we seek we already have and always have had. It is the love and grace of God that has been poured into our hearts (Rom. 5:5). Prior to his conversion, Augustine believed whatever meaning and peace he might have in life depended entirely on him. His happiness would result from his choices and his decisions, from how he took advantage of the opportunities before him. But that didn't work. Trying to arrange his life so that everything contributed to what he thought best for him left him famished. He kept missing happiness and remained a stranger to peace because he failed to understand that happiness begins in the gift of God's love—happiness is born from grace—and that he would be happy when he accepted, grew into, and conformed his life to the love from which he had been created. What stuns the reader about Augustine's conversion is that after so many years of toil and disappointment, Augustine's happiness happens so effortlessly. All it took was for him to recognize God speaking through the voice of a playful child. The educated, worldly-wise Augustine stumbles into happiness when he allows himself to be led by a child.

What does Augustine learn from his own life story? Augustine "puts on Christ" at Easter in the year 387 when he is baptized by Ambrose, bishop of Milan. A year later he writes a short theological work, *The Way of Life of the Catholic Church* (*De Moribus Ecclesiae Catholicae*). Augustine begins that work by noting, "Certainly, we all wish to live happily."[22] But he goes on to say that we will not be happy if we lack what we love, if we possess what we love but it is harmful, or if we have not learned to love what is best. This aptly describes Augustine's own odyssey. He realized early that happiness is a matter of possessing what we love. But he also discovered that having what we love does not bring happiness if what we love is bad for us or even if what we love is good, but not sufficient to complete us. We are restless and dissatisfied either because we choose the wrong things to love or because we love good things with disproportionate devotion.

Augustine learned that happiness comes to the person who both loves and possesses what is best for human beings. The essence of happiness, as *The Confessions* so poignantly demonstrates, is not a matter of having what we want unless what we desire is truly the most excellent good for men and women. Human beings have a natural attraction to the good, it is what we cannot help loving and desiring.[23] But we will not be satisfied with anything less than perfect goodness because only perfect goodness can complete us. As the Swiss theologian Servais Pinckaers says, "We could therefore define the human person as a being aspiring to perfection and the plenitude of goodness."[24] This is why the Christian moral life is best understood as an ongoing education into whatever is the most compelling, beautiful, and promising good for human beings. What Augustine learned from his own search for happiness was that happiness is not a matter of having my desires and preferences fulfilled regardless of what they may be. No, I *learn to be happy* by scrutinizing my desires and asking if what I have chosen to love possesses a goodness exquisite enough to complete me. Happiness is a *way of life* characterized by loving, possessing, and enjoying what is supremely good for us as human beings. Thus, for Augustine, anyone who fails to love and to live for what is best can never be genuinely happy.

As a Christian, Augustine finds that goodness in God. The happy life is to love God wholeheartedly and faithfully because God is the perfection of goodness, the supreme and most excellent good (*summum bonum*). There is no good greater than God, no good that surpasses God. The happy life, Augustine says, consists of seeking God through love in order to become one with him,[25] because we will know joy only insofar as we have intimacy and communion with what is best for us. What his own quest for happiness taught him is that the deepest and most relentless human aspiration is to find and to possess whatever good can bring peace to our hearts. Anything truly good brings a degree of joy and contentment to our lives, but even the best of human goods and the deepest of human loves are never enough for creatures like ourselves, who will be satisfied with nothing less than perfect goodness and perfect love. Every human good and every human love points to a surpassing good and love. Even the richest moments of intimacy hint of a deeper and more resilient union that can never be broken, never be lost. Fashioned from the goodness and love of God, we are drawn to the goodness and love of God and cannot have peace, fulfillment, contentment, or joy apart from them. Our happiness resides in flourishing in the love that made us and gives us life. As Augustine's journey taught him, apart from God the restlessness of our hearts can never be quieted.

What Does Augustine Teach Us about the Moral Life?

What lessons on happiness can we take from Augustine? First, the story of Augustine's journey demonstrates that happiness is inseparable from goodness. In order to be happy we must become good. Moral education should focus on teaching us how to become enchanted with goodness because if we are ever to be happy and fulfilled, we must be attracted to goodness more than evil, virtue more than vice. If we are to flourish and excel as human beings, we must find goodness compelling and irresistible. We must, in more traditional language, contemplate the beauty of goodness in order to be captivated by its radiance. This is why contemplation has always been a central practice of the Christian life. The purpose of contemplation is to open oneself to the goodness and beauty of God in order to be transformed by it. To see and not turn away from the good is an essential first step in moral formation because our growth and development as human beings hinge not only on finding goodness beautiful, but on becoming resplendent in goodness ourselves.

Second, Augustine's story suggests that the God who is our good wants our good. *God wants our good.* This fact should ground all consideration of the Christian moral life. Christian morality begins not with our initiatives and actions, but with the befriending activity of God. The God who befriends us in grace, Christ, and the Spirit, desires what is best for us and continually seeks to achieve it. The God who fashioned us *from* goodness and *for* goodness wants our happiness and works far better than we to accomplish it. The Christian moral life begins in God's grace, grows from that grace, and is sustained by that grace. We are called to respond to God's grace; to use our freedom, ingenuity, and intelligence to cooperate with it; and live according to it. But we are never solitary agents in the Christian moral life. We never "go it alone," because we always live and work in partnership with the gracious initiatives of God, and in partnership with others. The Christian moral life abides as a *response to grace*. It is our ongoing response, formed from gratitude, to the graced initiatives of God. We misconstrue the Christian moral life if we picture ourselves as autonomous, independent agents on whom everything depends. On the contrary, the language that best befits us is not the language of autonomy and independence, but of *receptivity* and *cooperation*. We thrive when we open ourselves to the grace, love, and goodness of God—when we allow God's spirit to move freely within us—and when we use our intelligence and freedom to work in harmony with God's grace, not against it or apart from it.

Thomas Aquinas

Our second guide on the subject of happiness is Thomas Aquinas (1225–1274). Aquinas could be the patron saint of every student who has ever felt his or her talents were overlooked or unappreciated. He is the perfect example of the student whose gifts were not immediately recognized. Quiet and shy by nature, Thomas was a boy who thought much but said little. And he was apparently a pretty big boy. One of his biographers described Aquinas as being "somewhat corpulent," which is a nice way of saying he was at least a little hefty.[26] As often happens with those who are reticent and reserved, and of lumbering physique, people concluded that Aquinas was not very bright; in fact, his youthful peers nicknamed him the "Dumb Ox." But Thomas's genius soon became known. One day Thomas dropped a sheet of his class notes in the corridor outside his room. A fellow student saw the notes and took them to their teacher, the famous Albert the Great. Glancing at the notes, Albert was so impressed that he remarked, "We call him the Dumb Ox, but the bellowing of that ox will resound throughout the world."[27]

Albert's prediction certainly was proven true, because the theology of this thirteenth-century saint and scholar has bellowed resoundingly for almost eight hundred years. Aquinas died before he reached fifty, but few have written more extensively and prolifically, or as astutely, as this man whose abiding desire was to help people understand the extent of God's goodness to us and how we should respond to it. Of all Aquinas's writings, the most important is his *magnum opus*, the massive *Summa Theologiae*, a stunning exploration of virtually every dimension of Christian theology, but a work Aquinas intended for "beginners." In the preface to the *Summa*, Aquinas said his aim "was to present those things that pertain to the Christian religion in a manner befitting the education of beginners, to present the fundamentals of theology briefly and clearly."[28] No work has shaped and impacted Christian thinking more than this "beginners book," and it is in its pages that Aquinas's most trenchant analysis of happiness is found.

Wrong Turns on Happiness

Like Augustine, Aquinas puts the human desire for happiness at the heart of the moral life. He begins his investigation of the Christian moral life with the simple declaration that happiness is our true good—the one good every person naturally seeks—and that we will not be satisfied until we possess a happiness that "essentially remains and is forever."[29] Seekers of happiness, we move through life in search of whatever we think will fulfill and complete us, something so exquisitely good that once we possess it there is nothing left for us to desire. Aquinas calls this consummate good our "ultimate end." Everybody has one because all of us set our hearts on something we believe will quench all of our desires.

The desire for happiness is natural, but knowing what will bring happiness is not. Aquinas held that real happiness and real peace come from possessing whatever good can bring us to our fullest and most perfect development. We will be happy, Thomas thought, when we not only possess, but are also transformed by, whatever good is capable of bringing us to our utmost possible excellence as human beings—the good or goods that enable us to be who we are created to be. But we are easily misled about where such fulfilling goodness is found. We are often more mistaken than astute about happiness. The common thread in all of our actions is the desire for happiness, but we seek happiness in different places and in different ways. This may be inevitable, but it is also costly because, Aquinas saw, wrong choices about happiness result in sadness and diminishment.

Consider, for example, what our society teaches about happiness. In a capitalist economy and a culture of consumerism, are we not bombarded with messages promising happiness through wealth and possessions? Aren't we every day indoctrinated by advertisements promising bliss through the clothes we wear, the cell phones we buy, and even the beer we drink? Or in our celebrity culture are we not taught to believe that fame and power, not service and commitment bring happiness? But if all these things really bring happiness, why are so many people depressed and discontent, angry and dissatisfied, and perhaps, amid all their comforts, slipping unknowingly into despair? Aquinas's response to our society's convictions about happiness would be that anyone who thinks wealth, fame, pleasure, or power can make us supremely happy is only imitating the "mass opinion of silly people" who are so misguided about happiness that we ought to pity them, not imitate them.[30]

But Aquinas was a realist. He knew how people think. Thus, when he begins his study of happiness he does not leap to the conclusion that God must be our ultimate good. No, the first candidate for happiness he offers is not God but money because, Aquinas notes, many people live as if money is their ultimate joy. Whatever we allow to win our hearts and master our affections is what we think will make us happiest, and for many people this is money. As Aquinas wrote, "For since happiness is man's final end it must be looked for where his affections are held above all. And such is wealth, as Ecclesiastes remarks, 'All things obey money.'"[31]

He also looks at honor and fame, power and prestige, bodily health, and pleasure as possibilities for our "ultimate end" because he knows the way we live. We are inclined to look for satisfaction in fame and prestige, to think pleasure will content us, or conclude that nothing matters more than being healthy and fit. And there is some truth to all of these claims. Aquinas does not study these possibilities only in order to dismiss them; rather, he acknowledges that there is something good about each of them and something important that they contribute to life. A certain amount of money and material goods are essential for a good human life. Having a good reputation does add something to our happiness and well-being. No one who has ever enjoyed a gourmet meal, a fine martini, or Italian ice cream will deny that such pleasures enrich us (sometimes more than our waistlines can bear). And no one truly alive will deny how powerful the pleasures of touch can be. A God who made all things good made these things good too. Aquinas agreed. He did not deny their goodness; in fact, he agreed that they are elements to a good and happy life. But he was also convinced that their goodness could only take us so far. Each of these things is unquestionably good, but insufficiently good. They go a long way to making our lives pleasant and fulfilled, but still fall short because none has the goodness necessary for bringing us to our optimum excellence as human beings. We may have all earthly goods and pleasures, Aquinas said, but we will still be dissatisfied—or we *ought* to be dissatisfied—because even when we have them in abundance we "recognize how incomplete they are and how far short of our highest good."[32]

For example, money cannot be our ultimate end any more than power, fame, health, or pleasure, because we will be brought to peace only by something whose goodness surpasses us, not by something less than us. Our happiness resides in something so superior in goodness that through desiring, loving, and possessing it we are brought to our highest possible excellence. The good that is our ultimate end, Aquinas reasons, is so perfectly good that it fulfills all desires.[33] Money and possessions cannot do this because no matter how much wealth we have or things we own we always want more. The same is true with power and fame and pleasure. We can have them all in abundance but will still be restless, still sense something is missing. Whatever will make us happiest must be able to do great things for us. It must be a good that stretches us, a good that can consistently carry us beyond previous levels of achievement and growth. Thus, for Aquinas, the happy person is not necessarily the woman or man who has all she or he desires; rather, the happy person is the woman or man who possesses the greatest possible good in the deepest possible way.[34]

Why Our Ultimate Happiness Is God

Such goodness is found only in God. Nothing other than God and nothing less than God can ultimately satisfy us because we are happy insofar as we possess the highest possible good, and that goodness is found in God alone, the source and perfection of all goodness. Human beings seek the unsurpassable good, "the good without reserve," Aquinas says, because we grow and flourish through goodness and are perfected and fulfilled through the highest goodness. Such unexcelled goodness cannot be found in any created thing, but only in God whose goodness is without defect and lacking in nothing.[35] For Aquinas, to be happy is to live in and from the most beautiful good, and to grow in the likeness of that good. "There is a drive within all things towards some likeness to God, who is their first beginning and their final end," Aquinas wrote. Thus, we cannot enjoy happiness unless we "become like God in goodness."[36] Throughout his analysis of happiness, Aquinas maintains that the ultimate end or supreme good of men and women is whatever brings us to our most proper and complete development as human beings. Union with God, sharing God's life intimately and continuously, is the true ultimate end for human beings because nothing less than God can appease our natural desire for the absolute good. Anything less than perfect communion with God will leave us dissatisfied and incomplete. Similarly, any account of happiness constituted by human goods alone will be both misleading and flawed.[37] Our aim, Aquinas insists, must be to "become like God in goodness."

But identifying our happiness in a life of friendship and fellowship with God creates a problem. How can we who are clearly other than God—finite, mortal, earthly, and sinful—possibly share in the life and goodness of God? How can we find happiness in a goodness that so infinitely surpasses us, a goodness that seems eternally out of reach? Like Augustine, Aquinas says such happiness must come through a gift. Left to ourselves we cannot possibly know intimacy with God, much less union with God, because God's goodness infinitely transcends us. The happiness we need is a happiness we cannot, by our own resources, possibly reach. But we can receive it as a gift. Human beings are fulfilled through a life of love, friendship, and communion with God—what Aquinas calls a life of *caritas* or charity. And this way of life is within our reach not because of our own powers or capacities, but because of God's grace. The God who wants our good gifts us with the happiness we seek.[38]

Aquinas's point is that we seek perfect happiness with God because from the beginning of our lives we, however imperfectly and incompletely, already know, share in, and live from that happiness. Aquinas says every human being begins life with a gift, namely, the gift of God's love and happiness poured into our hearts. God "communicates his beatitude" to us. What Aquinas means is that our lives originate in a grace, in the gift of God's very happiness infused into our hearts.[39] We cannot gain this happiness on our own, but we don't have to. It is the gift with which we begin our quest for happiness and the gift in which it is fulfilled. Like Augustine, Aquinas insists that the Christian moral life starts with a gift. It begins when God shares with us what we cannot possibly give ourselves, namely, the happiness and love that completes us. We cannot earn this gift, but we can open ourselves to receive it, and we can be increasingly conformed to it. In short, we seek the perfection of our happiness in God because the beatitude we anticipate we have, however dimly and imperfectly, already found.[40]

Christ—Our Preeminent Teacher in the Way of Happiness

But it is a happiness we can easily lose. This is why we need to be guided along the way of happiness. We need mentors who can show us the way. We need communities whose members are wise in the habits of happiness. It is the same in the moral life as in any other area of our lives. Even the most gifted athletes need to be trained, guided, and disciplined by coaches. In music, child prodigies still need to be taught and nurtured by teachers who recognize their gifts and tutor them so that they can become virtuosos. And the most brilliant scientists recognize the debt they owe to teachers who helped them develop their gifts to their optimum potential. The same holds true for the Christian life. Having a natural desire for happiness is no guarantee we shall find it. We need to be tutored in the happy life. We need wise mentors and skilled guides to lead us on our quest so that, when it comes to happiness, we don't keep showing up at the wrong place at the wrong time. We cannot miscalculate forever about happiness without ending up with a life we ultimately regret. We all make mistakes about happiness, errors about where real peace and meaning are found; but we cannot afford to be mistaken all of the time, year after year, decade after decade, if we want our life to be other than a colossal missed opportunity.

Augustine and Aquinas knew this. They recognized that if the heart of the Christian moral life is learning about happiness, then we begin the moral life not as experts in happiness but as apprentices. We are novices in the skills of happiness, not virtuosos, and novices need a teacher. In the Christian life our primary teacher in the way of happiness is Christ. He is our mentor; we are his disciples; and it is by observing him, listening to him, and learning from him, following his teachings and imitating his example, that we grow in happiness. Augustine taught that happiness is a way of life intrinsically connected to the life, teachings, and example of Christ. In Christ one sees the *path to happiness* and discovers the virtues and practices constitutive of happiness. This is why in the Christian moral life happiness comes not by having the freedom to pursue whatever we want; rather, for Christians, happiness requires being initiated into a way of life by which we gradually are conformed to the love, goodness, and beauty of God. Christian ethics is *training in happiness*, and in the Gospels we discover what that training involves. This initiation begins with baptism because in that sacrament Christians join their lives to Christ, promise to model their lives after Christ, and see themselves as lifelong disciples with Christ as their teacher. A life of discipleship is a training in happiness; and what disciples learn is that happiness comes as we learn to love our enemies, as we forgive rather than retaliate, and as we serve the least of all rather than lord it over them.

This goes against all our intuitions about happiness. We think we will feel better when we get even, not when we forgive. Seeking the good of our enemies seems the antithesis of happiness, not an essential ingredient of it. And we are taught to be the lucky people who are served, not the poor souls who do the serving. This is why so many, when introduced to the Christian life, turn away. We are reluctant to trust, much less commit ourselves to, a teacher who says an important first step to happiness is selling our possessions and giving what we have to the poor (Matt. 19:21). Most offensive of all is Jesus' promise that anyone who undertakes his path to happiness can count on daily crosses, certain tribulation, misunderstanding, and rejection. No wonder we are more likely to decline Jesus' invitation than accept it, and thus try our luck with happiness elsewhere.

Take the Beatitudes, the heart of Jesus' teaching from the Sermon on the Mount, where he sets out the way of life and the kind of community that will help bring about the reign of God (Matt. 5:1–12). For Augustine, the Beatitudes, as their name suggests, are the concrete practices by which Christians know happiness by being formed in the goodness of God.[41] But the Beatitudes, to say the least, present an unconventional understanding of happiness. Jesus promises happiness to those who are "poor in spirit," to the lowly and the humble, to those who hunger for holiness more than for power or wealth, to those generous with mercy and hesitant to condemn, to peacemakers who will suffer violence rather than inflict it, and to those who are insulted and persecuted because they refuse to renounce Christ. Who wants to take this road to happiness? The Beatitudes outline Jesus' path to happiness, and for generations Christian theologians and preachers have softened their blow by assuring discomfited believers that Jesus really didn't mean for us to take the Beatitudes seriously. They are, the argument goes, "eschatological ideals" that represent what Jesus would like the world to be but knows it never can be. Or perhaps they describe a perfectionist ethic for a special elite, but not something that could possibly be asked of everyone.

But Augustine thought otherwise. In his commentary on the Sermon on the Mount, Augustine suggests that Jesus' teachings on mercy, peacemaking, forgiveness, and justice are not impossible ideals too unreasonable ever to practice, but precisely the attitudes and actions that constitute happiness, because by practicing and embodying them we become godly. Augustine believed "the Beatitudes give us Christ's answer to the primary human question about happiness" because by living according to them we are conformed to the goodness of God and participate more completely in the life of God.[42]

Aquinas agreed. Like Augustine, Aquinas linked happiness with a life of discipleship, a life of following, learning from, and imitating Jesus. Christ is the center of the Christian moral life because we grow in the goodness of God and, therefore, know happiness, only in the measure that we more deeply possess and practice the virtues of Christ. Furthermore, for Aquinas, a life of discipleship is mediated through the sacraments, particularly baptism and the Eucharist. In the *Summa Theologiae*, Aquinas writes, "Baptism is required in order to begin the spiritual life; the Eucharist is necessary in order to bring it to its culmination."[43] The Christian moral life starts with baptism because baptism marks not only the beginning of a Christian's training in happiness, but also indicates what that training will involve. Baptism ritually expresses that happiness is learned *in community* as men and women apprentice themselves to Christ. But baptism also indicates that this training in happiness is never finished or complete. We never "finish our baptisms" because at no point do we achieve perfect conformity to the goodness of God. We strive for that goodness by claiming the Gospel as our rule of life, and we grow more deeply in that goodness as we follow the way of Christ, but we never equal or surpass it. Similarly, the Eucharist is an essential practice for the Christian moral life because it is the ritual through which our communal training in happiness primarily occurs. As apprentices in the life of happiness, at the Eucharist we *together* listen to the words and teachings of Christ and learn how to better model our lives on his. At the Eucharist we *together* eat the body and drink the blood of Christ—we consume Christ entirely—so that his attitudes and virtues might become our own. The Eucharist is the true center of the Christian moral life because it is the indispensable context for learning about happiness and for becoming people capable of happiness.[44]

Conclusion

In this opening chapter we have suggested that Christian ethics is best understood as an ongoing education or training in what constitutes authentic happiness for human beings. It would not be amiss to title a course on Christian ethics "How to Be Happy," because it is the main business of ethics to teach us this.[45] If human beings are made for happiness and have an ineluctable desire for happiness, it is important that we discover the kind of life most conducive to happiness. Our societies present a variety of understandings of happiness, and we can often learn from what they teach. But human beings want a happiness that lasts—and a happiness that does not deceive—and Christians believe that ultimately that happiness is found only in the love and praise of God, in what Thomas Aquinas described as a life of friendship with God. Viewing the Christian moral life as training in happiness is a different way of envisioning the enterprise of Christian ethics. It emphasizes the primacy of God's agency over human agency, of grace and gift over personal autonomy and achievement. It recognizes that the crucial truth from which the Christian moral life begins is that God wants our good and works for our good even if, as Augustine's life vividly captures, we are experts at undermining what God desires. And this approach to the moral life argues that we begin the quest for happiness as apprentices in need of a mentor. Christians find that mentor in Christ and call that quest a life of discipleship.

But we cannot take up the quest alone. The pursuit of happiness through goodness requires the company of friends. We need companions to take up the journey with us, communities where we find others who will not only support and guide us along the way, but who will rejoice in the quest with us. If the Christian moral life is an ongoing training in happiness, it must be lived in communities and sustained in friendships. It requires people who care for one another, help one another, and look out for one another. That is what friends, and good communities, do, and their role in the moral life is what we will next consider.

Some Questions for Reflection and Discussion

1. Prior to reading this chapter, what did you think Christian morality primarily involved? Why?
2. Does it make sense to you to envision the Christian moral life as "training" in happiness? Why or why not?
3. Do you think you can be happy without being good? Would you agree that good people are happy?
4. Was there anything about Augustine's story that connected with your own life's story? Have you ever, like him, feared happiness?
5. Thomas Aquinas said that every person has an "ultimate end." What do you see people choosing as their "ultimate end" today? How would you evaluate their choices?
6. Do you think happiness is something that has to be learned? And what in a Christian understanding of happiness do you find challenging? Agreeable or disagreeable?

Notes

1. Robert Ellsberg, *The Saints' Guide to Happiness* (New York: North Point Press, 2003), xi–xvi.
2. Etienne Gilson, *Moral Values and The Moral Life: The System of St. Thomas Aquinas*, trans. Leo Richard Ward (St. Louis, MO: B. Herder Book Co., 1931), 19.
3. Edmund L. Pincoffs, *Quandaries and Virtues: Against Reductivism in Ethics* (Lawrence: University Press of Kansas, 1986), 15.
4. Herbert McCabe, OP, *The Good Life: Ethics and the Pursuit of Happiness* (New York: Continuum, 2005), 9.
5. McCabe, *The Good Life*, 49.
6. Livio Melina, *Sharing in Christ's Virtues: For a Renewal of Moral Theology in Light of Veritatis Splendor*, trans. William E. May (Washington, DC: The Catholic University of America Press, 2001), 26. See also Servais Pinckaers, OP, *The Sources of Christian Ethics*, trans. Sr. Mary Thomas Noble, OP (Washington, DC: The Catholic University of America Press, 1995), 160.
7. Servais Pinckaers, OP, *Morality: The Catholic View*, trans. Michael Sherwin, OP (South Bend, IN: St. Augustine's Press, 2003), 75. As Pinckaers explains, "In the past, the good and happiness formed a single concept expressed by a single word: goodness, *bonum* in Latin. Happiness was the diffusion of the good, like the reverse side of a single quality."
8. Pinckaers, *Morality: The Catholic View*, 78.
9. Augustine, *The Confessions*, trans. Maria Boulding, OSB (Hyde Park, NY: New City Press, 1997), I, i.
10. Augustine, *The Confessions*, II, ii.

11. Augustine, *The Confessions*, III, i.
12. Augustine, *The Confessions*, III, iv.
13. Augustine, *The Confessions*, III, xx.
14. Augustine, *The Confessions*, III, v.
15. Augustine, *The Confessions*, VI, ix.
16. Augustine, *The Confessions*, VI, ix.
17. Augustine, *The Confessions*, VI, x.
18. Augustine, *The Confessions*, VIII, xii.
19. Augustine, *The Confessions*, VIII, xxv.
20. Augustine, *The Confessions*, VIII, xxviii.
21. Augustine, *The Confessions*, VIII, xxix.
22. Augustine, *The Way of Life of the Catholic Church*, trans. Donald A. Gallagher and Idella J. Gallagher (Washington, DC: The Catholic University of America Press, 1966), III, iv.
23. Pinckaers, *The Sources of Christian Ethics*, 409.
24. Pinckaers, *The Sources of Christian Ethics*, 412.
25. Augustine, *The Way of Life of the Catholic Church*, XI, xviii. Augustine writes: "To strive after God, then, is to desire happiness; to reach God is happiness itself."
26. James A. Weisheipl, OP, *Friar Thomas D'Aquino: His Life, Thought and Works* (Washington, DC: The Catholic University of America Press, 1974), 17.
27. Weisheipl, *Friar Thomas D'Aquino*, 45.
28. Cited in Weisheipl, *Friar Thomas D'Aquino*, 218.
29. Thomas Aquinas, *Summa Theologiae*, trans. Thomas Gilby, OP (New York: McGraw-Hill Book Co., 1969), I-II, 2,3. The edition of the *Summa Theologiae* used throughout this book is the Blackfriars' edition.
30. Aquinas, *ST*, I-II, 2,1.
31. Aquinas, *ST*, I-II, 2,1.
32. Aquinas, *ST*, I-II, 2,1.
33. Aquinas, *ST*, I-II, 2,7.
34. For an extended analysis of these points see Paul J. Wadell, *The Primacy of Love: An Introduction to the Ethics of Thomas Aquinas* (New York: Paulist Press, 1992), 44–62.
35. Aquinas, *ST*, I-II, 2,8.
36. Aquinas, *ST*, I-II, 2,4.
37. Pamela M. Hall, *Narrative and the Natural Law: An Interpretation of Thomistic Ethics* (Notre Dame, IN: University of Notre Dame Press, 1994), 66–67. As Hall explains, "Union with God constitutes the human end because no created good, or set of goods, can satisfy fully the human appetite for the true and the good. . . . The achievement of our good in strictly natural terms leaves us, according to the structure of our powers of intellect and will, 'metaphysically' unsatisfied; beyond this, the happiness accessible to men and women in this life is itself flawed."
38. Paul J. Wadell, *Friendship and the Moral Life* (Notre Dame, IN: University of Notre Dame Press, 1989), 122–26.

39. Aquinas, *ST*, II-II, 23,1.

40. Melina, *Sharing in Christ's Virtues*, 41.

41. For an earlier treatment of this point, as well as other points developed in chapter one, see Paul J. Wadell, "The Christian Moral Life: An Ongoing Education into the Nature of Authentic Happiness," *Anthropotes* 19, no. 2 (2003): 291–307.

42. Pinckaers, *The Sources of Christian Ethics*, 142.

43. Aquinas, *ST*, III, 73,3.

44. Melina, *Sharing in Christ's Virtues*, 152–54.

45. McCabe, *The Good Life*, x. In his introduction to *The Good Life*, Brian Davies, OP, notes that McCabe, while teaching at Oxford, entitled his introductory course in moral philosophy "How to Be Happy."

CHAPTER TWO

~

Not Going It Alone

Friendship and Community in the Christian Moral Life

High school reunions can make even the most self-assured a little apprehensive. A few years ago I attended my first high school reunion, roughly thirty-three years after my classmates and I grabbed our diplomas and walked away from one chapter of our lives, excited but uncertain about the future. Ours was not the typical high school experience. For four years we shared life together at a high school seminary, a boarding school in a tiny town about fifty miles west of St. Louis. We came from all across the country and for four years we navigated the perils of adolescence together in a community where we studied and prayed together, did our daily jobs together, played legendary practical jokes on one another, and talked as if we had all the time in the world. The world was just as turbulent and frightening and mystifying then as it is now, but in our communal life together we somehow managed to face it all with hope, even joy. The adventure came to an end with our graduation. The school closed that year, and our migration to new places and into new ways of life began.

That was the last most of us saw of each another until two former classmates decided we had waited far too long to gather together again. They went to work tracking everybody down, checking addresses, making phone calls, sending out e-mails. As word of the reunion spread, students in classes ahead of and behind us asked if they could come as well, so the "gates were thrown open" and "everyone was invited to the feast." Traveling to St. Louis in early October, it was as if all of us who had been scattered were being re-gathered, as if we who had been tossed apart were, if only for a weekend, coming back home. I had thought about a reunion for a long time, wondering if it would ever happen. But the closer my wife and I got to St. Louis, the more nervous I became. I wondered if this was all a colossal mistake. Would we come together, look at one another, be shocked at the change, and discover we had little to say to each another? Would the years apart leave us awkward with one another despite the life we had once shared? Would we be relieved when it all ended on Sunday afternoon, departing with the vow never to do this again?

Thankfully, none of that happened—besides the shock of having your memories of someone at seventeen or eighteen run smack into the reality of that person at fifty! It was as if for thirty-three years we had been waiting to get back together, waiting to reconnect, but also as if we had never been apart. We picked up conversations as if all those years had been only a momentary interruption. We joked as we had always joked, recalling elaborate pranks when our imaginations got the better of good sense. We reminisced, relying on another's memory to supply what our own hazy recollections lacked, and were shocked at how differently we remembered the same events. We made up for lost time by inquiring about the missing chapters of one another's lives, stories of college, marriages, job changes, children being born, and parents passing away.

And we prayed. With so much energy and emotion flowing about that weekend, we felt more than we understood. But everything became clearer at the Eucharist on Sunday morning. If the eyes of the disciples en route to Emmaus were opened when Jesus broke bread with them (Luke 24:31), gathered around the table of the Lord our eyes were opened too. We understood why gratitude and thanksgiving were the dominant emotions that weekend and why, after so many years of separation, the bond among us remained amazingly fresh and resilient, seemingly unbreakable. In his homily that morning, the priest, Fr. Randal, explained why. He had been our spiritual mentor and guide during those years, but also a true "father" and a friend since our own fathers were not at hand. He told us that so many years earlier we had left our families and our homes and journeyed to an out-of-the-way place in Missouri to answer the call of goodness. It was the lure of goodness that had drawn us together and that explained the power of those years. The desire to be and to do good were at the heart of that erstwhile adventure, and its appeal continued to speak to us that weekend. As adolescents we had come together to pursue the good, and what those years, recollected now three decades later, taught us is that we could not have done so alone. We needed one another to know and do the good. We needed a community in our quest for goodness because it is impossible to become good without others who have made that desire their own. Gratitude was the mantra of the weekend because we realized how indebted we were to one another. Our lives had been permanently changed, deepened, and enriched during those years precisely because of the people who had shared them with us. We came to say thanks and to wish one another well because we had learned that goodness cannot be achieved single-handedly. Whatever goodness and virtue there was in us was much more the handiwork of our friends than our own accomplishment.

Aristotle said that without friends no one would choose to live. It wasn't just because human beings are social creatures who find most things more enjoyable when they can be shared with others or because there is no way any of us could make it through life without friends to whom we could turn. All that is true, but the most important reason we need friends, Aristotle insisted, is because a life of goodness and happiness depends on having certain kinds of relationships. The moral importance of friendship and community is often overlooked. We may enjoy our friends and seek out communities, but we seldom think that the development of our character and our growth in happiness and goodness are inherently linked to them; in fact, we may see friendships as a pleasant escape from the moral life, not its core or center. But Aristotle represents a tradition that appreciated the central role of friendship in one's ongoing transformation in goodness and virtue. For him, friendship makes a life of goodness and happiness possible because there is no way our quest for goodness could be sustained, much less successfully completed, without the guidance and support of friends making that quest with us. If the moral life is an ongoing training in happiness, it absolutely requires certain kinds of relationships and communities in which such training can occur. And if our happiness is proportionate to our goodness, the moral life is a matter of growing together in the good in friendships and communities with people who also want to be good. For Aristotle, that is what happens in the best of friendships. And yet, their very importance makes us wonder if we can always count on such relationships in our lives, or perhaps question if we have ever known them. What happens if we lack the kind of friendships or communities we need to know, to grow in, and to enjoy the good?

In Christianity the horizons of happiness change. Thomas Aquinas took Aristotle's account of the centrality of friendship in the moral life, but radically reenvisioned it by suggesting that human beings are made not only for friendship with one another, but also for friendship with God—what he called charity or *caritas*. Our most exquisite happiness, Aquinas insisted, comes from all of us *together* seeking and enjoying a life of intimate friendship with God. Human beings are created for communion, we are fashioned for intimacy. But Aquinas realized the deepest truth of our being is that collectively we are made for intimacy and communion with God, and nothing less will content us. Friendship and community are a central element to the Christian moral life not just because we need and depend on one another, but more strikingly because our happiness, and therefore our goodness, pivots on all of us living in and from friendship with God. For Aquinas, the Christian life is a community's ongoing initiation into friendship with God; it is a community's sustained training in the happiness that is charity. This is one reason why there has to be a church, and it says something important about the kind of community churches need to be. The church should be the primary setting for learning, growing in, and being increasingly conformed to the happiness that is found in a life of friendship with God.

In this chapter we will explore the role of friendship and community in the Christian moral life by looking first at Aristotle's account of the place of friendship in the life of virtue and happiness, and then at the Christian claim that the most perfecting life is the communal life of charity, a life of deep, enduring friendship with God and one another. Through these investigations we will see why a life of happiness and goodness is impossible apart from certain kinds of relationships and certain kinds of communities. But we will also discover that the more deeply we are drawn into the happiness that Christians call friendship with God, the more radically we are called out of ourselves and into communion with others, even those we customarily call our enemies. Like my high school reunion, in the Christian life we will be happy only when "the gates are thrown open" and everyone, including our enemies, is "invited to the feast."

Aristotle—Finding Happiness through the Best Possible Life

For Aristotle, the purpose of ethics is to help human beings attain happiness by achieving their greatest possible good.[1] Aristotle named this unsurpassable good *eudaimonia*, and although it is commonly translated as "happiness," it more accurately refers to the best possible life or "the complete and perfectly satisfying life,"[2] one lacking nothing necessary for human flourishing. As Herbert McCabe said, for Aristotle happiness is "the state of the person who is living without hindrance the life that becomes a human being, the 'satisfactory' life (the life 'sufficiently made')."[3] In this respect, *eudaimonia* is not a single good, but includes all the goods and activities needed for men and women to grow into their most distinctive excellence as humans. If we were designing the best possible life for ourselves, what would it include? This is what *eudaimonia* seeks. In trying to grasp the content of Aristotle's understanding of a good life, we must ask questions such as these: What shape must our lives take if they are to reach their optimum development? How must our lives be construed if we are to be truly happy and fulfilled *as humans*? What would be, without qualification, the most satisfying life for us? Obviously, it would include such fundamental goods as food, clothing, health, and shelter. It would also have to include financial security, education and opportunity, satisfying work, as well as leisure and relaxation. These would all be necessary elements of *eudaimonia* because we could not have a truly good life without them.

But they would not be sufficient because with them alone we still could not cultivate our most distinctive and promising potential. The best possible life—which is what happiness really is—has to be one by which we can develop the quality or characteristic that best represents that for which we are made, and for Aristotle it is goodness. The supreme excellence of human beings is found in goodness, and goodness comes to us through the virtues. Each of the virtues manifests a particular dimension of goodness, and therefore is intrinsic to happiness. Justice is an expression of goodness and part of a happy life. Loyalty and faithfulness embody goodness and contribute to happiness, as do courage and perseverance, trustworthiness and honesty, and all the other virtues. For Aristotle the best possible life is the virtuous life because it is in developing and becoming skilled in all the various dimensions of goodness that we not only grow in our own special excellence as humans, but participate in it now.[4]

Aristotle expressed this by saying "happiness [*eudaimonia*] is some kind of activity of the soul in conformity with virtue."[5] He was not suggesting that the virtues are a *means* to the *end* of happiness, as if happiness were the consequence of virtue or the reward of virtue. Rather, a life of happiness is *constituted* by the virtues because the virtues make us good.[6] In *Christians Among the Virtues* Stanley Hauerwas and Charles Pinches say that with Aristotle "we cannot see happiness as some ideal final state, realizable only in the distant future. For happiness is not so much the end, but the way. Happiness comes as we acquire and live the virtues."[7] The most satisfying life for human beings cannot be one in which happiness is forever out of reach, something to which we continuously move but never truly know. That would be a life of bitter disappointment and futility, not satisfaction, and it is why Aristotle suggests we participate in happiness now, however imperfectly and incompletely, to the degree that we grow in goodness through the virtues. Again, a virtuous life is not the means to happiness, but the very form and substance of happiness. The most satisfying life for humans is the virtuous life embraced as completely as possible now.

In Aristotle's schema of the moral life, *eudaimonia* and the virtues are intrinsically connected. We cannot know happiness or human well-being apart from the virtues because such creative and diverse goodness most fittingly represents who we truly are—or at least ought to be. Aristotle explains this by saying everything that exists has its own special function or purpose. Planets and plants have a special purpose, each of the animals does, but so do human beings. A thing's proper function (*ergon*) is whatever activity makes it what it uniquely is, and not something else. The proper function of human beings is whatever distinctive activity sets them apart from other creatures and helps bring them to their own distinctive flourishing. Our special function—our lifetime job description, if you will—is to grow in goodness because it is only through goodness that our most distinctive excellence is achieved.[8]

But obviously such goodness cannot be accomplished all at once any more than perfect happiness can be instantaneously achieved. We strive for goodness, we struggle to acquire it, and we grow into it, but we also fall away from it and sometimes reject it completely. This is why we must understand the life of virtue as a quest, an unfolding but never completed odyssey toward the good. We can share now in the good we seek, but never completely and perfectly. And because acquiring the virtues is difficult, sometimes even painstaking, it is easy to grow disheartened. Whether we struggle with our own weaknesses and imperfections, with setbacks and disappointments, or simply with the fact that becoming good takes time, the temptation is to forsake the quest for goodness for something more manageable, something less taxing, and perhaps even more appealing.

This is why *eudaimonia*, the best possible life for humans, not only involves the virtues, but also requires friends. In Aristotle's ethics, happiness, the life of virtue, and the companionship of friends are all inextricably connected. We cannot know happiness without becoming good, but we cannot acquire the virtues necessary for goodness without friends. "The supremely happy person is the good person," theologian Gregory Jones notes, "and in order to be both good and happy one needs and desires the presence of friends."[9] We need friends because there is no way we can grow in goodness without the guidance, counsel, and support of others. For Aristotle good friends are more than comforting accessories to the life of virtue. They are quintessential elements to it because we cannot acquire the virtues without them. The moral life is a partnership, a truly communal and cooperative enterprise, because we will know the happiness that comes in goodness only in companionship with others who seek it with us.

How Friends Help Us Become Good

How then do friends help one another become good and grow in happiness? What is their role in the moral life? There are many ways to answer this, but four ways friends contribute to one another's moral development seem especially important. First, friendships are essential components to the moral life because every real friendship draws us out of ourselves and teaches us how to care for others for their own sake.[10] A fundamental and indispensable quality of every true friendship is to seek the good of the friend and to delight when that is accomplished. Friends want what is best for one another and they work to make that possible. We would hardly count anyone our friend if he was indifferent to our well-being or only halfheartedly committed to our good; or, what is worse, if he tried to persuade us to do something unworthy of ourselves. The focus of friendship is on the true good and happiness of the friend. People who want what is best for us only when it is convenient for them or who are only occasionally concerned for our good cannot be considered real friends. Friends care about one another over time; their commitment to what is best for one another endures.

There are different ways to express this important dimension of friendship. Sometimes it is called *benevolence*, a word that means to wish well for another and to desire their good. Sometimes it is described as *beneficence*, which means actively to seek and to work for another's good. If benevolence describes a fundamental attitude of friendship, beneficence is its fundamental activity. Together they characterize a relationship in which each person is wholly committed to the good of the other and finds meaning and joy in being so. As the British theologian Liz Carmichael writes, "Friendship exists where each wishes well to the other for their own sake, and is willing to act on that goodwill, and is aware of the goodwill of the other; and a 'friend' is a person involved in such a relationship."[11]

As abiding qualities to the life of any true friendship, benevolence and beneficence contribute to our formation in goodness because they teach us to live for something more than our own gratification or self-interest. Friendships (and good communities too) call us out of ourselves and challenge us to see beyond the pinched horizons of self-concern and self-interest by asking us to identify with another person and her good. An ongoing challenge in the moral life is to continue to grow by enlarging our capacity for generosity, justice, and compassion. But an ongoing temptation is to resist this challenge by turning in on ourselves and allowing anxiety, self-absorption, fear, or insecurity to reduce the moral landscape of our world to whatever is most advantageous or most comforting for us. The life of any true friendship works against this narrowing by summoning us to invest in another's good and to remain devoted to her best interests even when doing so requires sacrifice from us. Friendships teach us what it means to be faithful and fair. They deepen our capacity for generosity and thoughtfulness. They show us why being truthful and trustworthy matters. This is why the ordinary life of an ordinary friendship is morally important. Indispensable qualities of character are chiseled into us in the crucible of friendship. More than anything, friendships teach us the requirements of love.

We may not often reflect on how good friendships form our character, but consider what happens in the life of such a relationship. Friends demand time of one another. Friends count on each other to be present and available, not only when there are successes to celebrate and accomplishments to savor, but also in times of failure, hardship, and difficulty. We want and rightly expect the presence of our friends amid all the circumstances of our lives precisely because friendship is a matter of sharing in the life of another as completely as possible, but not just when doing so is easy or agreeable. Friends count on one another and depend on one another. But cultivating this kind of loyalty, faithfulness, and trustworthiness is difficult. Standing with others when they are struggling, failing, or just not very easy to be with is hard. It is hard to attend to the needs and well-being of another person over time, but this is what real friendship teaches and it is an important moral skill. Anybody can be occasionally attentive to the good of another, especially when doing so is pleasing or convenient. At the beginning of any friendship there is nothing we want more than to be with our friends and to do good for them. But extending that care for another over time—both "in season and out of season"—is what true friendship demands, and none of us finds that kind of faithful love easy.

For instance, the longer we remain friends with someone the more we come to know about them. But what we discover is not always easy to embrace. Suppose we find that the friend we once knew as thoughtful, kind, funny, and considerate can also be petty, hurtful, and depressingly moody? What if the "free spirit" we initially found so appealing in her can also lead her to be careless and thoughtless? What does it mean to seek the good of another then? Friendships are important settings for our growth in goodness because they tutor us in the hard lessons of love. Sometimes love must take the form of patience as we bear the shortcomings of another and care for her despite her imperfections. No real friend abandons another at the first intimations of human frailty and weakness; in fact, to remain faithful and committed to a friend, and to continue to seek her good despite that discovery, is proof of real friendship.[12]

At some point in any real friendship benevolence and beneficence must be expressed through forgiveness. Can we really be committed to what is best for a friend if we are unwilling to work through the hurts and disappointments that are part of any friendship? Do we really want our friend's happiness if we allow her failures to obscure the good we once saw in her? Friendships are morally praiseworthy because in order for them to grow, deepen, and be sustained over time, a variety of virtues must be developed in the friends. Friendships cannot last unless the friends become skilled in justice, generosity, and patience. They have no future without the virtues of loyalty, trustworthiness, care, and forgiveness. These are all exquisite expressions of goodness, and they are regularly acquired through the life of good and lasting friendships. They are part of what it means to commit ourselves to seeking the good of another for his or her own sake. And they are one important reason why friendships play a significant role in our moral development.

A second way friendship facilitates our growth in goodness is that through our friends we come to know ourselves better.[13] If the overall purpose of the moral life is to help us grow in goodness and to acquire the qualities of character necessary for human excellence, then we need to be aware of the tendencies and dispositions in us that might work against this. But oftentimes we are not. We are not always the best judges of our character, especially when it comes to our shortcomings. Our self-knowledge is limited, but also selective and sometimes deliberately cloudy. I don't want to see, much less to admit, that I can be stingy, stubborn, or self-righteous. I don't want to recognize my tendency to be judgmental and harsh and intolerant. And maybe I have become very skilled at denying how anger and resentment can control me or how envy can make me devious. In all of us there are impediments to goodness—attitudes, tendencies, and habits that drag us down and turn us away from the good. It can be arrogance in one person, greed in another, vindictiveness in a third. We need to know these unflattering aspects of ourselves because unless we address them we will be stalled in our quest toward the good. Or, what is worse, we will turn away from the good because we shall no longer recognize where it can really be found. We think we'll find happiness by holding on to a grudge or by nursing resentments. We think it will be better always to put ourselves first, to be manipulative when necessary, or to lie when the truth might inconvenience us.

This is where our friends can help us. If a friend really does want what is best for me and truly is committed to my good, she must tell me the truth. She must care enough about me to point out any attitudes or behavior I may have that turn me away from the good instead of toward it. I may not always want to know what she recognizes in me, but I need her insight and her guidance to help me wrestle with my own worst tendencies. Friends are patient with each other, but they must also be truthful with each other. I do not serve a friend well if I see him courting attitudes or habits that really are not good for him, but say nothing. I don't give up on him as he struggles with these shortcomings, but neither do I merely accept them. A true skill and requirement of friendship is knowing how to tell a friend that he or she needs to change. This takes courage, and it only works where trust is strong, but it is an essential element of benevolence and beneficence because we cannot want the best for our friends if we stand by and say nothing when we see them developing habits we know will only hurt them.

Thus, friends must feel free enough to offer each other guidance and counsel, but also correction. If I see a friend becoming quite casual about lying or dishonesty, I need to call this to his attention and warn him about its effects. If he sees me blaming others for my own mistakes or becoming better at naming others' faults than being honest about my own, he must tell me. In this way, friends, aware of each other's shortcomings as well as their strengths, help one another grow toward the good. They recognize that as they pursue what is best they may stumble and lose their way more than they stay on the path. So they steady one another by encouraging each other to grow in their best qualities and to wrestle with their worst. They know that the moral life is a quest, an unfolding adventure, so their growth in goodness takes time. But they also know that it requires an honest appraisal of themselves, the good along with the bad, and often only friends see this clearly enough to offer that assessment. This is another reason a happy life is impossible without them. Although it is hard to admit, we cannot be happy without someone willing not only to support and encourage us, but also to tell us where we may have gone wrong. What is lost to us if we lack such friendships in our lives? Or if we refuse to allow them to develop?

A third way that friendship—and good communities too—aid our growth in goodness and our quest for happiness is that friends help us stay focused on and committed to what is best and most promising.[14] If we envision the moral life as an ongoing training in goodness, it is easy to imagine how anyone could grow weary and disheartened. The good we seek is hard to attain and never completely in our grasp. We grow in this goodness, but we never completely possess it. This is particularly true in the Christian life because here the goodness we aspire to is the unexcelled goodness of God. If, as Christians believe, our happiness depends on sharing in and being transformed by God's goodness, then our training in happiness always stands unfinished. None of us can ever surpass the goodness we see in God. We approach this goodness, but we never master it. We grow in its beauty, but we certainly never exhaust it. In the Christian life we remain seekers, people on a quest.

The difficulty with this approach to the moral life is that if the goal of the quest continually eludes us—and if it asks so much of us—it is easy to become discouraged and to begin to look for more congenial ways of living. Perfect friendship with God may be the most promising possibility of our lives, but it is also the most demanding. Even if our most exquisite happiness resides in intimacy and communion with God, it is hard to sustain ambition for such a life, not only because so many things pull us away from it, but also because in this world we can never know it fully or completely. When the good we seek perpetually transcends us, we are tempted to direct our attention to other more attainable goals or to be lured by more comfortable and achievable understandings of happiness; in short, it is easier to be a profligate consumer or a polished pleasure seeker than it is to be a faithful Christian. Too, we grow disillusioned as we wrestle with setbacks and disappointments or with our own weaknesses and failures. In fact, a Christian account of happiness almost ensures occasional disillusionment because it argues that our happiness depends on a radical change of ourselves, a thorough conversion of our hearts that will always be incomplete. How then do we sustain an ambition for goodness—how do we continue to find goodness attractive—when growing in it is more than the work of a lifetime? How do we persevere when there are so many rival understandings of happiness and so many conflicting views about what counts as a good life?

It is impossible without the support and companionship of friends or the encouragement we find in healthy, strong communities, hopefully the kind of communities we find in our churches. Aquinas described perseverance as "prolonged endurance in any good which is difficult,"[15] which is an apt description for a life of Christian discipleship. He agreed that it is hard to remain committed on our journey toward the goodness found in God, hard to persevere in our quest for its happiness. Thus, Aquinas, like Aristotle, knew we cannot persevere alone, we can only persevere together. Anything difficult is more easily managed when others share in it with us. Whether it is finishing a challenging task, getting through a difficult semester, or suffering through periods of adversity and darkness, anything seems more manageable when we are not forced to face it alone. Without the support, presence, and encouragement of friends and communities, we are easily defeated. Without others to turn to, we lose hope. Any difficult undertaking demands perseverance, but we can hardly persevere without others who struggle with us precisely because they believe the goal we seek, no matter how difficult, is worth the effort it requires. As Stanley Hauerwas and Charles Pinches write, perseverance or constancy is "a communal virtue. It is not something one of us possesses alone, but something we share and into which we help each other grow."[16]

Their point is that "good people help keep each other good."[17] And they do this by reminding each other of the value of the quest. The value of anything is both sustained and enhanced when others share in it with us. This is why the Christian life of discipleship requires good friendships and good communities—why, in fact, it requires a certain kind of church. Even when the goal of the journey is friendship and happiness in God, we need others to assure us of its value, others to remind us that seeking God must always be the core commitment for our lives. It is what Christians in their friendships and in their faith communities ought to do for one another. Churches ought to be communities in which the "friends of God" steady one another when any are tempted to give up. They ought to be communities where one person is able to supply the energy, zeal, and commitment another might occasionally lack. Whether through humor, counsel, encouragement, or simply their presence, Christians should do for one another what good friends always do: They should help one another remain resolute in the pursuit of the most promising good for our lives.

Finally, friends and communities are indispensable elements to the moral life because the best and most enduring friendships, and the strongest and healthiest communities, provide the very form of life necessary for growing in goodness and acquiring happiness.[18] We do not become good haphazardly, much less single-handedly; rather, we become good by participating in ways of life that form us more deeply in the good. Friendship and community are integral elements of such a way of life because we grow in goodness and know happiness only by spending time with good people and by seeking what is best together with them. This is why friendship is more than just a comforting relationship. It is also a moral enterprise because we come to embody the good not directly, but in and through relationships with others who are seeking the good as well. Aristotle touched on this when he noted that we need friends "only to provide what we are unable to provide for ourselves."[19] His point was precisely that the one thing we cannot provide ourselves is goodness and happiness. Goodness and happiness cannot be attained on our own because both are, as it were, a community endeavor, a group project. Put differently, if the moral life is a quest for happiness and goodness, we must not see ourselves as solitary sojourners. Such a life can only be undertaken, and sustained, in certain kinds of relationships and communities that foster habits and practices that nurture goodness.

Similarly, if the Christian moral life requires the transformation of ourselves in the goodness of God, it has to be a cooperative enterprise because such a radical and ongoing transformation can occur only with others who desire that goodness as well, and through a way of life that makes it possible. This is why friendships do more than make our training in goodness pleasant or interesting. Friendships—or certain kinds of moral communities—make a life of goodness possible because the only way for us to grow in goodness, and thus know happiness, is with people who share a love for what is best and are committed to helping one another grow in it. We need others to create a way of life in which together we can move toward God by being conformed more completely to the goodness of God. This is what friends and community members provide for one another. It is not just that they help one another better understand the attitudes, habits, and practices that are conducive to goodness and holiness; rather, it is that through the disciplines, rituals, and practices of a shared way of life, they acquire all those things together. In order to flourish in goodness, particularly the goodness of God, we need people who embrace a shared conception of life. We need people who agree on what is most important in life and why it demands our wholehearted devotion. But we especially need people who want to aspire to these things with us because there is no other way for us to reach our good. Good friendships and vibrant, strong communities are the settings in which we acquire, exercise, and flourish *together* in the goodness that is God. In more theological language, it is why we need a church and what, at its best, ought to be happening in our churches.

Charity—Seeking Happiness through Friendship with God

We are happy when we possess our true good. But for Christians the true good is not an abstract idea but a personal relationship. Christianity teaches that we are made for communion with God and will be fulfilled only by sharing in the life of God. Nothing less than being drawn together into the triune life of God will make us happy. Thomas Aquinas spoke of this intimate, personal relationship with God as a friendship and described this friendship in the language of charity.[20] The life of happiness *is* the communal life of charity because living in friendship with God is the deepest and most complete way for us *together* to participate in the goodness of God. We rightly think of a person of charity as one who is kind, considerate, and thoughtful. But for Aquinas charity, while including such behavior, involves something far more compelling and inviting, but also something far more demanding.

For him, charity is not just a singular virtue, but a communal way of life whose rituals, habits, and practices form its members in the being and character of God. Put differently, a life of friendship with God ought to result in a community whose members learn to love as God loves *and* find happiness in doing so. Consequently, charity describes the most expansive community possible because it links us not only to God, but also to every man and woman who, like us, is loved into being by God and called to communion with God.

For Aquinas, a life of friendship with God does not narrow our world but dramatically expands it. We misunderstand the meaning of charity as *friendship*, but also as *happiness*, if we think it refers only to one's individual relationship with God. The friendship with God that is our happiness is never between God and ourselves alone because the more we grow in friendship with God, the more we are challenged to extend the parameters of our love to others. In the Christian moral life, happiness demands participating in an ever-growing community of love that is centered in intimate and abiding friendship with God, and from that friendship reaches out to others. It is never a matter of me alone sharing in the highest possible good, but of all of us *together* partaking of that good and, in doing so, learning to befriend others.

In shaping his understanding of happiness, Aquinas essentially follows Aristotle's logic. In his *Nicomachean Ethics* Aristotle claimed that happiness is not so much a state, but whatever activity or set of activities brings about the fullest possible development of human beings. Happiness is not so much something that we are, but something that we do. Aquinas agreed. Like Aristotle, he argued that the most satisfying happiness for human beings depends on achieving the special excellence proper to human beings. But Aquinas differed from Aristotle in what he took this excellence to be. For Aristotle, the greatest possible happiness was found in communities of the virtuous, communities in which true "friends of the good" flourished together in a *strictly human* good. Aquinas envisioned happiness similarly to the extent that it involved people flourishing together in community, but for him the center of this shared life was the divine good of charity, the supernatural good that is friendship with God and that is offered to everyone.[21]

As mentioned in chapter 1, the life of charity rests on a gift. If friendship with God is our happiness, it is possible only through grace. We can live together in friendship with God only because through grace we already partake in God's life now. To paraphrase 1 John 4:16, we can abide in friendship with God only because God, from the beginning of our lives, abides intimately in us. Aquinas captured this by saying the life, goodness, and happiness of God are "communicated" or "infused" in us through charity. As Liz Carmichael writes, "The Latin word *communicatio* similarly denotes sharing, participation and fellowship, but it can also mean the act of communicating the ability to participate. Thomas employs its entire range of meaning: God imparts or communicates his 'beatitude,' his joyful life to us; and through this transforming gift we are enabled to share the divine life actively with him."[22] Perhaps the pivotal truth of charity is that God *chooses us* for friendship. God seeks us, and even desires us, more than we may seek or desire God. Or as 1 John 4:10 puts it, "In this is love: not that we have loved God, but that he loved us." Charity is a gift of grace, a truly supernatural endowment, never something we can merit or achieve on our own. If the highest good for us is to become like God by together growing in the goodness of God, this is possible only because we have first been befriended by God.[23] Our most perfect happiness is a gift, something bequeathed to us, and not the result of our own strategies or calculations.

Charity—A Distinctive and Challenging Way of Life

But it is a gift that is meant to grow. No more than Aristotle's friends possessed goodness instantly do we ever live in perfect friendship with God. Grace begins the life of friendship, but like any relationship it can either deepen or weaken over time. Too, as with any relationship, we can neglect friendship with God, be indifferent to it, or completely reject this understanding of our lives. The most promising relationships can die and so can one's relationship with God. We cannot take the gift of charity for granted. To truly receive it is to begin to live according to it by allowing our love for God to inform everything we do. Like a couple in a marriage whose constant aim is to strengthen the gift of their love, one's abiding intention in the Christian life must be to grow more deeply in friendship with God. And just as the gift of a marriage requires that spouses give a particular shape to their life if that gift is not to be lost, so too does friendship with God call us to a distinctive way of life.

One danger of the language of friendship with God is that it can sound so abstract—so vague and ethereal—that it can seem to have no practical consequences. But charity is not meant to be an impractical and unreachable ideal; rather, as *the way of happiness* it is an actual, distinctive, and very challenging way of life. The grace of charity introduces us to a new kind of existence. It summons us to take up a new way of life with its own particular expectations and practices, and one that is meant to be embraced not just occasionally, but daily. To enter friendship with anyone is to take up a new way of life because every friendship in some way reorders our lives and gives us new commitments. Every friendship makes a visible difference in our lives inasmuch as our lives begin to be structured around certain persons and projects rather than others. This is also the case when we live together in friendship with God. Charity does not take us out of the world, but calls us to live in the world differently by embracing all of the commitments and all of the characteristics of a friend of God. A life of friendship with God, if it is to be more than vacuous piety, has to be visibly displayed. There must be behavior and practices through which friendship with God not only can be known, but can grow and deepen.[24]

What would such a life look like? What would it involve? One way to answer this is to reflect on the kind of life made possible for us by Christ. If Jesus is the definitive example of a life lived in friendship with God, then we should turn to him—and the saints who came after him—to learn what the life of charity might entail. In his book *Life on the Vine*, theologian Philip Kenneson says Christians are called to cultivate love, to cultivate joy, peace, patience and kindness, to cultivate goodness, faithfulness, gentleness, and self-control, because each of these "fruits of the Spirit" (Gal. 5:22–23) were virtues of Christ.[25] We grow in friendship with God when we imitate the goodness made visible in Christ. A life of friendship with God cannot be one that is ruled by anger, dissension, harshness, bitterness or sadness, envy or jealousy. Not only are these things incompatible with the goodness of God, but they also, as Jesus taught, draw us away from God, as well as from one another. Similarly, lying, betrayal, cynicism, and cruelty have no place in the community of charity because they contradict the actions by which Jesus teaches that we live as the friends of God and, therefore, are happy. Love, joy, peace and patience, kindness and goodness, faithfulness, gentleness, and self-control are communal ways of being that form us in friendship with God and thus constitute happiness.

The life of Jesus illustrates that happiness comes to us when our lives are conformed to the goodness of God. Jesus reveals what that goodness is and how it is "made flesh," what it requires and the diverse ways it can be embodied in our ordinary lives. Jesus calls his followers to "put on" virtues such as truthfulness, justice, compassion, mercy, and forgiveness because through them we are "trained" in the goodness of God and live as the friends of God. All of the virtues to which Jesus calls us in the gospels are constitutive of happiness because in exercising them we share in the goodness and holiness of God. On the other hand, Jesus warns about the dangers of greed and pride and arrogance, of harshness, deceit, and vindictiveness, because such ways of being draw us away from God. By cultivating these things we remove ourselves from a life of friendship with God and therefore become strangers to happiness.

Charity—Expanding the Circle of Love

An important critique of using friendship with God as a metaphor for the Christian life is that wrongly understood it can seem to reduce the Christian life to something that is always comfortable and consoling, and something about which we are always in control. God, the "friend," is there to support and reassure us, but never to challenge us. God pleases and is always nice, but never demands. Friendship with God is then seen not as a radically demanding way of life, but one that asks nothing of us while assuring us that everything about us is fine. In this understanding of friendship with God, God must conform to us, not we to God. As Liz Carmichael warns, the danger of speaking about God as friend is that God becomes "a cozy and tolerant companion, one among many whom we might care to collect as a friend, a congenial item to add when constructing a 'designer spirituality' for ourselves. That reduces God to the status of an existent among other existents, trivializing a relationship that if real, affects and transforms our whole being."[26]

A "dark side" of any friendship, including friendship with God, is to allow friendships to narrow and collapse our world because they extend only to those who agree with us, who think the way we think, and never challenge us to change.[27] But the friendships practiced by Christians, if they are truly modeled on God, should never shrink our horizons of love. In the Gospels, Jesus commands us to love, but not in the way we ordinarily think about love. He intensifies the summons to love by saying we must love not as the world teaches us to love, but "As I have loved you, so you also should love one another" (John 13:34).[28] God's love alive in Christ becomes the rule for human love, and this is what makes charity a risky and ultimately revolutionary kind of love, and perhaps a very unnerving understanding of happiness. True friends of God can never restrict their love. A life lived in friendship with God does not allow our love to become calculating or safe. We are to befriend others as God has befriended us; thus, our love can never be choosy or selective. We may like some more than others, and certainly be attracted to some more than others, but we cannot choose to love some while hating others if we are to imitate the befriending love of God.

God befriended us in Christ and continues to befriend us in the Spirit. But the only way God could reach out to us in friendship was if the horizons of God's own love would expand. God could not have befriended us if God had chosen to keep the divine circle of love safely closed. As Paul intimated in his famous "Philippians' hymn" (Phil. 2:6–11), when God became one of us in Jesus, the divine circle of love burst open. In Jesus God's love moved beyond its Trinitarian life, entered our world, and was offered to all.[29] In the same way, a life of friendship with God summons us to move beyond our safely chosen parameters of love. Like the divine love, our love too is to burst open to include the different and the disagreeable, the hostile and the strange, because in Christ God befriends us all.

This is how a community of the friends of God is to love in order to continue God's ways in the world. This is how they are called to understand happiness. Through their love for others, even their enemies, friends of God show the world how God has loved us. In this way the distinctive life of charity is most visibly, poignantly, and hopefully displayed. It is easy to dismiss such a capacious love as impossibly idealistic. We know how hard it can be faithfully to love one who loves us, so how can we really love the unlikable and the strange, much less our most fervent enemies? But the very credibility of a life of friendship with God hinges on Jesus' radical command of love being a real possibility. A life of friendship with God is uselessly sentimental if it lacks the power to remake the world according to the plans and purposes of God. If the love of the friends of God cannot help transform the world in hope and joy by working to overcome hostilities and divisions, then such a life is a consoling illusion, not an invitation to find happiness in furthering the creative and redemptive activity of God.

Christians can love as Jesus loved, however fragile and imperfect their efforts may be, because God's love for us makes such love possible. The conventional understanding of love is that we restrict our love to people we like and enjoy, and especially to people who love us in return. The problem with practicing such love alone, however, is that it lacks the power to change anything; it cannot make anything new. The love of charity is decidedly unconventional, but also decidedly innovative and hopeful because it has the power to move us beyond the comfortable and familiar boundaries of love in order to create something new. Because God transcended "the conventional limits of love and friendship" in the life of Jesus, and particularly in his death and resurrection, we can love in more creative and hopeful ways now.[30] For Christians, love and friendship are transformed by the grace of Christ, and that opens previously unthinkable possibilities for both. What before was seen to be absolutely impossible—to love one's enemies—becomes, thanks to Christ, not only thinkable, but also commanded! The aim of a life of friendship with God is to create a community where we extend to all the love, goodwill, and forgiveness that God offered to us.[31] In the Christian life, to create a community of "universal friendship" whose love is centered in God and offered to all is happiness. This is the kind of community churches are called to be.

Obviously, the kind of world envisioned by charity and constitutive of happiness is not easily achieved, and for many people not even plausible.

More than anything, it's risky and costly because it does not allow us to narrow the boundaries of love. Friendship with God demands that we wrestle with the fear, hurt, mistrust, hostility, rejection, and suspicion that fragment communities and separate us from one another. It summons us to tear down walls that divide, rather than hide behind them. But we are often much more accustomed to alienation and estrangement than we are to reconciliation and community. Consider the trajectory of our own lives. As children we tend to be more open and trustworthy than we are as adults. But as we grow, our lives typically become "progressively narrower and more regulated . . . containing enemies as well as friends, jealousies and disillusionment as well as trust."[32] The hurt, betrayal, and disappointment we suffer and inflict counsel us to live cautiously and guardedly; they teach us to narrow the circle of love, not extend it. We learn not to trust, not to befriend, but also not to risk and, therefore, not to grow. The happiness found in living in friendship with God can open us to further hurt and disappointment because of what it will ask of us, but what is the cost of not taking that risk?

People striving to follow the life of charity do not deny the multiple ways we both inflict and receive hurt from one another, nor do they deny how skilled we can be at failures in love. But they refuse to allow these breakdowns in love to prevail, because they know that happiness is impossible for all of us if they do. They believe that "the deep meaning of society is that people should 'live as friends with one another.'"[33] And they also believe that this is God's fundamental work in the world. The ministry of God in Christ and the Spirit, and hopefully also through us, is a ministry of peacemaking and reconciliation, a ministry of healing, restoring, and making one. Charity is a revolutionary love, not a safe and cautious one, and friendship with God is a risky and challenging way of life precisely because it commits us to fashion our lives according to the risk-taking love of God that we see dramatically embodied in Jesus. But it is also an eminently joyous and hopeful way of life that is guided neither by the hurts of the past nor the shortcomings of the present, but by a vision of the future reign of God, that community of perfect and eternal mutual love. "Universal friendship becomes reality in heaven, the 'perfectly ordered and completely harmonious fellowship in the enjoyment of God, and of each other in God,'" Liz Carmichael writes. "There we shall see each other full of God, for God will be all in all. 'Who,' Augustine asks, 'does not long for that city, from which no friend leaves, into which no enemy enters?' There all our loves, too often one-sided or painful in this life, are fulfilled in eternal friendship and true peace."[34]

Conclusion

This is the happiness for which a life of friendship with God trains us. It's a life worth living because of what it makes possible for ourselves and for the world. Still, it is an odd and even unnerving way to think about happiness because we are not accustomed to think that happiness requires nurturing a "friendship to all the world,"[35] including the world of the unlikable, the seemingly unlovable, and the hostile. We assume our love must be sparingly given if we are to avoid the "slings and arrows" that bring us sorrow. We assume bliss will come not when the circle of love becomes ever more expansive, but when we remain at its center. But if our ultimate good and happiness is found in God, and if it is in "loving as I have loved you" that we most resemble God, then Jesus' command to love all our neighbors (not just the likable ones) is indeed the path to happiness.

It is not an easy path to take up, and it surely is not one we can navigate alone. A life devoted to friendship with God requires community because we need others—especially the holy ones who have gone before us—to instruct us in the ways of this radical love and to support us in our struggle to achieve it. The church should be such a community, a true fellowship of charity. It isn't always, but it should teach us that real happiness is a quest we pursue together, a true "cooperative enterprise" through which we help one another grow together in the holiness and goodness of God. In this life, our happiness will always be imperfect and incomplete because our transformation in God's goodness is never finished. But those trained in the love, goodness, and happiness of God envision a happiness where love beats unhindered and unimpaired in the perfect community where God's befriending love is extended to all and received by all.

This chapter began with the recollection of a high school reunion where long-ago friends were reminded that a good and happy life is something we pursue together. But they also realized that the bond of their friendship was fresh and resilient—unbreakable for more than thirty years—because the happiness they had been formed in was charity, the daunting but joyous life of living together in friendship with God. That is a rich and good life, and it is an immeasurably hopeful and joyous one. But it is also full of setbacks, discouragement, periods of disillusionment, and even moments of defeat. If we align our lives with this quest, we certainly need the companionship of friends, but we also need to be equipped with the expertise and skills of the virtues. There is no way we can be steadfast in the good and rich in happiness without them, and they are the subject of chapter 3.

Some Questions for Reflection and Discussion

1. Do you think there is a "best possible life" for human beings? If so, what would it include for you? How do you think most people would understand this?
2. What do you see as the necessary qualities for good friendships? What has been the role of friendships in your own life?
3. What are some of the good things that friends do for one another? Are there friends who have made you better? If so, in what way? Are there ways you have made your friends better?
4. How would you see the role of friendship in the moral life? Do you think such relationships are hard to find? Are they rare?
5. How would you understand a life of friendships with God? What might be some of the rewards of such a life? What might be some of its challenges?
6. Has this chapter changed what you think a church should be?

Notes

1. Liz Carmichael, *Friendship: Interpreting Christian Love* (London: T & T Clark International, 2004), 15.
2. J. L. Ackrill, "Aristotle on Eudaimonia," in *Essays on Aristotle's Ethics*, ed. Amelie Oksenberg Rorty (Berkeley: University of California Press, 1980), 28.
3. Herbert McCabe, OP, *The Good Life: Ethics and the Pursuit of Happiness* (New York: Continuum, 2005), 7.
4. Paul J. Wadell, *Friendship and the Moral Life* (Notre Dame, IN: University of Notre Dame Press, 1989), 35–41.
5. Aristotle, *Nicomachean Ethics*, trans. Martin Ostwald (Indianapolis, IN: Bobbs-Merrill Educational Publishing Co., 1962), 1099b25.
6. McCabe, *The Good Life*, 6.
7. Stanley Hauerwas and Charles Pinches, *Christians Among the Virtues: Theological Conversations with Ancient and Modern Ethics* (Notre Dame, IN: University of Notre Dame Press, 1997), 13.
8. McCabe, *The Good Life*, 50.
9. L. Gregory Jones, "The Theological Transformation of Aristotelian Friendship in the Thought of St. Thomas Aquinas," *New Scholasticism* 61, no. 4 (1987): 374.
10. Lawrence A. Blum, *Friendship, Altruism, and Morality* (London: Routledge & Kegan Paul, 1980), 67–71. See also Paul J. Wadell, *Becoming Friends: Worship, Justice, and the Practice of Christian Friendship* (Grand Rapids, MI: Brazos Press, 2002), 67–68.
11. Carmichael, *Friendship*, 16.

12. Carmichael, *Friendship*, 59.
13. Wadell, *Becoming Friends*, 69–71.
14. Wadell, *Friendship and the Moral Life*, 59–61.
15. Thomas Aquinas, *Summa Theologiae* (New York: McGraw-Hill, 1966), II-II, 137,1.
16. Hauerwas and Pinches, *Christians Among the Virtues*, 36.
17. Hauerwas and Pinches, *Christians Among the Virtues*, 36.
18. Nancy Sherman, *The Fabric of Character: Aristotle's Theory of Virtue* (Oxford: Clarendon Press, 1989), 127.
19. Aristotle, *Nicomachean Ethics*, 1169b8.
20. Aquinas, *ST*, II-II, 23,1.
21. Paul J. Wadell, "Growing Together in the Divine Love: The Role of Charity in the Moral Theology of Thomas Aquinas," in *Aquinas and Empowerment: Classical Ethics for Ordinary Lives*, ed. G. Simon Harak, SJ (Washington, DC: Georgetown University Press, 1996), 148.
22. Carmichael, *Friendship*, 111.
23. Hauerwas and Pinches, *Christians Among the Virtues*, 46.
24. For further elaboration of this point, see Wadell, "Growing Together in the Divine Love," 154–58.
25. Philip D. Kenneson, *Life on the Vine: Cultivating the Fruit of the Spirit in Christian Community* (Downers Grove, IL: InterVarsity Press, 1999), 32–34.
26. Carmichael, *Friendship*, 165–66.
27. Carmichael, *Friendship*, 198.
28. Hauerwas and Pinches, *Christians Among the Virtues*, 45.
29. Hauerwas and Pinches, *Christians Among the Virtues*, 45.
30. Carmichael, *Friendship*, 39.
31. Carmichael, *Friendship*, 51.
32. Carmichael, *Friendship*, 178.
33. Carmichael, *Friendship*, 179.
34. Carmichael, *Friendship*, 61.
35. Carmichael, *Friendship*, 139. Carmichael is citing Jeremy Taylor.

CHAPTER THREE

~

Facing Shipwreck and Bandits

Virtues and the Quest for Happiness

We are pilgrims, people on the way.

Thinking of the moral life as a journey is fitting because from the moment our lives are set in motion at birth we are on a pilgrimage searching, exploring, reaching out for whatever we think will bring us joy. Initially, the objects of our quest are small—as babies we'd crawl to the first thing that caught our eye. Later, taking our feeble first steps, we'd stumble across the room for a stuffed animal or a doll to content us, but only momentarily because soon something else would grab our attention and we'd set forth anew. As the years unfold, the geography of our journey changes and we take up more expansive adventures. We leave home to chase after dreams. We venture off to schools; fall in and out of love; try our luck with various careers; succeed, fail, and try again. We get lost, sidetracked, and sometimes even ambushed on our journeys, but short of death, the pilgrimage never ends because to be human is to be a wayfarer, a people on the move.

The philosopher Josef Pieper calls this our *status viatoris*, the "condition or state of being on the way,"[1] and says it is the "innermost core" of what it means to be a creature.[2] As human beings we are never anything other than pilgrims because we never fully possess what we desire. We move toward wholeness, but we never know it completely. We strive for happiness and satisfaction, but are never so content that we don't reach out for more. Pieper calls it the "inherent 'not yet' of the finite being,"[3] that inescapable condition of being orientated to fulfillment but never quite knowing it completely. And so the infant's gesture of reaching out defines us throughout our lives.

The objects of our attention change, but we never stop wanting, desiring, and striving. We make progress toward our goals, but no matter what we achieve, we press forward because there is always something better that calls to us, always something more that beckons.

This is especially true when what we are reaching for is the love and goodness of God. The Christian life is a pilgrimage, an always unfolding quest whose destination is lasting communion with God. But it is a happiness that must always be pursued, but never fully possessed, because it requires the ongoing transformation of ourselves in the goodness of God, and at no point is that conversion complete. We strive for this goodness, we grow more deeply into it, but we are never perfectly conformed to it. The "not yet" character of life abounds in the Christian life because the remaking of ourselves in holiness will always be unfinished. At what point can we exhaust the goodness of God? When can we say no further growth in God's goodness is possible for us? Moreover, sometimes we tire of the quest because it is difficult, wander away from God, and chase other possibilities. We explore other paths, pursue countless dead ends, and sometimes lose our way so completely that we have no idea what we should be seeking and no idea that we are lost. When the geography of one's quest reaches not for the stars but for the kingdom of God, there is no shortage of ways to get sidetracked, no lack of opportunities to be discouraged. In the Christian life the pilgrim's destination is happiness in communion with God, but that is a long and challenging quest that is easily forsaken for less demanding possibilities.

This is why we need the virtues. We need skills and qualities of character that will keep us focused on what is best for us. We need "habits of being" that strengthen us in our pursuit of excellence lest we fall short of the happiness that is meant to be ours. But there are so many ways that can happen. When writing about the virtue of courage, Thomas Aquinas said that a "brave man . . . does not shrink from a journey . . . because of fear of shipwreck or bandits."[4] We can imagine this as the courage one needs to travel through a dangerous country or to undertake a perilous voyage. But we can also imagine it as an apt metaphor for the journey of life, a journey no one can complete without bravery and perseverance, because it is fraught with perils too. Think of the times we are "shipwrecked" by disappointment, discouragement, or adversity. Think of how suffering, whether from illness, great loss, or terrible sorrow, can be a "bandit" that steals away our happiness and convinces us the good we seek will never be ours. Think of how we are shipwrecked by choices that turn out badly, by foolish decisions and wasted opportunities. Too, there may be "thieves" along the way who rob us of hope and confidence, thieves whose cynicism, thoughtlessness, or casual maliciousness beats us down and steals life from us. But we are also ransacked by our own misunderstandings of the good, by our weaknesses and sinfulness, by our refusals to change, and by clinging stubbornly to evil. There are many ways a life can go wrong, because even though we are called to goodness there is no guarantee we will seek it, learn to love it, and live to become one with it.

In the Christian life, training in happiness is also necessarily training in the virtues. In this chapter we will examine the connection between goodness, happiness, and the virtues by considering first what virtues are and why we need them, how they are acquired, and what they do for us. But since the Christian life is a pilgrimage on which we together seek happiness and fulfillment in God, we will secondly inquire about what specific virtues we need to develop if we are to enjoy the happiness that is found in friendship with God. No matter how well we plan and prepare for a pilgrimage or journey, much happens that we never anticipate. The most memorable journeys are full of surprises, wrong turns, momentous challenges, and unexpected events, and this is especially true with our pilgrimage to God. As we make our way, we pass through periods of darkness, times marked more by chaos and confusion than clarity, moments when we understand little and doubt much. What habits and skills must we possess if we are not to be "shipwrecked" by all that comes our way? What virtues will help us persevere? Lastly, how do we pursue happiness in a world marked by so much suffering and pain? If, as Christians believe, any one person's happiness is tied up with the happiness of others, can we make our way in friendship with God without befriending the suffering? Can we enjoy the happiness of God if they are left behind? We'll conclude our analysis of the virtues by suggesting that in the Christian life there is no happiness without compassion.

Virtues—Developing Our Potential for Excellence

Human beings are fulfilled in goodness. And goodness describes the excellence that inheres in anything that is what it ought to be. There is a "goodness" to flowers that bloom, to tomatoes that are plump and juicy, to Kentucky bourbon that has been aged in charred white oak barrels just the right number of years. There is "goodness" to a Mozart symphony, to a Michelangelo sculpture, or to a Jane Austen novel. There is "goodness" to predators swift enough to seize their prey and "goodness" in creatures skilled in eluding them. And there is goodness in human beings who have achieved what for us constitutes excellence and perfection. "In its most proper sense," Jean Porter writes, "'goodness' applies to *perfected* being, to whatever is, insofar as it is what it ought to be. A good pen is a pen that writes well, a good desk is sturdy and even, and a good woman is healthy, wise, and virtuous."[5] Porter, taking a cue from Aquinas, notes that there is an innate drive in any creature to seek whatever represents the perfection of its nature. Perfection comes to a creature that has achieved the "full actuality of existence, in accordance with one's potential as a member of a given species."[6] This means one thing for an eagle, something else for a horse, and something altogether different for us. To understand anything's potential perfection, we have to know what it would mean for it to be "good." But in every case something is good when it has developed as much as possible its own distinctive potential for excellence. As Porter writes, to say that "every creature seeks the good" means "that every creature is oriented toward its own goodness, that is, its fullness of being in accordance with the ideal of its species."[7]

The difference, however, between every other species and ourselves is that everything else in existence achieves its perfection naturally or instinctively. All things considered, a flower will grow to bloom, a thoroughbred to be swift, and a retriever to retrieve. Each of them will naturally achieve some degree of goodness because they cannot be totally other than what they were created to be. But we can. We can become something other than what a "good" human being ought to be because, given our ability to deliberate and to choose, we have an active role in our development that other creatures lack. In the proper environment, animals will grow and develop as they ought—they will naturally realize their own distinctive goodness. But our growth and development, as well as our corruption and decline, are primarily not the work of instinct but of our own moral agency. Through our reason, imagination, and free will we are able to fashion ourselves in ways other creatures cannot. This is part of our nobility, but it can also lead to our demise because through the intentions, attitudes, and habits we foster we can turn away from our true good, neglect the potential that is most fittingly ours, and, therefore, ultimately waste our lives. Like every creature, we have an instinctive inclination toward goodness, a fundamental hunger to achieve our distinctively human potential. But there is no guarantee that we will. There is a gap between what we are now and what we need to become; however, unlike other creatures, that gap is closed not naturally but largely through the ongoing actions of our lives. Through the most consistent intentions we adopt, through the way we think, perceive, feel, and act, we can know happiness by realizing our unique human excellence that resides in friendship with God and with all God loves. But we can also choose to widen that gap, by thinking, perceiving, feeling, and acting in ways that draw us increasingly further away from what we were created to be. We can tragically misdirect our lives.

This is why we need the virtues. Sometimes when we hear a person described as virtuous we picture someone who is afraid to enjoy life, someone overly cautious, a bit uptight, and way too respectable. We imagine a person who plays by the rules and never takes chances. Who of us, if told we were about to spend the day with an exemplar of virtue, would conclude that might be fun? But to think this way is to misunderstand what the virtues are. The virtues are the qualities, attitudes, intentions, feelings, and habits we need to develop in order to have a rich and authentically good human life. They are the qualities of character we must possess if we are to achieve the excellence most properly ours. For instance, an athlete must develop certain habits and skills that enable her to achieve excellence in a sport. She must be disciplined, practice diligently, take instruction well, and cooperate with others. For a student to achieve excellence, at the very least he needs the virtue of responsibility, the virtue of perseverance, the virtue of intellectual curiosity, and the virtue of honesty. The virtues matter because they are the habits and skills by which we achieve excellence in any particular field.

But we also need to achieve excellence in life, excellence as persons and as communities, and for this we need certain habits and skills as well. To achieve excellence as human beings we need to be skilled in the virtue of justice because we have to learn what it means to live well with others. This is true whether you are sharing a room in college, part of a family, working in a business, or a member of a church. To achieve excellence as human beings we need expertise in love because even though we are called to love all of our neighbors, we cannot love them all in the same way. Parents recognize this when they learn loving every child equally does not mean loving every child identically. Teachers wrestle with the requirements of love (as well as justice) when they wonder if a student really does deserve another chance. To achieve excellence as human beings we need the virtue of prudence because as we make our way through life we are confronted with many situations in which what it means to do good is not always clear. To achieve excellence in life we need courage and patience and hope because anyone lacking these virtues will be defeated by difficulties or destroyed by adversity. To achieve excellence in life we need to be skilled in forgiveness because even the best relationships weaken through misunderstanding, hurts, and everyday failures in love.

Thus, the virtues do not repress us, they develop us in all the right ways. They are the quintessential humanizing qualities because through them we grow more deeply in our most exquisite excellence as individuals and as communities. The virtues constitute a humanizing way of being and living because through them everything about us, our passions and emotions, our intelligence and our reason, our imagination and our perceptions, our freedom and our choices, even our memories, work together to help us achieve the good. The virtues integrate and direct all our capacities so that everything about us is disposed to attaining the excellence that counts for happiness, the excellence Christians find in friendship with God. As Gilbert Meilaender puts it, with the virtues "we have begun to approach the furthest potentialities of our nature, . . . we are living life characteristic of flourishing human beings."[8] Why do we need the virtues? Because through them we move from simply being oriented or disposed to the good, to consistently embodying and doing the good, and even flourishing in the good. In more theological language, the virtues bring happiness because as we acquire them, are changed by them, and possess them more completely we reach the perfection that is most properly ours, the perfection of radiating the love and goodness of God in everything we do. Through the virtues we become good persons who know what it means to live a good life, a "life that is becoming to a human being"[9] in every possible way. As Russell Connors Jr. and Patrick McCormick summarize, "virtues are those good moral habits, affections, attitudes and beliefs that lead to genuine human fulfillment, even perfection, on both personal and social levels."[10] They are characteristic, habitual, and insightful ways of being and acting that make both who we are and what we do good.

Vices—Habits That Impair Happiness

But there are also characteristic, habitual, and less than insightful ways of being and acting that make who we are and what we do less than good, even evil, and these are the vices. Vices are "poor moral habits, affections, attitudes and beliefs which hinder human fulfillment or perfection, both personally and socially."[11] Vices impair, and ultimately prevent, happiness and fulfillment because cultivating them not only turns us away from the good, but also forms us into persons who can no longer recognize, much less enjoy, the good. If the virtues are habits that form us in the various characteristics of goodness (e.g., justice, love, compassion, generosity), vices are habits that deform, corrupt, and pervert because they train us in habits and practices that are incompatible with human flourishing. Vices make us ill suited for a truly good life. For example, if I become skilled in the vice of selfishness instead of the virtue of generosity, I cannot thrive as a person because my habitual disregard for others will deny me the kinds of relationships I need to be happy. If I have more expertise with envy and jealousy than gratitude, I will be so resentful of the gifts and achievements of others that I will never appreciate my own. Or if I become more adept at imprudence than prudence,

I will wreak havoc in my life and the lives of others because my behavior will be careless and impetuous.

Certain attitudes, intentions, feelings, and actions are incompatible with happiness and a flourishing human life because they undermine the proper development of ourselves in goodness. The vices leave us morally and spiritually malformed. With them we cultivate not excellence, but mediocrity and moral decline. If the moral life is a journey, with the vices we lose our way and ultimately forget what the journey is about. Vices not only sidetrack our pursuit of the good, but also leave us pursuing things that are not good; with them we relinquish the only truly worthwhile human quest in favor of adventures that may initially appear promising but ultimately corrupt and destroy. Take, for instance, the vice of greed. Living to attain as much money as possible is an enticing option. In order to achieve such a goal, one would have to become skilled in greed and enchanted by wealth. But where would pursuing such a life take one? What other goods and possibilities would it deny a person? What is lost to me if I consistently opt to invest my time and energy in attaining wealth rather than in caring for my marriage? What is lost to me if I am so habitually concerned with possessions that I never take time to know the soul of the person who loves me?

Or consider the vice of revenge. It is easy to nurture the habit of revenge because it is always appealing to settle a score by inflicting a little harm on those who have harmed us. But does this bring excellence? Does revenge make us happy? And what if we become so skilled in revenge that we are characteristically vindictive, even cruel? Vices corrupt, vitiate, and destroy; they disfigure us morally and spiritually. They, not the virtues, are the truly oppressive (and ultimately enslaving) habits, because gaining expertise in the vices forms us into the kinds of persons who have no idea what their true good is. The cumulative effect of their ongoing deterioration is to make us strangers to happiness because with the vices everything about us works against our true good. Developing qualities such as pettiness, laziness, dishonesty, greed, malice, cynicism, or unfaithfulness leads not to wholeness and contentment, but to our moral and spiritual disintegration. With them we become fatally unsuited for life.

Virtues—Skills for Completing the Journey

We need the virtues in order to be good human beings. But we also need them to successfully deal with all we will encounter during the course of our lives. If the moral life is a journey, an unfolding odyssey in search of the goods that complete us, the virtues are the skills we need to complete the journey successfully.[12] As people on the way, we confront a variety of challenges, situations, and opportunities. Some assist us in achieving our goals, but others hinder and sometimes even threaten us. On any journey we are confronted by the unexpected. Sometimes the surprises of life work in our favor, but other times they are woefully unsettling. Too, as we move through life we encounter all kinds of persons. Some are cooperative, well intended, and kind, but others are crafty and manipulative, even malicious. Some have our best interests at heart, others are exploitative and untrustworthy. The path of any life is never a completely blessed trajectory. We deal with setbacks and disappointments, painful failures and terrible losses. Loved ones die, cherished relationships end, illness besets us. There is an inherent fragility to any life because the well-being and stability and success we work so hard to achieve can be easily demolished by bad luck, misfortune, or the malice of others.[13]

If we are not to be undone by the challenges and setbacks of life, we need virtues such as courage, hope, patience, and perseverance. When we leave home for the first time, when we begin a new job, when we are confronted with illness, we need courage to help us deal with our understandable fears; otherwise those fears master us and eventually defeat us. Inevitably, we face difficult situations where people, groups, or institutions work against us; without patience, discouragement triumphs and we begin to lose hope. The nature of any quest—particularly the quest of a human life—is to expose us to peril. We see this when we listen to a person's life story. No matter how blessed with security, good fortune, love, and support, no one moves through life unscathed. There are the normal bumps and bruises of life that come from slights, hurtful words, and occasional misunderstandings. But there are far greater calamities that can easily defeat us if we lack the fortitude and resolve necessary for finding our way through them. This is what the virtues give us. They are the attitudes, habits, and qualities of character that enable us "to respond creatively to new situations or unanticipated difficulties."[14] They are the skills we need to negotiate successfully all we might encounter as we take up life.[15]

Every worthwhile quest exposes us to dangers. Many of those dangers are external to us, but sometimes we discover "dangers" within us, elements in ourselves that can sabotage our pursuit of the good. When we are tired or stressed, maybe we learn that we are not as patient and kind as we had thought; or maybe we seek relief in behavior that is not healthy. When things do not go our way, perhaps we grow bitter and resentful and angry. Maybe the tinge of envy we feel reminds us we are not quite gracious enough to rejoice at a friend's success. Or when we are pressured by others to conform, do we discover that we are not strong enough to follow our own convictions? These inner revelations can defeat us if we allow our own weaknesses and imperfections to convince us that aspiring to what is best is impossible for us. And so instead of battling with these "dangers" we surrender to them. We let our weaknesses get the best of us and settle into a moral and spiritual malaise that is not only beneath us, but also prevents our happiness. Unless we develop qualities of character that help us deal with the inevitable perils of the journey, whether external or internal, the quest defeats us. This is why we "cannot leave home" without the virtues.

Acquiring the Virtues—How to Become Experts in Goodness

How then do we acquire the virtues? No one is naturally virtuous, because a virtuous person is someone who does the good consistently, skillfully, insightfully, and even delightfully. Becoming this sort of person takes time. All of us have inclinations to goodness, but an inclination to goodness is not enough because it does not ensure that we will actually do good, especially when doing so is costly or difficult. We have an initial capacity for virtue because as human beings we are oriented to the good, but in order to acquire true expertise in goodness that tendency to the good has to be developed into a habit, a firm, stable, and predictable quality of being and acting. When this occurs we become virtuous persons, persons who are "experts" in goodness because the distinctive qualities of all the various expressions of goodness have become enduring qualities of ourselves. We do the good skillfully and characteristically, not haphazardly or occasionally, because we are good.[16]

Developing a virtue is like developing a talent. Even the most naturally talented musician still has to devote years to practicing if she is to become a true virtuoso in her field. The great artists whose works we admire today did not paint masterpieces from the start. They gained excellence in their field as they experimented, worked diligently, took counsel from others, and learned from their mistakes. Simply having a talent is not enough to assure excellence in a field because that talent has to be honed and deepened over time—the gift must become a true expertise. The same is true in the moral life. We have a capacity for justice and generosity and mercy and courage, but that is not enough to assure goodness because it does not guarantee we will act justly or generously or mercifully or courageously at any particular moment. We possess a virtue only when our disposition for a particular feeling, attitude, or action has developed into an abiding characteristic or habit. When that occurs we can be counted on to be kind or just or compassionate because each of those expressions of goodness has become an enduring quality of ourselves. We are just, generous, merciful, and courageous people because we bear those qualities within us. In this respect, the virtues are not added to an already formed identity, like ornaments on a tree, but are true expressions of that identity.

To describe a virtue as a habit does not mean a virtuous person does the good in a rote or mechanical way. The language of habit can be misleading if we take it to mean that doing the good becomes so second nature to a person that he does what is right almost thoughtlessly and impersonally. On the contrary, the virtues make goodness "second nature" to a person in the same way that throwing a touchdown is "second nature" to a professional football player or having perfect pitch is to an opera singer. Virtuous persons do not think twice about acting justly, because they have become truly just persons. They do not hesitate to tell the truth, because years of refusing to lie have made them genuinely truthful persons. We expect them to be truthful because they have become the kind of persons who would never harm others (or themselves) with a lie. Consequently, to say they characteristically tell the truth simply means honesty and truthfulness are constitutive of who they are as persons.

We acquire a virtue by acting a certain way over time. Virtues are developed by repeated activity, by practice. I become compassionate by regularly making myself available to the needs and sufferings of others. I become generous by recognizing my tendencies to selfishness and refusing to succumb to them. The more accustomed we are to thinking, feeling, and acting a certain way, the easier it will be for us to live that way. The virtues facilitate doing good because the more we practice a particular way of doing the good, the more it becomes part of who we are. And that is because the quality of a particular expression of goodness gradually becomes a quality of ourselves. For example, one act of kindness does not make one a genuinely kind person. But making a practice of kindness will, because the quality of kindness that forms the act gradually transforms the person, making him into the sort of person we expect to be kind because by "practicing kindness" he has become kind. Kindness "becomes him," or even better, he has "become kindness" because what once was only occasionally a quality of his actions is now a true expression of his self. The virtues habituate us in goodness because they imbue not only our acts, but also our character, with goodness. Any habit we develop will "mark" us as persons because a habit represents how we have been formed and shaped through our actions.[17] The virtues are habits that enable a "becoming" of ourselves in the good, while the vices describe a "becoming" of ourselves in habits that diminish and corrupt.

Virtues change us because they are transformative activities. But the extent of that change depends on the degree of goodness we hope to possess. If I simply want to be decently good or conventionally good, the change demanded may be slight; however, if the measure of goodness I seek is found in God—if that is my understanding of excellence—then at no point is the conversion of the self complete. Aquinas expressed this when he said a virtue represents a change or "modification of a subject."[18] But he also noted that the virtues change us in "accord with a standard," and that through them we are brought to the full "term of our development."[19] If the "term" or endpoint of our moral and spiritual development is found in our being conformed to the love and justice and mercy and goodness of God, then acquiring the virtues is truly the work of a lifetime. When virtues are measured according to the goodness of God, I can never perfectly possess them because I can always grow more deeply in their goodness.[20] In his *Summa Theologiae* Aquinas captured the inexhaustible potential of virtue in the Christian life by speaking about the virtues of beginners, the virtues of those well on their way, and the virtues of those who have finally arrived.[21] Those "who have finally arrived" are the saints. Until that final transformation of ourselves in God's goodness, we remain pilgrims on a quest. As we journey toward God, we grow in God's goodness, but we never fully possess it.

Aquinas's analysis of the stages involved in the development of the virtues reminds us that we only understand what a virtue is about when we remember the excellence it is meant to help us achieve.[22] The purpose of any virtue is to help us realize a potential good. For Aristotle this might consist in being a virtuous citizen in Athens. For people in business today it could mean advancing in the corporate world. For athletes, monks, or scholars it will be something else. What counts for excellence varies according to the different roles that characterize our lives and the goals and purposes peculiar to those roles. The form a virtue must take will depend on what it means to achieve excellence and to flourish in a particular role, whether in marriage and family life, in friendships, or in one's professional life. But beyond these particular roles, the most basic purpose of the virtues is to help us succeed at life by achieving excellence as human beings. Christians believe that excellence consists in growing in the goodness of God. In the Christian life, this is what counts for excellence, and if it explains why our goodness is always incomplete, it also explains why our happiness can always increase.

Facing Shipwreck and Bandits—Virtues That Help Us Prevail

Identifying happiness with partaking in the love and goodness of God offers a powerful and compelling way of understanding our lives. But the epic dimensions of this ambition can also leave us skeptical of its realization. We may believe that envisioning our lives as a quest for happiness that is fulfilled in the ongoing transformation of ourselves in the love and goodness of God is the most promising way of understanding our lives. But the costs and challenges involved in this conception of happiness can tempt us to lessen our ambitions by focusing on more easily attainable goals. Sharing in the love and goodness of God may be our most exalted possibility, but it is an endlessly challenging goal and one that always surpasses us.

And so we grow weary and restless, and a little disillusioned. We are tempted to give up on the quest for this kind of happiness and this kind of goodness, and to seek other more congenial adventures. We want a journey whose destination will be more easily reached and whose joy will be more immediately attained. We want less demanding ambitions, less costly loves. This is understandable, but if we lower our hopes and opt for a more comforting account of life, we also deny ourselves our most promising good. If the Christian life is a pilgrim's journey to beatitude with God, we must learn not to be "shipwrecked" by discouragement or "robbed" of our most exquisite hope by struggle or disillusionment. We need virtues to sustain us on the journey to God. Several are necessary, and more will be examined in subsequent chapters. But if we are not to be waylaid in our quest to share in the love and goodness of God, three virtues seem especially crucial: magnanimity, courage, and compassion.

Magnanimity—Sustaining an Aspiration for Greatness

One of the reasons it is easy for us to forsake the quest for ever-deepening friendship with God is that we live in a world that increasingly no longer believes in the value of such a life. To make holiness one's life ambition can seem foolish, even incomprehensible, in societies that teach us to aim for little more than "comfortable survival."[23] As Brian Hook and Russell Reno observe, Christianity is alien to many people today not because it may be hard to believe in God; rather, Christianity is alien because "it pursues excellence without limit and seeks glory everlasting."[24] It is the heroic ambition of Christianity that puts us off, the vastness of its hope that unsettles us. And so instead of aspiring for excellence in God's goodness, we are taught to seek economic success, social acceptance, material comfort, and pleasure. Or we are told through advertising and endless commercials that we need not aim for anything higher than our own gratification, so we immerse ourselves in distractions and trivialities. We think a mistaken life is not one that falls short of goodness, but one that lacks novelty and excitement. In many societies today people are implicitly taught that a life of calculated self-interest is wiser than a life of service. To know success in the world, we have to put ourselves first. As Hook and Reno summarize, "our age is allergic to heroic ambition and inured to the attractions of excellence."[25]

But it is a costly allergy because adopting such ways of living leads not to happiness but to superficiality and emptiness. This is why *magnanimity* is an indispensable virtue for anyone being trained in a happiness that is found not in wealth or power or pleasure or celebrity, but in God. Magnanimity, which literally means to be of "great soul" or "great spirit," is the virtue that trains us to reach for what is best in every dimension of our lives. Josef Pieper says "Magnanimity, a much forgotten virtue, is the aspiration of the spirit to great things."[26] The magnanimous person always aspires to what is best, always strives for what is truly excellent and worthy of our lives, and refuses to settle for less. "Someone is called magnanimous," Aquinas writes, "because he aspires to things which are great simply and absolutely,"[27] and notes that the magnanimous person particularly seeks excellence in goodness and virtue.[28]

Through the virtue of magnanimity our attention remains fixed on the most promising possibility of our lives. The magnanimous person is not deterred by the lure of more immediately appealing possibilities. She does not allow difficulty, fear, or discouragement to dissuade her from persisting in her quest for moral and spiritual excellence. A magnanimous person has "the courage to seek what is great and become worthy of it." She always "decides in favor of what is, at any given moment, the greater possibility of the human potentiality for being."[29] She will not be cowardly in her hopes or puny in her ambitions. She insists on being as great in goodness as she possibly can because she knows happiness is found in risking something heroic. More than anything, she accepts the greatness to which God calls us and for which God has made us capable.[30] She knows our fundamental error is not that we hope for too much, but that we settle for so little. Refusing to abandon her hope, she steadfastly orientates her life to fulfillment in God and is confident that God will help her achieve this end.

The opposite of magnanimity is *pusillanimity*, a vice that is hard to spell and even harder to pronounce, but important to avoid. In writing about this vice, Aquinas described pusillanimity as a "pettiness of mind" by which a person turns away from excellence.[31] If the magnanimous person looks to what is best, the pusillanimous person lowers his sights by consistently opting for what is easier or more appealing. Pusillanimity is a dangerous habit to acquire because through it we not only lose our taste for what is truly good, but also grow comfortable with mediocrity. A magnanimous life will always challenge us, but a pusillanimous life asks nothing of us. The pusillanimous person never has to grow, never has to change or be challenged, because he avoids any goals or commitments that would call him beyond himself in sacrifice, goodness, or love. Comfort and complacency characterize the pusillanimous person, not heroism and excellence. But cowardice befits him as well. The pusillanimous person turns away from any aspirations to greatness because he fears them. He lacks the courage a magnanimous life requires. He is afraid to be as great as God calls him to be, and thus flees from the most exalted possibility for his life. In his analysis of this vice, Aquinas noted that for Aristotle pusillanimity was one of the most damaging habits to develop because by it a person "withdraws from what is good."[32] To withdraw from what is good is an enduring temptation in the Christian life and one the virtue of magnanimity helps us resist.

Courage—For All Those Times We Need to Be Brave

Second, there is courage, the virtue that helps us deal with the fears and difficulties of life. A few years ago I was making a retreat. One of the participants on the retreat was a Native American woman from northeastern Wisconsin. On the last day of the retreat she brought a gift for all of us, a small red cloth pouch that was filled with a few herbs and spices. As she passed these around to each of us, she said that in her tribe you would hold this little pouch in your hand any time you needed "to be brave." Those words—and her gift—have stayed with me because I know how many times I am challenged "to be brave." We need to be brave when we are faced with difficult situations, especially ones that continue over time. We need to be brave when we face obstacles in our lives, whether from other people, institutions, or problems that are not easily solved. We need to be brave when suffering visits our lives, or the lives of people we love. We need to be brave when we face situations we would much rather flee but know we must confront. When we look back over our lives we recognize moments when fear easily could have conquered us, whether the fear came from dealing with intimidating people, threatening situations, or the loss of persons close to us. If we had allowed fear to get the best of us, our lives would have shut down in sorrow, discouragement, and perhaps even despair. Fear stymies us. It keeps us from moving forward because if we are controlled by fear we are unable to confront the everyday obstacles of life. Courage gives us the energy, resolve, and ingenuity necessary to move through the tribulations of life so that they do not deter us on our quest.

But it is easy to be deterred because it is easy to lose heart. When writing about the virtue of courage, Aquinas said courage helps us deal with all that opposes us in life,[33] with all that shakes our confidence or convinces us that the good we seek is either impossible to attain or not worth the hardship it involves. This "opposition" may come from other persons, from the betrayal of friends, from physical difficulties, from financial stress, or from our own limitations and weaknesses. It may come during times of transition, during periods of disillusionment, from the failures of others or the foolishness of ourselves. No matter how fortunate we may be, eventually we struggle with anxiety, stress, and discouragement. No matter how strong our convictions, at some point adversity makes us question them. The traditional model for courage is the battlefield because if our greatest fear is the fear of death, no one wrestles with this more than the soldier under attack. But sometimes the "battlefield" is an appropriate metaphor for our lives. There are so many ways we too can feel under attack. The obstacles we face may not be as mortally perilous as those of a soldier, but they are nonetheless real. And just as any soldier cannot be paralyzed by fear if he or she wishes to survive, neither can we be ruled by fear if we hope to survive life's challenges and grow in life's good. This is why there is no happiness apart from courage.

There are two parts to courage, *perseverance* or *patient endurance*, and *daring*. Perseverance is the aspect of courage that helps us "persist to the end of a virtuous undertaking"[34] when doing so is hard. This "virtuous undertaking" may be trying to live a life of truthfulness, kindness, and integrity. It may refer to our commitment to treat others justly, even when that requires sacrifice from ourselves. It may involve our intention to remain faithful to people we have promised to love, whether as friends, spouses, or parents. In the Christian life, the "virtuous undertaking" is our desire to grow in the goodness of God. It is hard to persevere in a good life because many forces weaken our resolve and lure us away from the path. Like a devious gravitational pull, we are lured from goodness when there is pressure on us to compromise our beliefs. We are lured from goodness by the temptation of more immediately appealing possibilities. And we are lured from goodness because if moral excellence is our goal, it sometimes seems we will never reach our destination. Without the perseverance that courage brings, we easily grow discouraged and our zeal for goodness dims.

It is hard to remain steadfast in the good—hard to persevere—because so much weakens our resolve. Think of how hard it is to tell the truth when others want you to be silent or when you know being truthful may come at great cost, something both prophets and corporate whistleblowers can attest. Think of how hard it can be to refuse to join your peers in something you believe is wrong. Or consider the times when being fair might lessen your popularity with others, whether colleagues, other employees, fellow students, or family members. Any person willing to "be steadfast and not turn away from what is right"[35] needs the perseverance that courage brings. A common failure in the moral life is to turn away from what is right because of fear or difficulty. This may be a typical temptation, but it is one we cannot afford to grow comfortable with because if we flee what is right whenever embracing it is costly, we will move progressively further away from the goodness happiness requires. Ordinarily, we turn away from the good on account of fear or difficulty not all at once, but gradually. But this is precisely the danger. We may hardly notice the effect of moral cowardice on our character, but it must be resisted if our ambition for excellence is not to die. This is why persons of courage, regardless of the obstacles they face, "cling most bravely to what is good."[36]

The second part of courage is daring. Perseverance has to be balanced with daring because the aim of courage is not only to help us endure difficulties, but also to overcome them. Without daring, courage can look like resignation. There may be some hardships we can only suffer through, but endurance should not be our first response to hardship, and certainly not our only response. Initially, courage works not to endure adversity, but to conquer it. With daring we attack all that stands in the way of the good. We don't simply endure injustice, we speak out against it. We don't simply pray for the poor, we denounce the structures, institutions, and policies that perpetuate economic injustice. We do not simply hope that corporations, governments, or churches will be more just, we openly call them to change. Daring is not recklessness or carelessness; rather, it is the insight, imagination, energy, and determination we need to confront and to overcome the "oppressing difficulties" of life whenever we can, and not only for ourselves, but for others as well. We need daring to know how to deal with people who make life a constant battle for us, whether they are peers, intimidating professors, belligerent spouses, or unethical supervisors. Martin Luther needed to be daring when, in the sixteenth century, he spoke out against abuses he saw in the church. And four hundred years later, Dr. Martin Luther King Jr. certainly needed this aspect of courage when, at the cost of his life, he called for an end of racial discrimination. Persons and communities cannot persevere in the quest for goodness without daring. If we are not adept at this dimension of courage, we easily grow complacent with evil, allowing what is not right to become the norm, rather than the exception.

Daring serves the Christian life by helping us attack anything that thwarts our quest for God. As we journey to God we encounter many obstacles or "dangers" that threaten the successful outcome of our quest. These dangers can come from temptations, from the presence of evil in our world, from other persons as well as from ourselves. If we are not to be undone by all the things that impede our growth in the goodness of God and in our flourishing together in the life of charity, we need to be daring. In his analysis of courage Aquinas said, "But courage ought not merely to endure unflinchingly the pressure of difficult situations by restraining fear; it ought also to make a calculated attack, when it is necessary to eliminate difficulties in order to win safety for the future."[37] The "future" Aquinas had in mind was eternal beatitude with God and the saints in heaven. We cannot afford to allow fear or difficulty or opposition to stop our progress to God or to leave us abandoning that quest altogether. As pilgrims on our way to God, we must make "calculated attacks" on anything that might defeat us, eliminating them so that we "win safety for the future." Courage is an essential element to our training in happiness because without it we too easily give up on the quest instead of, with God's help, seeing its completion.

Compassion—Making Suffering Productive of Good for Ourselves and for Others

And then there is compassion. Without this virtue, to speak of the Christian moral life as a quest for happiness can sound too self-interested and egotistical. Without compassion, the Christian moral life easily collapses into concern for one's goodness, one's holiness, one's salvation, as if we could secure any of these without concern for someone else, especially those who suffer. Compassion expands the horizons of our world by reminding us that any genuine understanding of happiness has to take into account the pain and suffering of others. This is especially true in the Christian life because Christians believe the whole of humanity constitutes a body, and as members of this body each person's happiness is inseparably connected to the happiness of every other person. We cannot pursue a life of moral excellence without compassion because a constitutive element of such a life is attending to the plight of others. This is why any training in happiness must include being trained in compassion. Opportunities for learning this virtue abound because on our pilgrimage to God we encounter many along the way who are afflicted and distressed, many who are wounded and broken. A Christian understanding of happiness cannot overlook them.

If magnanimity is the virtue by which we confront temptations to mediocrity and courage the virtue by which we wrestle with fear and discouragement, compassion is the virtue that helps us deal with suffering, whether our own or that of others. No one wants to suffer, and no one should ever seek to suffer. There is a natural tendency in us to want to flee suffering because suffering is fundamentally (if not ultimately) a negative experience. We may endure suffering, but we do not choose it, because by its very nature suffering "restricts, victimizes, oppresses, and deprives."[38] Like an unwelcome guest, suffering displaces us. It intrudes upon our life, upsetting our plans and overturning the order of our world. Something as simple as trying to study for an exam or finish a paper while being plagued with the flu illustrates this. Much more seriously, consider what happens to the person who has just been diagnosed with cancer. Or who has just lost her job. Or whose life has been ravaged by misfortune. We have goals we want to accomplish and we have hopes for the future, but suffering distances us from those goals and weakens those hopes. Suffering can turn our world upside down and make us question everything.

Suffering is a stumbling block on the way to happiness because suffering, at least in some sense, impedes our attainment of happiness.[39] Any experience of suffering is difficult because suffering comes between us and the life we would hope to have. As Sebastian MacDonald comments, "Suffering is the experience of an intrusion into the usual sense of well-being and functioning of a person, inflicting tension, conflict or ill at easeness."[40] Suffering distances us from fundamental goods of life, goods such as health, peace, or security. Most of all, suffering reminds us of the fragility of life, of the limits of our powers, and of our own inescapable mortality. It exposes what we least want to admit, namely, our lack of control, our dependence on others, and our own eventual diminishment. Suffering represents "the lack of something good that should be present, but is not," MacDonald elaborates. "Suffering is undesirable, and one seeks to avoid it, if possible, or else eliminate or diminish it. It is negativity, involving absence, loss, limitation, restriction."[41]

Suffering may be undesirable, but it is hardly unavoidable. No matter how well we plan, as we make our way through life suffering will visit us. It is an unwelcome but inevitable part of every person's journey. If suffering is not to defeat us, there has to be a way for us to suffer well instead of poorly. Put differently, if suffering comes to all of us, there must be "a good way of being human" in the face of suffering.[42] There must be a way for us to seek excellence and achieve good even amid suffering. Patricia McAuliffe describes suffering as an "unchosen negativity," but also notes that "suffering can serve to humanize as well as dehumanize." If suffering is not to dehumanize, "We must make it productive of good."[43]

This is the work of compassion. Compassion makes suffering "productive of good." Compassion is the "solution" to the problem of suffering. This does not mean that with compassion we can necessarily end suffering or remove its causes. But it does mean that compassion teaches us how to grow in love and goodness not only despite suffering, but also through suffering. Compassion helps us make progress in the good life even when suffering persists. Every virtue is a power for being and doing well, and the particular power of compassion is to give us wisdom and strength in relation to suffering. It is through compassion that we learn to suffer well instead of poorly, that we bear our sufferings in hope instead of bitterness. All suffering changes us in some way, but not necessarily for the better. How suffering affects us depends on how we as moral agents respond to it. We have likely had moments when suffering led to self-pity, resentment, and bitterness. But these responses to suffering, no matter how understandable, are ultimately self-defeating not only because they give suffering increased power over us, but also because they shape us in ways that are at odds with goodness. We must learn how to suffer so that the experience, no matter how negative, might change us for the better. This is not to romanticize suffering or to minimize its difficulty. But it is to say that we give suffering more power over us than we ought when we allow it to diminish us morally and spiritually.

Compassion gives us skill and expertise in relation to suffering so that we remain moral agents in our suffering, not simply victims to suffering. As moral agents, we can give meaning to our suffering and determine how we will respond to it. For example, suffering can prompt us to reassess our lives and our priorities. It can lead us to a clearer sense of identity and give us a much keener and truer perspective on life. Suffering can induce a healthy reevaluation of what matters most to us and what we want most to achieve; thus, it can be a means to moral and spiritual conversion. Many people who have endured great suffering say it taught them that nothing matters more in life than loving those entrusted to us, that nothing matters more than kindness, goodness, generosity, and faithfulness. They were not claiming that their suffering was good, but they were insisting that it could be productive of good depending on how they chose to respond to it. Their suffering led to a richer understanding of themselves and their place in the world. Perhaps most importantly, instead of narrowing their world, suffering deepened their sensitivity to others and connected them to fellow sufferers throughout the world. Thus, suffering may be a fundamentally negative experience, but it does not have to be finally negative because goodness accrues to the person who allows her suffering to deepen, not diminish, her humanity. Sebastian MacDonald captures well the excellence that can come from suffering. "To have survived well means that one has remained wholesome through it all, not beaten into defeat, or hardened by bitterness," MacDonald writes. "The results of this development appear as a refinement occurring within the inner recesses of a person's character. This refinement can reflect a certain excellence about the person, who has learned to bear well the suffering, with its duration and intensity, and to utilize the helps one has received to sustain it, on behalf of other sufferers."[44]

As MacDonald's comment illustrates, instead of allowing suffering to isolate us from others, the virtue of compassion deepens our connectedness to others, especially those who suffer. The power of any love is to unite us to the persons we love. Compassion is the form love takes in the face of suffering because instead of abandoning those who suffer, compassion unites us to them by drawing us into their lives.[45] Too, because we know what it is to suffer, compassion enables us to identify deeply and sympathetically with others who suffer. Through compassion we *choose* to enter into the sufferings of others because, having undergone suffering ourselves, we know what suffering does to a person. And because we know the debilitating effects of suffering, we do not want them to suffer alone. We want to be with them in their sufferings and we want to help them. In *Choosing to Feel: Virtue, Friendship, and Compassion for Friends*, Diana Fritz Cates notes, "Compassion is, in part, a disposition deliberately to receive and respond to persons in pain *as if* they were persons with whom we share our lives. That is to say, it is partly a disposition to experience in the presence of persons in pain a sense of 'mutual indwelling' or oneness that makes it possible for us to say meaningfully that we experience something of the same pain that they experience (and we therefore desire and seek the alleviation of that pain as partly our own)."[46]

Compassion empowers us to turn our own familiarity with suffering into a gift for others. Because we recall the frustration, fear, vulnerability, pain, and fatigue that accompanies suffering, we are not only able to understand well what another sufferer is experiencing, but we also are more attuned to knowing how to help alleviate their suffering.[47] The person of compassion has gained a certain expertise in relation to suffering and chooses to use that expertise to benefit others who suffer. In fact, because suffering marked some of their own journey in life, they want to befriend others who suffer in order to help these fellow pilgrims along the way. In this respect, just as our own suffering displaces us by taking us out of the normal routines, comfort, and security of our lives, persons of compassion choose to be displaced a second time by deliberately deciding to be with those who suffer.[48]

For Christians being trained in the happiness of God, compassion is not an optional virtue but a quintessential way of imitating God and, therefore, of becoming like God. In his study of the virtue of compassion, moral theologian James Keenan links compassion with mercy and defines it as "the willingness to enter into the chaos of others so as to answer them in their need."[49] But if one were to ask why should we be merciful and compassionate, Keenan says it is because God was merciful and compassionate to us. In becoming one of us in Jesus, God entered into the chaos and suffering of our world in order to help us in our need. Jesus is God's compassion incarnate,

God's merciful presence in person. If in Jesus God was immersed into the pain and suffering of the world, then in imitation of God we should enter into the pain and suffering of others not only to comfort them in their suffering, but also, like Jesus, to do what we can to alleviate it and to eliminate the causes for it.[50]

Practices of compassion have to be part of our training in happiness because by imitating this central characteristic of God, we grow more fully in the goodness of a God who in Jesus became a fellow sufferer in our world. The virtue of compassion makes us like God because nowhere is the character of God more fully revealed than in God's willingness to enter into the tears, pains, and sufferings of our world. It was God's willingness to be "displaced" by becoming one of us in Jesus that guides our own displacement on behalf of those who suffer. As Keenan observes, "Mercy is so important because it is, above all, the experience we have of God. In response to that mercy, we become imitators of the God in whose image we are made."[51] No account of life that is founded in the goodness of God can neglect compassion. If the God we strive to imitate did not ignore the sufferings of others, then neither can we seek fullness of life by neglecting the afflicted among us. Any initiation into a good and happy life has to include education in compassion because in the Christian life we cannot know the happiness of God if, as we make our way, we ignore our brothers and sisters who suffer.

Conclusion

We have traveled far in this chapter. And perhaps all this talk about life as a quest, about ourselves as pilgrims forever on our way, and of virtue and excellence is wearying. Wouldn't it be enough just to become moderately good rather than to frustrate ourselves by aiming for the elusive goodness of God? Isn't it acceptable to lower our sights a little, to aim for simple human decency instead of holiness? The problem with an ethics of virtue, especially in the Christian life, is that it connects happiness with becoming great in goodness, specifically with imitating and ultimately resembling the goodness of God. Most of us do not want to be that great; most of us do not want to pay the price for that kind of happiness. We prefer being ordinary over being great, being average over being excellent. But what do we lose when we refuse to be our best? When we flee from heroic ambitions? What happens to us and to our world when we are no longer able to risk the happiness of the saints?

In a postscript to *Man's Search for Meaning*, Viktor Frankl's famous memoir recounting his years in the death camps of Nazi Germany, Frankl came to an interesting conclusion. This Jewish psychiatrist, who had beheld and suffered the most unimaginable atrocities, would have every reason to despair of humanity's potential for goodness. But it was precisely his exposure to the worst of humanity that convinced him that nothing less than aspiring to greatness in goodness would give the world hope. In the closing lines of a 1984 postscript to the book, Frankl wrote, "You may of course ask whether we really need to refer to 'saints.' Wouldn't it suffice just to refer to *decent* people? It is true that they form a minority. More than that, they always will remain a minority. And yet I see therein the very challenge to join the minority. For the world is in a bad state, but everything will become still worse unless each of us does his best."[52]

Some Questions for Reflection and Discussion

1. How would you explain what a virtue is and why we might need them? And which virtues would you see as most important for your life now?
2. What can make developing a virtue difficult?
3. How would you explain the "cost" of developing vices? What would you see as some of the more destructive vices in persons and societies today?
4. Have you ever known a *magnanimous* person? What struck you about him or her? Do you think our society encourages us to be more *pusillanimous* than *magnanimous*? Why or why not?
5. Can you think of times in your life when you especially needed the virtue of courage? What happens to us if we lack courage? And what are some ways that individuals, churches, and societies might need to be more "daring" in courage today?
6. How would you explain the importance of compassion in "the good life"?

Notes

1. Josef Pieper, *Faith, Hope, Love*, trans. Richard and Clara Winston, and Sr. Mary Frances McCarthy, SND (San Francisco: Ignatius Press, 1997), 91.
2. Pieper, *Faith, Hope, Love*, 92.
3. Pieper, *Faith, Hope, Love*, 93.
4. Thomas Aquinas, *Summa Theologiae* (New York: McGraw-Hill, 1966), II-II, 123,5.
5. Jean Porter, *The Recovery of Virtue: The Relevance of Aquinas for Christian Ethics* (Louisville, KY: Westminster/John Knox Press, 1990), 37.
6. Porter, *The Recovery of Virtue*, 38.

7. Porter, *The Recovery of Virtue*, 49.

8. Gilbert C. Meilaender, *The Theory and Practice of Virtue* (Notre Dame, IN: University of Notre Dame Press, 1984), 12.

9. Herbert McCabe, *The Good Life: Ethics and the Pursuit of Happiness* (New York: Continuum, 2005), 11.

10. Russell B. Connors Jr. and Patrick T. McCormick, *Character, Choices and Community: The Three Faces of Christian Ethics* (New York: Paulist Press, 1998), 25.

11. Connors and McCormick, *Character, Choices and Community*, 25.

12. Alasdair MacIntyre, *After Virtue: A Study in Moral Theory* (Notre Dame, IN: University of Notre Dame Press, 1981), 135.

13. Martha C. Nussbaum, *The Fragility of Goodness: Luck and Ethics in Greek Tragedy and Philosophy* (Cambridge: Cambridge University Press, 1986), 1–21.

14. Meilaender, *The Theory and Practice of Virtue*, 9.

15. Meilaender, *The Theory and Practice of Virtue*, 9.

16. Paul J. Wadell, *The Primacy of Love: An Introduction to the Ethics of Thomas Aquinas* (New York: Paulist Press, 1992), 116.

17. Wadell, *The Primacy of Love*, 113.

18. Aquinas, *ST*, I-II, 49,2.

19. Aquinas, *ST*, I-II, 49,2.

20. Aquinas, *ST*, I-II, 61,5.

21. Aquinas, *ST*, I-II, 24,9.

22. MacIntyre, *After Virtue*, 172–73.

23. Brian S. Hook and R. R. Reno, *Heroism and the Christian Life: Reclaiming Excellence* (Louisville, KY: Westminster John Knox Press, 2000), 212.

24. Hook and Reno, *Heroism and the Christian Life*, 212.

25. Hook and Reno, *Heroism and the Christian Life*, 211.

26. Pieper, *Faith, Hope, Love*, 101.

27. Aquinas, *ST*, II-II, 129,1.

28. Aquinas, *ST*, II-II, 129,4.

29. Pieper, *Faith, Hope, Love*, 101.

30. Pieper, *Faith, Hope, Love*, 119. In this respect, *acedia*, one of the seven deadly sins, is a vice that opposes magnanimity. A person caught in *acedia*, Pieper notes, "lacks courage for the great things that are proper to the nature of the Christian. . . . One who is trapped in *acedia* has neither the courage nor the will to be as great as he really is. He would prefer to be less great in order thus to avoid the obligation of greatness."

31. Aquinas, *ST*, II-II, 133,2.

32. Aquinas, *ST*, II-II, 133,2.

33. Aquinas, *ST*, II-II, 123,2.

34. Aquinas, *ST*, II-II, 137,1.

35. Aquinas, *ST*, I-II, 61,3.

36. Aquinas, *ST*, II-II, 123,6.

37. Aquinas, *ST*, II-II, 123,3.

38. Patricia McAuliffe, *Fundamental Ethics: A Liberationist Approach* (Washington, DC: Georgetown University Press, 1993), 30.

39. Sebastian K. MacDonald, CP, *Moral Theology and Suffering* (New York: Peter Lang, 1995), 49.

40. MacDonald, *Moral Theology and Suffering*, 2.

41. MacDonald, *Moral Theology and Suffering*, 5.

42. Diana Fritz Cates, *Choosing to Feel: Virtue, Friendship, and Compassion for Friends* (Notre Dame, IN: University of Notre Dame Press, 1997), 4.

43. McAuliffe, *Fundamental Ethics*, 30.

44. MacDonald, *Moral Theology and Suffering*, 19.

45. MacDonald, *Moral Theology and Suffering*, 22.

46. Cates, *Choosing to Feel*, 231.

47. Cates, *Choosing to Feel*, 231.

48. Cates, *Choosing to Feel*, 214.

49. James F. Keenan, SJ, *Moral Wisdom: Lessons and Texts from the Catholic Tradition* (Lanham, MD: Rowman & Littlefield Publishers, Inc., 2004), 124.

50. MacDonald, *Moral Theology and Suffering*, 42.

51. Keenan, *Moral Wisdom*, 127.

52. Viktor E. Frankl, *Man's Search for Meaning* (New York: Pocket Books, 1984), 179.

CHAPTER FOUR

~

Every Person's Truth

Made in the Image of God, Called to Do the Work of God

Dead Man Walking tells the story of Sr. Helen Prejean's work with prisoners on death row at Louisiana's Angola State Prison. One of the men she visits is Robert Willie, who, along with Joseph Vaccaro, raped and murdered eighteen-year-old Faith Hathaway. Vaccaro was sentenced to life in prison, Willie to death. It was not the first of Robert Willie's crimes. No childhood saint, by the time he was fourteen Willie had been involved in numerous thefts and break-ins, was guilty of driving while intoxicated, of carrying a concealed weapon, and of aggravated assault on a police officer. At twenty he was back in jail for burglary, and from 1972 to 1979 he was arrested thirty times. While serving time at the federal penitentiary in Marion, Illinois, Willie joined the Aryan Brotherhood, a white supremacist group whose membership badge was two tattoos, one of a swastika, the other of a skull. Without a doubt, he knew more about hatred than love, and his misguided life had left a legacy of brutality, violence, and incalculable harm. For Vernon and Elizabeth Harvey, Faith's parents, Willie was the monster who took from them what they most loved and guaranteed that their lives would be marked by mourning and loss.

Sr. Prejean does not deny any of this. She speaks truthfully to Willie about the evil he has done, and challenges him to stop lying to himself and to accept responsibility for his deeds. She knows he is self-absorbed, shallow, full of resentments, and in desperate need of repentance. He is a liar, a thief, and a thug; an often cruel, vicious man; and a murderer. But for her he is also something more. There is another truth to Robert Willie, a truth he must claim if the story of his life is not to climax in bitterness and be forever defined by hatred. Sr. Prejean wants to open his eyes to the whole truth of who he is. This involves claiming his identity as a rapist and murderer, but something else as well. He must see himself as he has never done before. Sr. Prejean confronts Willie with this other dimension of his self when she visits him one day on death row. She tells him "that despite his crime, despite the terrible pain he has caused, that he is a human being and he has a dignity that no one can take from him, that he is a son of God." Stunned by these words, Willie's usually hardened face melts into a smile. "Ain't nobody ever called me no son of God before," he tells Sr. Prejean. "I've been called a son-of-a-you-know-what lots of times but never no son of God."[1]

Who are we really? How should we think of ourselves? Sr. Prejean sees what everyone else sees in Robert Willie, but she also sees something more. He is a murderer, but for her that is not his only identity and is not, despite its awfulness, the most important truth about him. She sees another truth in him, a deeper reality, and appeals to him to claim that identity too so that the terrible evils he has done do not remain the only fact about him. If, in the last days of his life, he can claim this deeper truth about himself, perhaps he can uncover his capacity to love, and perhaps that capacity to love will enable him to see the wrong he has done and die not cursing those who want his death, but asking their forgiveness. Willie can give a hopeful ending to what has hardly been a hopeful life if, in the waning days of his life, he lives from this other truth and allows this truth to change not only how he has always seen himself, but also how he has obviously seen others. It's not just that Willie had never thought of himself as a child of God before, but that he clearly had not seen Faith Hathaway that way either. Sr. Prejean knows everything about Robert Willie but refuses to abandon him, because as a Christian she will not let his identity as a sinner be the only truth about him. There is another truth buried beneath all his misdeeds and transgressions, and it is this truth, both hopeful and disturbing, that insists that Robert Willie, the rapist and murderer, is also a child of God, and as a child of God remains a person with dignity. In the eyes of most he is a moral monster deserving death. But to Sr. Prejean, Robert Willie is a murderer who was, nonetheless, fashioned in the image of God, and this fact marks him for life.

What makes us persons? What gives us dignity? What is it that sets us apart from other creatures? These are the questions that will be explored in this chapter. Philosophers and theologians have wrestled with these questions and suggested different ways for determining what constitutes us as persons. But the trouble with so many of their answers is that somebody is always left out, pushed to the margins of humanity and excluded. For instance, there is a long-standing tradition that has argued it is our rationality, our capacity to think, reason, and deliberate, that distinguishes us from other creatures and makes us persons. But what then happens to infants who have not yet developed these capacities or to Alzheimer's patients who have lost them? If rationality makes us persons, this would suggest that infants are not fully human and that victims of Alzheimer's no longer are. Are they then expendable? Of less account than the rest of us? Others argue that it is our freedom, our capacity for self-determination that constitutes us as persons. We are human because we can choose and through our choices give shape and direction to our lives. This sounds compelling, but what about people whose capacity for self-determination may be limited because of mental or physical disabilities, or because of political and economic realities? Are they less than human and, therefore, less worthy of consideration? We may seem on safer ground if we claim it is moral awareness or conscience that makes us persons, but this could suggest that we can, in good conscience, kill people such as Robert Willie, terrorists, or other miscreants who seem to have no conscience. Many would argue that we not only can, but should rid society of such people. But the danger of eliminating any person or group on the basis of them no longer being human is that such elimination, no matter how seemingly reasonable, ultimately diminishes ourselves. When Sr. Prejean insisted that Robert Willie remained a child of God despite all the evil he had committed, she did so to protect her humanity as much as his own. She realized that denying anyone the dignity of being a person not only strips something sacred away from him or her, but nurtures something dangerous in us as well. A good bit of history's horrors are the result of one group deciding they had the power to determine who was truly human and worthy of life, and who was not.

This is why Christian theology, at its best, insists that the key point is not *what* makes us persons, but *who* makes us persons.[2] The problem with focusing on what makes us persons, whether it be our rationality, our freedom, our call to be responsible, or our conscience, is that anyone who appears to lack any of these criteria can be removed from human consideration. Whatever they lack is reason for excluding them or even eliminating them. But if we ask who makes us persons instead, this opens to a completely different way of understanding ourselves, what it is that gives us dignity, and why it is that every person *without exception* is worthy of moral consideration. Beginning with the question of who makes us persons teaches us that our lives are gifts, not our own possession, and that our human dignity does not depend on us possessing any particular capacity, talent, or ability. Dignity and sacredness is something we receive, not something we earn or achieve, and this is why even the worst of us remain, like Robert Willie, a child of God.

We will not succeed in our quest for happiness unless we rightly understand who we truly are. This is why any consideration of the Christian moral life must include some account of what it means to be a person. How I understand happiness, how I see others, and what I take my life to be will all be shaped by what I think it means to be a self. From a Christian perspective, if our quest for happiness is to succeed, we must recognize three fundamental truths about ourselves: we are creatures, we are made in the image and likeness of God, and we are called to do the work of God. What these claims might mean for us, and what difference they make, is the subject of chapter 4. We will conclude by giving some attention to how a Christian account of the person might influence our stance on ethical issues that pertain to the beginning and end of life. In other words, we will consider how Christian convictions about who God is and who we are might be relevant for how we think about bioethics.

Creatures—What It Means to Live from the Generosity and Goodness of God

The first claim that Christianity makes about human beings is that we are creatures brought to life by the love and goodness of God. We do not give ourselves life; rather, we receive life from the God who brings everything into existence. The core principle of a Christian theology of creation is that all life begins in God and nothing lives apart from God or independently of God. The biblical stories of creation in the book of Genesis capture this by emphasizing that God alone is creator, God alone gives life. Everything that exists, from the galaxies to the smallest atom, the plants and the animals, and especially ourselves, is the handiwork of God, dazzling expressions of God's ingenuity and love. It is God who calls everything into existence, God who summons everything from nothingness to life. God says, "Let there be light," and there is light. God says, "Let the earth bring forth vegetation," and it happens. God looks at the empty seas and the empty skies and, like a playful artist, fills them with fish and birds. God wants there to be creatures who can enjoy his creation and care for it, and so the first human beings appear.

Genesis presents God as an amazingly prodigious artist bringing beautiful things to life, ingeniously fashioning into being creatures of astonishing diversity, delighting in them and declaring all of them good. The stories of creation attest to the goodness of creation, but they also make it clear that God alone creates, that God alone can do this. Everything else that exists, including human beings, are not creators but creatures, not the authors of life but *receivers* of life. Like everything else that lives, we are not self-constituting, autonomous beings; rather, from the first to the last moment of our lives we are radically dependent, creatures whose lives originate in God and at every moment are sustained by God. The opening words of Genesis proclaim a truth that is echoed throughout the Bible's narrative of creation, fall, and redemption: In the beginning there was nothing, a "formless wasteland," and that there is anything at all testifies to the love, generosity, and goodness of God. A God who did not have to create transformed that wasteland into a garden teeming with life. We live from the superabundant energy of God in a universe where everything articulates the diffusive love, wisdom, and creativity of God. Perhaps most tellingly, we live because God does not want to be all there is.

What does this tell us about ourselves? A Christian theology of the person says our lives are not our own, they are God's gift to us. And at every moment they remain God's gift to us because the God who once fashioned us into being continually sustains us in life. Contrary to customary ways of thinking, my life is not my own because the self I am is continually being given me by God; at every moment, God's love constitutes and sustains me. I can never be truly autonomous because I have no self apart from God, no self that is strictly my own. I remain a creature tethered to God, a being with an inseverable lifeline to God. Like everything else in existence, I live from a love I cannot give myself but can only receive. The Christian understanding of the person changes what it means for any of us to say "I am." As the theologian Arthur McGill wrote, "I am no longer that part of reality which has been delivered over to me, which now belongs stably to me. Rather, I am by virtue of a constant receiving. My 'I am' exists by virtue of an activity that constantly comes from beyond myself. . . . My 'I am' necessarily and constantly includes God's activity of constituting me."[3] A Christian theological anthropology claims we live not from our own power, but always from the endlessly creative love of God. We live because it is the nature of God to engender and communicate life.

And we live because we are loved. We speak often about how the love of others sustains and strengthens us. We tell those close to us that we could not live without their love. We let them know we are indebted to them because the gift of their love has brought us more fully to life. But the claims we make about the necessity of human love are even more applicable for the love we receive from God. God does not create and then abandon us. God does not draw us to life only to leave us on our own. From beginning to end God's love is the innermost principle of all existence, the gift from which everything lives. As Michael Himes explains, "Why is there being rather than nothing? . . . The Christian tradition's answer, as I understand it, is, 'Because it is loved.' The reason that anything exists is that it is the object of love. All things that are, are loved into being. The fundamental ground for anything is that it is called into being because God loves it."[4] This is what it means to be a person, someone who is forever receiving her life as a gift of divine love. "When we have this sense of ourselves as what we constantly receive from God's free giving, what do we experience when we experience ourselves? *We experience love*,"[5] McGill writes. Love is the ground of our being, the divine gift continually sustaining us. We are creatures held in life by God's love. This is not to deny the importance of human love for mediating God's love in our lives. But it is to say if we were not loved divinely, we would not be. As Himes summarizes, "Not to be loved by God is not to exist. Everything that is, to the extent that it is, is loved."[6] We exist because God is related to us in every instant of our being and in every dimension of our being.[7] It is a relationship of creative, life-giving love.

Resting in a Gift—Living from a Love We Cannot Give Ourselves

In a Christian theological anthropology, to be a person is to rest in a gift. Everyone (and everything) exists in virtue of a love they cannot give themselves, but also a love that cannot be denied them or ever taken away from them because it is God-given. It is not rationality, freedom, self-determination, or moral awareness that makes us persons. It is God's love, and that is something everyone has. The trouble with defining what constitutes us as persons in terms of some quality or qualities we might have is that anyone who lacks these qualities or who is judged to have them to a deficient degree risks being assessed as less than human or not truly a person. Obviously, all sorts of harm can result if we decide who counts as persons and who does not. But if our unique identity as persons is the handiwork of God's love, and this is something everyone receives, then every human being is a *person*. No one is expendable. Everyone deserves respect and is worthy of consideration. One's dignity and identity as a person are not measured in terms of intelligence, talent, physical ability, wealth, creativity, or even goodness; instead, they are determined by a love that never leaves them. The yet to be born, the not so talented, the limited or infirm, the poor and the elderly, even the reprobate and the depraved *count as persons* because just like the healthy and the wealthy and the good, they are held in life by a love that delights in them.

We can bristle at this understanding of ourselves because we rebel against the idea of being needy and dependent, and are often affronted by the thought that our life is neither our possession nor achievement, but a gift. We want to be self-possessed and self-sufficient, not creatures who are inherently and inescapably indebted because we live always from the power of God's generosity, not from our own strength, ingenuity, wealth, achievements, or resourcefulness. We typically see dependence as a liability, an unwelcome concession to finitude, and think to the degree that we must depend on anyone (perhaps especially God) that we are not free. Dependence and need, we think, are something we should grow out of and spend the best years of our lives working to avoid. We aim for autonomy and independence, and think the less vulnerable we are the better. This is why we fear illness, infirmity, any disability, and aging. They spell a loss of autonomy and a diminishment of freedom.

But it is actually the case that our freedom begins the moment we acknowledge and embrace our dependence. Accepting my life as a gift frees me from the burden of having to establish myself or from having to give my life stature and legitimacy. I do not have to make myself count, I do not have to make myself matter. I matter because I am loved, and I live on account of that love. Too, knowing that life is something I continually receive means I do not have to cling desperately to my self in the fear that any giving will always result in a loss of self. I cannot lose what I never truly possess, but I can freely share what I know I will always receive. Once I claim this identity, this understanding of myself, I can begin to live freely and joyously because I am spared the impossible task of having to be the source and sustainer of my existence. Instead of seeing my life as an easily depleted resource I cannot afford to share, I can be extravagant in giving myself because I know whatever I expend, I am always receiving. I can be open and free and generous in my relations to others, even if they hurt me, because whatever life they take from me God is always giving to me.

This is what it means to live in the freedom of love. Knowing we are loved, knowing that "the love that passes understanding is available to us in the very act of our being, because we are constantly receiving that from our God,"[8] frees us to reach out to others in love. We do not have to live cautiously and craftily, hiding ourselves from others lest they steal life away from us, for they cannot take from us the gift that is always there for us. We live from a never-ending abundance of love. In a Christian theological anthropology, this is what it means to be a creature, a human being, a person, and it is why we can make a gift of our lives in love instead of clinging to them in fear. As McGill concludes, "In short, in all my relations with other people I am freed from the anxiety of having always to keep possession of my own identity in order to be."[9] If the Christian moral life is training in happiness, an essential part of that training is coming to see that like God, we are most ourselves when we make a gift of ourselves in love.

Images of God—Bringing God to Life on Earth

The second claim Christianity makes about us as persons is that every man and woman is created in the image of God. Based on several passages from the book of Genesis (1:26–27; 5:1–3; 9:6), this teaching has so consistently informed a biblical and theological understanding of the person that it has virtually become the standard Christian definition of who we human beings are. Christianity holds that every human being without exception is a living, breathing likeness of God, a unique manifestation of God, or, as the Quakers say, a "spark" of the divine. Each one of us articulates something of God, each one of us brings something of God to life in the world. And that there are so many differences among us—physical differences, racial and ethnic differences, cultural and religious differences—means that no one of us alone can adequately express God. It is all humanity together, stretched across the generations, who image God. Our ancestors, our contemporaries, and those yet to be born bring some word of God to life on Earth. Every person who has lived or who will ever live embodies something unique of the goodness and beauty of God. Every person is a once-in-a-lifetime, never-to-be-repeated expression of God. The doctrine of the *imago Dei* means that if we have "eyes to see," we can find God in everyone we meet.

To be an image of God means not only that some aspect of God is entrusted to us as uniquely our own, but also that our true identity is found in whatever this distinctive image is. And the reason is that the image of God in us represents the unique way God sees us, the special and immensely personal way God's love envisions us. Our true self—our most promising and blessed identity—is what God's love has fashioned us to be. We come to our true self, and therefore to happiness, not when we flee from this identity or suppress it, but when we grow more deeply into it. Our innermost identity is this image of God in us because it is what makes us ourself and not anybody else. What Christianity claims makes each of us persons safeguards our identity because it suggests that each one of us is truly an original, a novel expression of God come to life in the world. The German theologian Jurgen Moltmann captures this by saying the Christian teaching of the *imago Dei* means that God wants to be present on Earth through each one of us.[10] Christians believe God was most fully present in Jesus, but not exclusively present in Jesus. Jesus may be the most perfect image of God, but he is not the only image of God. As God's images, each of us is a person in whom God can be encountered and made known. Each of us, in our blessed singularity, re-presents God to the world. Jesus did this more completely and exquisitely than any of us can; Jesus re-presented God flawlessly. But as God's images, we too are to make God present on Earth, each in our own unrepeatable way.

A Critical Task—Learning to See the Dignity and Sacredness of Every Person

Many things are entailed by this second component of Christianity's understanding of the person, but three seem most important. First, if every person is the image and likeness of God, this means that every human being has an inherent dignity and sacredness that must be respected and can never be exploited or violated. In the Christian tradition, the fact that every human being *without exception* images the life, goodness, and loveliness of God is the foundation for human rights and reverence for life. Our value as persons is bestowed on us by God. We have a sacredness and dignity that must be respected and can never be taken away. And it is not a matter of the gifts and talents we have, the contributions we make to society, our wealth or our health, or even our moral character. It is not a functional dignity that is determined by social standards and achievements, but an inherent, inviolable dignity that is imprinted in our being by God.[11] We are *given* dignity by God. We do not earn or merit it any more than we determine its presence in ourselves or in another. Our role is not to say which person or group has dignity. Our responsibility is to recognize and respect the dignity that is already and always there.

The teaching of the *imago Dei* means the wealthy and the powerful have no more dignity than the poor and the weak, the healthy and strong no more than the disabled and infirm, men no more than women, people who are straight no more than people who are gay. But this is not the way we usually think. We live in a society that may claim everyone is equal in dignity and worthy of respect. But we do not always act that way. We act as if the beautiful, the wealthy, the powerful, and the strong image God more than the ordinary and the plain, more than the poor, the weak, and the broken.

I once heard a sermon that poignantly captured how important it is to see everyone as God's image and act accordingly. The gospel that Sunday was the famous story from chapter nine of the gospel of John, the story of the man born blind whose sight is restored by Jesus. The priest who presided at the Eucharist that morning worked on a college campus and told a story that was both riveting and painful to hear. One of the students who lived on campus was blind. On a weekend in March a group of other students, under the guise of friendship, invited the young man who was blind to go out with them to some of the bars in the neighborhood surrounding the campus. Eager for companionship and happy to be included, the blind student accepted. But for the students who invited him, the aim of the evening was not fellowship but cruelty. Their plan was to get the young man drunk, something they knew would not be difficult since he seldom drank. He thought his companions that evening were drinking along with him and wanted to believe that they really had befriended him, but the only thing they desired that night was the prospect of his humiliation and the joy they would take from it.

When it was clear that the blind student was drunk, they left the bars, shoved him into a car, and drove him through the streets of the area. By constantly changing direction, they knew he would be confused and disoriented. The blind student was known for being able to find his way around the campus very well. Perhaps the other students resented that he would not let his blindness determine everything about him. Perhaps they wanted him to know he was not like them and should never think of himself as their equal. And so when they were sure he was thoroughly drunk and had no idea where they were, they drove halfway across a bridge passing over a river near the campus, stopped the car, shoved him out onto the sidewalk, and said if he was such an expert at finding his way around, he should have no trouble getting back to his dorm. The priest, who lived in the dorm that year, was awoken by the sounds of someone sobbing. He opened his door, looked down the corridor, and saw the blind young man curled on the floor, weeping loudly, broken and humiliated.

Just as the passage from the gospel of John makes the hearer wonder who in the story is really blind and in need of healing, the priest that Sunday morning asked us who in this narrative of humiliation and abuse was truly unable to see? The other students were trapped in greater darkness—theirs was the most damaging blindness—because they were unable to see that this student born blind was as much a living, breathing image of God as they were. The priest's story made us uncomfortable because it prompted us to wonder when we too might have been blind to the image of God in others and how our lack of sight had hurt them. How we act toward others depends on how we see them. If we see them through a vision twisted by cruelty, arrogance, superiority, or coldness, we will never be just or respectful to them. If we see them through eyes weakened by fear, fear for whatever in them is different and therefore threatening to us, we will be reluctant to claim them as God's images too. This is why in the Christian moral life our training in happiness has to include lessons in learning to see the dignity and sacredness that God gives to all creatures. It must form in us the vision needed to recognize God in every person we meet.

Imaging a God Who Is a Partnership of Love

Second, as God's images, human beings are called to live in relationship with God, one another, and all of life. We are made for intimacy and communion with God and one another. We are, to the depths of our being, essentially social, persons made to find happiness and life not by turning in on ourselves, but by opening our lives to others in love. As Catholic moral theologian Richard Gula says, "To be is to be in relationship. . . . Humanity and relatedness are proportional so that the deeper one's participation in relationships is, the more human one becomes."[12] This is why breakdowns in love, no matter how common, must be overcome. It is why self-centeredness, a temptation for everyone, always impoverishes. Selfishness is never a path to life because it denies us the relationships we need to be drawn more fully to life. Moreover, our inescapable need for others explains why we naturally fall in love and are happiest when we are loved and loving. Nobody needs to be taught how to fall in love. We may need to be taught how to stay in love, but falling in love comes easily to us because our need for intimacy and communion is bred deeply within us. We are programmed to love, fashioned to find happiness and completeness through being with others and, to be sure, through being with God. It is not an optional feature of life, but an absolute requirement for life. And it is why nothing is deadlier than never learning to love or never experiencing love.

But why is this so? Why in *Tuesdays with Morrie* did Morrie Schwartz, echoing the poet W. H. Auden, tell Mitch Albom, "Love each other or perish. . . . Without love, we are birds with broken wings."[13] Perhaps because we are spitting images of a God who is not a single, isolated deity, but a perfect communion of love.[14] The need for intimacy and communion is bred into us because we are modeled after a God whose innermost being is relational. Christians express this by speaking of God as Trinity. The doctrine of the Trinity means not that there are three gods, but that in one God there are three persons bonded together in love. God is a communion of unbreakable love, an everlasting partnership of love. God is not three isolated individuals; rather, God is the solidarity of unbreakable love. To speak of God as Trinity is to hold that at the very heart of God we find not solitude and isolation, but intimacy and community. And it is a communion of persons characterized by life-giving, mutual love. In God, each person's love gives life and identity to the others. The love of the Father gives life and identity to the Son, and the love shared between them gives life and identity to the Spirit. For Christians, God is the "giving and receiving" of love, the ongoing dance of love that is perfect, joyous life.[15] Or as Michael Himes puts it, "The central point of the doctrine of the Trinity is that God is least wrongly understood as a relationship, as an eternal explosion of love."[16]

As God's images, there must be some correspondence between what is true for God and what will be true for ourselves. Love, intimacy, communion, and friendship are not optional elements to a life of happiness but absolute requirements, because if the God in whose image we are made only exists relationally, then the same holds true for us. If God is a partnership of love, we will find life, happiness, and fulfillment in whatever measure we imitate such love in our own lives. Love and life go together because the very possibility of developing and prospering as persons hinges on cultivating in our families, friendships, churches, and communities something resembling the generous, affirming, joyous love that is God.

We are brought to life through love and we live through love. This love can take the form of friendship, marriage, or parenting. It can be expressed in service, compassion, faithfulness, playfulness, affection, patience, or forgiveness. But it has to be present for us to live because the core truth of God's being is the core truth of our own. And deep down we know this. We know we are happiest not when our lives are guided by excessive self-concern, but when we are part of relationships and communities where people care for one another, watch out for one another, support one another, and are faithful to one another. We are happiest and most fulfilled when we make a gift of our self to others and receive the gift of their selves in return. Like God, our happiness comes from being part of the ongoing dance of love. If not, as Morrie Schwartz said, "we are birds with broken wings."

Growing into the Image of Christ

Third, if we are created in the image of God (*imago Dei*), we are perfected in the image of Christ (*imago Christi*).[17] The unique image of God in us is not a static, unchangeable reality, but one that is meant to grow and develop in order to reach its most complete expression as an image of Christ. The *imago Christi* is what the *imago Dei* strives for and intends because Christ is the fullness of God in person, the fullness of God *enfleshed*. We need an example of what it would mean to image and re-present God, and this is what Jesus shows us because Jesus was not simply an extraordinary religious figure or unusually good man, but the very embodiment of God. Every person is called to re-present God on Earth, but none has done so more perfectly and fully than Jesus. In his attitudes and actions, in his teachings and ministry, Jesus so completely exemplified the love, justice, and compassion of God that Christians believe he was not only God's anointed one, but also divine. This is why the *imago Dei* in us cannot be understood apart from the *imago Christi*. Jesus is the exemplar of the *imago Dei* and so it is in him that we most fittingly learn what it means to image God in our own lives.

We are made in the image of God, but we are also entrusted with an image of God. This unique expression of God in us is our most precious possession. But it is an identity that needs care and attention. Whether or not we present our image of God to others depends on how we live. Since God endows us with this image it cannot be finally destroyed in us, but it can be obscured, it can be diminished and disfigured, which is what happens in a life of sin. Even in murder the image of God remained in Robert Willie, but it was overshadowed by the darkness of his sin. Through contrition and repentance, through the work of grace and the power of Christ's redemption, that faint image of God in him could be restored,[18] but it did not stand unaffected by the evil he had embraced in his life. Like Robert Willie, we can live in contradiction to the image of God in us and choose another identity. We can even renounce that image of God by habitually choosing to bring evil into the world instead of good. But we cannot completely erase God's insight about who we are meant to be, and that is our hope. We live into that hope when we take the image of God entrusted to us and bring it more fully to life through our imitation of Christ. Sr. Helen Prejean did this for Robert Willie. She showed him what it would mean for him to live according to God's image in him. She reminded him of who he was called to be and could be. It was an identity he finally embraced in death.

Called to Do the Work of God—The Responsibilities of Stewardship and Vocation

What makes us persons? What gives us dignity? So far we have answered these questions in two ways, both of which underscore that it is God's actions toward us that make us persons. Nonetheless, we are given life for a purpose and this brings us to the third dimension of a Christian understanding of the person: We are creatures fashioned in the image and likeness of God who are called to do the work of God. In Christianity, a key dimension to our dignity is that we are called to responsibility. For Christians, to be a person is to be entrusted with a task. God calls us "to participate in his work, in his project of love and salvation,"[19] a work that extends to all of God's creation. God entrusts us with the well-being of creation, both human and nonhuman. We are called to care for one another, to draw each other more fully to life through love, compassion, and kindness. But we are also called to care for Earth, for the other species God has created, and for all the resources of the planet. We are not to be careless with Earth any more than we are to be careless with one another.

As God's representatives on Earth, we are given the moral responsibility of *stewardship*. To speak of stewardship suggests that our special status as human beings is one of moral responsibility, not privilege. We are to watch over and care for God's creation, not abuse or destroy it. From a biblical and theological perspective, stewardship refers to how God's love and care for all creation (human beings, plants and animals, all Earth's rich resources) are to be expressed and promoted through us. Stewardship means that we use our intelligence, imagination, and freedom to respect, protect, and care for everything that God, from the beginning, declared good. God gives us life and places us on Earth so that we can serve his plans and purposes. As Brennan Hill observed, "Creatures who have been made in the image and likeness of God do not exercise the privilege of lording it over creation as superior beings. They come to creation, rather, as servants of a loving and creative God, stewards acting in God's place."[20]

A Christian view of the person challenges how we understand ourselves and how we see our place in the world. It starts not by asking, "What do I want to do?" or "How might I be fulfilled?" but "How does God need me?" or "What is the particular work God has designed for me?" In a Christian theological anthropology, each of us is called to re-present God on Earth. But we do this not only by imaging God, but also by contributing to the work of God. Or better, we best image God when we do the work of God. Christianity teaches that every person is called to actively participate in the creative and redemptive activity of God. Traditionally, Christian theology has referred to the distinctive work God calls a person to do as his or her *vocation*. It is not uncommon, particularly for Roman Catholics, to associate vocation with the priesthood or religious life, or marriage; similarly, other Christian denominations connect vocation to one's primary work in life. But vocation can also be understood more broadly as the call to use whatever gifts and talents we have to further God's work in the world. It is the unique way each of us is accountable to God. Germain Grisez and Russell Shaw capture this understanding of vocation when they write: "Each one of us has something important to do. Each has a particular set of gifts, opportunities, and other attributes—including weaknesses and strengths—that is uniquely our own. And each of us is obliged to examine that package to determine its potential for communicating God's truth and love, confronting evil (including the evil in ourselves), and dealing with it. This is to say we should examine what we have received for its redemptive potential."[21]

God calls us because God needs us. This is a stunning claim because it means that the God who created the heavens and Earth "doesn't go it alone." God works through us. God counts on our cooperation and assistance. A theology of vocation underscores the absolute importance of human responsibility for carrying forward God's creative and redemptive activity in the world. God has plans and purposes, but God needs our cooperation and assistance for those plans and purposes to be fulfilled. God wants to bring love, justice, and goodness to the world, but chooses to do so through the work of our hands. We may seldom consider that the God of the universe might need us for anything or that we could possibly be useful to God. But a Christian understanding of the person claims that God calls us because God depends on us. The work of creation begun by God is to be nurtured and cared for by us, whether we are nurturing another human being through love, caring for the sick, serving those in need, or nurturing Earth. There is supreme humility to God, because as Yahweh's covenant with Israel, and Jesus' call to his disciples, indicate, God cares for the world, its peoples, and the whole of creation through us. "God has chosen to work in this world through the agency of human hands," Lee Hardy writes. "He chose to create a world where we, as God's representatives, are involved in the ongoing business of creation and the repair of creation—a world where we assume responsibility for the well-being of the earth and all who inhabit it. . . . In responding to our callings, we are actually participating in God's care for humanity and the earth. We are God's co-workers."[22] This is a tremendous affirmation of every person's dignity and importance. Every person matters because every person has an irreplaceable role to play in furthering God's work in the world.

We ordinarily do not think of ourselves or of our contribution to life as that significant. We may want to do good, but what does doing good in the ordinary circumstances of our ordinary lives have to do with the creative and redemptive work of God? Of helping build the kingdom of God? A vocation refers to how we are to do the great work of God (to love our neighbor, to seek justice, to serve one another, to care for all life) not in some imagined world, but in the less than perfect world that is our home now. Seeing our lives through the lens of vocation does not take us outside of our ordinary settings in life, but challenges us to see them differently. A person who looks at life through the lens of vocation asks, "How can I do good here? How am I needed? How can I help?" Such a person knows we can be "useful" to God no matter where we are. We do the good work of God in the fabric of our everyday lives, if we are ever to do it at all.

The language of stewardship and vocation reminds us that every person, regardless of his or her state in life, is "providentially situated"[23] to carry on the work of God. Traditionally, providence refers to how God "provides" for the world. But ordinarily God provides for the world *through* us. Just as God once entered into history in Jesus, God continues to enter into the world through our goodness, our compassion, our service, and our thoughtfulness. God ministers to the needs of the world through our gifts.[24] Wherever we are, we are called to use our talents and gifts to do good. The theologian Karl

Barth captured this when he spoke of "places of responsibility."[25] By this he meant that in any circumstance or at any moment in life we can cooperate with God in doing good. Barth recognized that human beings are capable of great things, but we are called to do great things in the regular roles and responsibilities of our lives. This means one thing for a student away at school. It means another for a parent or grandparent. It means something else for a doctor, a restaurant owner, a mechanic, or a store clerk. But no matter where we are we can make a lasting contribution to life through acts of ordinary goodness and love. It is in this marriage, with these friends, with these coworkers, or with these roommates that God counts on me to touch the world with his love, to redeem and make holy.

And it happens all the time. I teach at a college where every day I see students "do the work of God" by being there for one another, by helping each other through hard times, by making each other laugh, by being faithful friends to one another. It happens in marriages when spouses comfort one another, are patient with each other, and challenge one another. Parents "do the work of God" when they love their children for who God made them to be, when they patiently and lovingly navigate them through the perils of adolescence, or when they challenge their children to live for something more than themselves. Men and women in business share in the creative and redemptive work of God when they are honest and fair, when they are unfailingly just, and when their work serves the common good. Every day each one of us is "providentially situated" to bring God's love to life in the world. Put differently, as images of God we are called to re-present God. And we do this best when we understand that our greatest legacy lies not in fame or celebrity, not in power, wealth, or prestige, but in how we have increased goodness, in how we have worked with God to make all things whole.

Life Is Good but God Is Better—How Should We Think about Matters of Life and Death?

Throughout this chapter we have reflected on how Christians might think about who they are and their place in the world. Such theological convictions have important ethical implications, perhaps especially when wrestling with questions that pertain to the beginning and end of life. Bioethics is a relatively recent field,[26] but certainly a rapidly developing one, and one with enormous consequences for how we understand ourselves and our place in the world. Forty years ago, who would have thought that today we would be pondering issues such as genetic engineering, cloning, stem cell research, assisted reproduction, genetic therapy, or euthanasia? Where will advances in medicine take us? What possibilities await us in the future? How should we think about these matters? A Christian theology of the person provides us with a helpful framework for considering how to respond to advances in medicine that can be both promising and daunting.

First, Christians should approach issues in bioethics by remembering that we are *creatures*. This means we do not possess our lives; they belong to God. This is why we are not absolutely free to do with our lives as we please.[27] Too, to be a creature means we exist *only* in relation to God, and from the beginning to the end of our lives remain dependent and indebted, men and women who continually receive their lives as a gift from God. Christians, for example, have consistently rejected euthanasia and suicide as moral options because both belie the fundamental fact that our lives are gifts entrusted to us by God in love. Furthermore, as creatures we must remember our distinctive place in creation and the limits that accompany our status, particularly the limits of bodily life. Our true humanity is displayed (and preserved) when we remember that as creatures we are above the beasts, but we are not God. We are gifted, intelligent, free, ingenious, creative, and daring, but we stand, Gilbert Meilaender enjoins, "where one who is truly human ought to stand—between the beasts and God."[28] It is important to keep this in mind when considering the power medical technology can give us over our lives and the lives of others. As Meilaender warns, "the temptation to be more than human may leave us less than human."[29] Thus, our actions regarding matters of life and death are more likely to be wise and truly humane when they are informed by an understanding of what it means to be a creature.

Analysis of bioethical issues today tends to revolve around four fundamental principles: autonomy, nonmaleficence, beneficence, and justice.[30] But of these four, autonomy is customarily seen as the most important principle for determining how we should think on issues of life and death. As James Walter and Thomas Shannon note, "we have relied almost exclusively on autonomy as the cornerstone of ethical analysis."[31] This is not surprising "for autonomy is the 'All American' value. Almost from conception we have had drummed into us the message that we must be the master of our fate, the captain of our ship, the one to forge our own destiny with our own hands, and that we are the one solely responsible for our own fate."[32] Autonomy may be an "All-American" value, but it is not (at least as we commonly understand it), a Christian value because its emphasis on independence, individualism, and self-determination is at odds with what it means for us to be creatures. Autonomy cannot "reign supreme" for Christians because choice and self-determination are not what make us persons; rather, we are made persons by the creative love, goodness, and generosity of God. Furthermore, if autonomy means (as it is often upheld) that all "choices are private" and therefore immune from any social or moral evaluation,[33] then this cannot be endorsed by Christians either. Our choices are not private because we are accountable to God and because our lives are enmeshed in communities and relationships with others. Both our relationship with God and our relationships with others create moral bonds, obligations, and responsibilities that are easily obscured and transgressed when we act as if autonomy is the only principle that matters. Autonomy may be an important moral principle if it calls our attention to the dignity of individual persons and the justice and respect that are owed them. But it is not the only relevant moral principle for bioethics and will lead us astray in dangerous and worrisome ways if we allow it more prominence than it deserves.

Second, we gain clarity and wisdom in issues of bioethics when we remember that we are both *finite* and *free*. We are given freedom to grow and develop intellectually, morally, and spiritually. We are given freedom so that we may use our intelligence, ingenuity, and creativity in service to the good of others. And we are given freedom so that we can ultimately transcend ourselves in love and communion with God. But we are also "finite beings, located in space and time, subject to natural necessity,"[34] and mortal. Too, as humans we are open to God and fulfilled in God, but we are also accountable to God. This means our freedom must always be constrained by moral limits, and thus there are times when we ought not to do everything we can do. We have our freedom from God, but we must resist "playing God." It is hard not to be impressed by the stunning advances in medicine over the past few decades. But it is also hard not to worry that our technological abilities tempt us to forget that we are fallible, that we do not always know all that we need to know, and that we can be overly confident about the consequences of our actions. Gifted by God, we are capable of making astonishing advances for human well-being, but we are also easily sabotaged by a Promethean pride. If medicine is not to lead to dangerous illusions about who we are and the mastery we either can or ought to have over our lives, we must steadfastly resist a "morally blind technology."[35] We need to "beware of the tyranny of the possible, the pressure to suppose that we ought to do whatever we are able to do."[36] Many things may be possible for us, but that does not always mean they are good for us.

Third, there may be nothing more urgent in bioethics today than to remember that human beings are *mortal*. No matter how hard we try, no matter how carefully and wisely we live, our lives "will be marked by illness, injury, aging, decline, and death."[37] To be human is to be mortal, and no advances in medicine can ever erase this fact. Medicine may be able to prolong our lives, but it cannot overcome the fact that ultimately death will triumph and our biological lives will be over. It is no secret that many of us live in cultures and societies today that persistently encourage us to deny our mortality. But this is a dangerous subterfuge that results in idolatry. If my fundamental objective in life is to avoid death, or even to stay alive as long as possible, I forget that life is "not a god, but a gift of God," that it is a good, but it is not the highest good.[38] Christians believe life is sacred, but they do not believe it is the greatest good. They believe human life is "a profoundly high and important value, but not an absolute or unqualified, supreme value."[39] Put differently, Christians are not "vitalists" who believe that human life is the highest good and therefore must always be preserved regardless of the costs.[40] This is why most Christian ethicists hold that although it is not permissible to aim at or intend another person's death (e.g., euthanasia, assisted suicide), we are not obliged to do everything possible to keep a person alive.[41] When it is clear that "a possible treatment seems useless or (even if useful) quite burdensome for the patient, we are under no obligation to try it or continue it."[42] Treatment can be withheld, withdrawn, or refused when it is clearly of no benefit to a patient.

Similarly, a denial of our mortality can turn medicine, science, and technology into gods. Health is an important human good, but like sheer physical existence, it is not the greatest good.[43] We should appreciate what medicine and technology make available to us, but we ought not to worship them. Ultimately, what "the human heart desires is not simply more years," Meilaender writes, but "something qualitatively different. . . . Even were we to master aging and dying, we would not have achieved the heart's desire; for the longing for God is not a longing for more of the same, more of this life."[44]

Christians believe that death is evil—and that even after Jesus' resurrection it remains an enemy—but they do not believe it is "the worst thing that can happen to us."[45] The worst thing that can happen to us is to live lives bereft of meaning, goodness, and love. The worst thing that can happen to us is to live apart from God and from others. This is why for Christians the most pressing question is not *how long* we live, but *how* we live.[46] Christians should be free from the tyranny of death because thanks to Jesus' resurrection they believe that in God there is a love that is stronger than death. If death could not contain Jesus, neither can it contain us who are baptized into his body and who live in and from God's love. A central message of Christianity is that God's love overcomes death. That is why death brings grief and mourning and loss, but not despair.[47]

To forget this is to give death much more power over us than it deserves. Death cannot be banished from life. To attempt this will not only make us slaves to technology, but less than human. Our primary ambition in life should not be to avoid death, but to love well, to care for one another, to seek God, and to increase goodness. Our overriding concern should not be how medical technology might one day enable us to conquer death, but "How should I want to live in order that I may die well?"[48] If we forget this and allow fear of death to dominate our lives, we likely try to be in control of our lives—and everything that happens to us—in ways that are not healthy. To be human is to be frail, vulnerable, finite, and mortal. We have some control over what happens to us in life, but it is limited. As Daniel Callahan astutely warns, to make maximum control a fundamental aim in life is not a desire that will serve us well.[49] Moreover, Christians believe our ultimate security comes not when we are in total control, but when we are in God. "Because we come from God, belong to God, and are destined finally to return to God, we need not fight without restraint to control all the circumstances of our existence, or to preserve our lives as they near their end, or to control absolutely the circumstances of our dying."[50] Because we come from God, belong to God, and are destined finally to return to God, we need not live in fear. We should cherish our lives and live them as fully as possible, but we should not cling to them as if our future as persons depended on our continued biological existence. Our future as persons is found not in our bodily existence, but in the love and goodness of God that brought us into being in the first place.

Conclusion

What makes us persons? What gives us dignity? In this chapter we have suggested that our lives are not something we possess, but are gifts we continually receive from the abundant and creative love of God. We are made persons by God and given dignity by God. Living from the love and goodness of God frees us because it means we do not have to make ourselves count. If my life is a gift, I do not have to establish its value and dignity. I do not have to make myself matter. If my life is a gift, I can live free from fear and anxiety because I know I will always matter to the "gift giver."

At the same time, if we count *for* God, God also counts *on* us. God depends on us for furthering the plans and purposes of God. In a Christian account of the moral life, each of us has a vocation, a specific role to play in fostering the well-being of God's creation and in helping to bring that creation more fully to life. In our training for happiness we have to discover what our vocations might be because our happiness hinges on knowing how we are called to make a gift of our lives in service of something greater than ourselves. It is a question really of what we should do with our freedom, and that is the subject of chapter 5.

Some Questions for Reflection and Discussion

1. Why can it be hard to accept the fact that we are creatures? And that we are continually receiving our lives as gifts?
2. Why is it sometimes difficult to see the image of God in others? And why can it be even harder to claim the image of God in ourselves?
3. How did you react to the story about the student who was blind? What are some examples of "blindness" in our world today?
4. What does the word "vocation" mean to you? Does anything change in your life if you think of yourself as called? As entrusted by God with special responsibilities? What do you think your vocation is?
5. Can you recall any time in your life where you felt you were "providentially situated" to do good? How are you "providentially situated" today?
6. How does a Christian theology of the person assist you in wrestling with issues of life and death? Where do you see the denial of death at work in our society today?

Notes

1. Sr. Helen Prejean, *Dead Man Walking* (New York: Vintage Books, 1993), 162.
2. Ian A. McFarland, *Difference and Identity: A Theological Anthropology* (Cleveland: The Pilgrim Press, 2001), 9.
3. Arthur C. McGill, *Death and Life: An American Theology* (Philadelphia: Fortress Press, 1987), 51.
4. Michael J. Himes, "'Finding God in All Things': A Sacramental Worldview and Its Effects," in *As Leaven in the World: Catholic Perspectives on Faith, Vocation, and the Intellectual Life*, ed. Thomas M. Landy (Franklin, WI: Sheed & Ward, 2001), 97.
5. McGill, *Death and Life*, 51.
6. Himes, "'Finding God in All Things,'" 98.
7. McGill, *Death and Life*, 51.
8. McGill, *Death and Life*, 52.
9. McGill, *Death and Life*, 52.
10. Jurgen Moltmann, *Man*, trans. John Sturdy (Philadelphia: Fortress Press, 1974), 109.
11. Dennis P. Hollinger, *Choosing the Good: Christian Ethics in a Complex World* (Grand Rapids, MI: Baker Academic, 2002), 72–73.

12. Richard M. Gula, SS, *Reason Informed by Faith: Foundations of Catholic Morality* (New York: Paulist Press, 1989), 65.

13. Mitch Albom, *Tuesdays with Morrie: An Old Man, A Young Man, and Life's Greatest Lesson* (New York: Doubleday, 1997), 91–92.

14. International Theological Commission, "Communion and Stewardship: Human Persons Created in the Image of God," *Origins* 34, no. 15 (September 23, 2004): #25.

15. Catherine Mowry LaCugna, *God for Us: The Trinity and Christian Life* (San Francisco: Harper, 1991), 243–305.

16. Himes, "'Finding God in All Things,'" 96.

17. International Theological Commission, "Communion and Stewardship," #13.

18. International Theological Commission, "Communion and Stewardship," #47. The document reads: "Understood in the perspective of the theology of the *imago Dei*, salvation entails the restoration of the image of God by Christ, who is the perfect image of the Father. Winning our salvation through his passion, death and resurrection, Christ conforms us to himself through our participation in the paschal mystery and thus reconfigures the *imago Dei* in its proper orientation to the blessed communion of Trinitarian life."

19. International Theological Commission, "Communion and Stewardship," #57.

20. Brennan R. Hill, *Exploring Catholic Theology: God, Jesus, Church, and Sacraments* (Mystic, CT: Twenty-Third Publications, 1995), 92.

21. Germain Grisez and Russell Shaw, *Personal Vocation: God Calls Everyone by Name* (Huntington, IN: Our Sunday Visitor Publishing Division, 2003), 99.

22. Lee Hardy, "Investing Ourselves in the Divine Economy," *Christian Reflection: A Series in Faith and Ethics* 4, no. 1 (2004): 30, 32. See also John Paul II, "Laborem Exercens: On Human Work," in *Catholic Social Thought: The Documentary Heritage*, ed. David J. O'Brien and Thomas A. Shannon (Maryknoll, NY: Orbis Books, 1992), #25.

23. Douglas J. Schuurman, *Vocation: Discerning Our Callings in Life* (Grand Rapids, MI: William B. Eerdmans Publishing Co., 2004), 39.

24. John C. Haughey, SJ, "The Three Conversions Embedded in Personal Calling," in *Revisiting the Idea of Vocation: Theological Explorations*, ed. John C. Haughey, SJ (Washington, DC: The Catholic University of America Press, 2004), 10.

25. Schuurman, *Vocation*, 28.

26. Albert R. Jonsen, *Bioethics Beyond the Headlines: Who Lives? Who Dies? Who Decides?* (Lanham, MD: Rowman & Littlefield Publishers, Inc., 2005), 14.

27. Gilbert Meilaender, *Bioethics: A Primer for Christians* (Grand Rapids, MI: William B. Eerdmans Publishing Co., 2005), 2.

28. Gilbert Meilaender, *The Freedom of a Christian: Grace, Vocation, and the Meaning of Our Humanity* (Grand Rapids, MI: Brazos Press, 2006), 121.

29. Meilaender, *The Freedom of a Christian*, 127.

30. Jonsen, *Bioethics Beyond the Headlines*, 17.

31. James J. Walter and Thomas A. Shannon, *Contemporary Issues in Bioethics: A Catholic Perspective* (Lanham, MD: Rowman & Littlefield Publishers, Inc., 2005), 49.
32. Walter and Shannon, 50.
33. Walter and Shannon, 30.
34. Meilaender, *Bioethics*, 4.
35. Walter and Shannon, *Contemporary Issues in Bioethics*, 24.
36. Meilaender, *Bioethics*, 90.
37. Daniel Callahan, *The Troubled Dream of Life: In Search of a Peaceful Death* (Washington, DC: Georgetown University Press, 2000), 123.
38. Meilaender, *Bioethics*, 66.
39. Callahan, *The Troubled Dream of Life*, 86.
40. Meilaender, *The Freedom of a Christian*, 168.
41. Meilaender, *The Freedom of a Christian*, 169.
42. Meilaender, *The Freedom of a Christian*, 169.
43. Joel Shuman and Brian Volck, MD, *Reclaiming the Body: Christians and the Faithful Use of Modern Medicine* (Grand Rapids, MI: Brazos Press, 2006), 20.
44. Meilaender, *The Freedom of a Christian*, 126.
45. Shuman and Volck, *Reclaiming the Body*, 124.
46. Meilaender, *The Freedom of a Christian*, 162.
47. Shuman and Volck, *Reclaiming the Body*, 133.
48. Callahan, *The Troubled Dream of Life*, 148.
49. Callahan, *The Troubled Dream of Life*, 117.
50. Shuman and Volck, *Reclaiming the Body*, 123.

CHAPTER FIVE

~

Freedom

Exploring a Dangerous Topic

What's so great about freedom?

It seems a silly question to ask because we assume the importance of freedom is self-evident. Doesn't everyone know freedom is essential for a good human life? Have you ever known anyone who said he did not want to be free? And when so many people have suffered and died for the sake of freedom, isn't it almost blasphemous to question its value? We may take our freedom for granted, but we don't want to imagine life without it and we'll fight anyone who tries to take it away from us. Nobody likes being controlled by another. Nobody who is healthy would ever choose to be oppressed, dominated, and victimized. It's why we cheer when tyrants are deposed, when the oppressed revolt, and when democracy is won. Who of us would not have wanted to take a sledgehammer to the Berlin Wall?

It is no wonder that we cherish and celebrate our freedom. Freedom gets to the heart of what it means to be a person. We need freedom to live. We need freedom to discover who we are and to become what we are called to be. Freedom and life go together because without this power we cannot guide and direct our lives. Without freedom we cannot make choices that give our lives meaning, substance, and even nobility. Without freedom we cannot ultimately be responsible for our lives. We need freedom to grow, we need freedom to love and to do good, and we need freedom in order to die well. Freedom is a hallmark of what it means to be a person. It is a fundamental human right because it is key to our dignity and our identity. Not to respect another human being's freedom is to violate her soul. Slavery does this, oppression and violence do too, but so does any relationship characterized by manipulation and control. If we are going to flourish, we have to be free. Surely any account of the moral life centered in happiness has to have a privileged place for freedom.

But the question persists: What's so great about freedom? It is a question we need to probe and one whose answer may not be as obvious as we think. We cherish freedom, but what do we mean by it? How do we understand it? What should freedom empower us to do? How we think about freedom makes all the difference because our understanding of freedom will impact our lives and the lives of others. Does freedom mean always doing what I want? Does freedom mean never being restricted? Is freedom nothing more than the liberty to pursue my desires? Theologian Reinhard Hütter says freedom is a "dangerous topic." "If we get freedom wrong," he insists, "our mistake will ultimately kill us."[1] Mistakes about freedom are morally and spiritually deadly because they misdirect our lives, damage our communities, and ultimately deform our souls. It is precisely because the effects of freedom are so powerful that we have to understand well freedom's purpose. From its beginnings Christianity has recognized the absolute importance of freedom, insisting that it was for freedom that Christ set us free (Gal. 5:1). But from its beginnings it has also recognized that freedom is indeed a dangerous topic because there are so many ways we can go wrong in how we understand and use this precious gift. We cannot live without freedom, but we can also be destroyed by it. This is why any account of the Christian life has to be clear about the meaning and purpose of freedom. If Christ set us free for the sake of freedom, what are we to do with this gift?

This is the question that will guide our analysis of freedom. We'll begin by examining contemporary understandings of freedom and then explore a Christian theology of freedom. What we will discover is that freedom is a precious but fragile possession that can easily be lost, and even destroyed, if we do not rightly learn what freedom means and how it ought to be used. Contrary to our ordinary assumptions, in a Christian account of freedom we are not naturally free. For Christians, freedom is both a gift and a virtue. We have a natural capacity or disposition for freedom, but as with any virtue we must develop that disposition into a skill. We must learn to be free. We must work at growing in freedom by reckoning with all that diminishes it. And because it is so crucial that we come to understand and embody freedom correctly, we need to be apprenticed in freedom by those who have achieved its excellence. Who is the freest person you know? What makes that person free? These are important questions to ponder as we begin our exploration of freedom. What we shall discover is that the freest people are good people, the people who have used the gift of freedom to grow in the goodness of God. This may be contrary to our initial thinking about freedom. And that is why, for the sake of happiness, freedom requires a particular way of life.

Contemporary Accounts of Freedom

We can come to a rudimentary understanding of freedom by first considering what most represents the opposite of freedom.[2] Most of us would agree that freedom, at the very least, means the absence of coercive interference from others. I am not free when I am ruled, controlled, or unduly restricted by another. Slavery would be an example of such coercive interference, but so would be torture, intimidation, brainwashing, or imprisonment. In each case something is done to a person that is a direct attack on his or her ability to be free. This bedrock understanding of freedom is sometimes called *negative freedom* because its focus is on the absence of freedom, situations of bondage or oppression that constitute the antithesis of freedom.[3]

These examples of negative freedom remind us that certain minimal conditions must be met for freedom to be a real possibility for a person. For instance, two basic requirements of freedom would be the *space to act* and the *power to act*. Having space to act refers to "the chance or the opportunity to do what we have a mind to do. The circumstances of our world must be such that action is a real possibility."[4] As a prerequisite of freedom, having space to act means "a person can truthfully say this action, this way of life is open to me, it is something I really *may* do. There is nothing preventing me from doing it."[5] One reason that a person in slavery or in prison lacks freedom is that so many actions are not real possibilities for him. A slave or a prisoner cannot do what he has the mind to do; in fact, his life is intentionally circumscribed by so many restrictions and limitations that he is continually reminded that he cannot do what he would like to do. Similarly, there is no real freedom without a certain degree of power to act. A person has power to act when she or he "can truthfully say this action, this way of life is something I really *can* do."[6] Again, anyone enslaved, imprisoned, or held captive lacks this second prerequisite of freedom because so many basic expressions of freedom such as freedom of movement or freedom to choose how one spends one's time are denied persons in these conditions. A slave cannot truthfully claim that choosing not to work for the day is a real possibility for him any more than a prisoner can truthfully say this afternoon he will walk to the closest mall. In the case of slavery the restriction of freedom is obviously unjust, whereas the prisoner's loss of freedom may be deserved; but in both cases a striking characteristic of their lives is the absence of freedom.

Nonetheless, are space to act and power to act sufficient for freedom? Is that all freedom involves? A fuller understanding of freedom focuses on the freedom to choose, act, and decide as we wish. This is freedom of choice, the freedom of knowing what we want to do and being able to do it. We would hardly consider ourselves free if we were never able to make good on an intention or to achieve a goal that was important to us. We logically connect freedom with choices because it is through such intentional behavior that we direct our lives every day. But is this all freedom is? Is being able to choose enough to make me free? It is an important question because many of us see choice as the quintessential element of freedom. We think freedom consists in being able to choose whatever we want and often assume that the decisive value at stake in any contested moral issue is the right to choose. We may not like the choices people sometimes make, but we agree that what matters is the freedom to make them. This view identifies the essence of freedom with individual liberty. Freedom is about individuals being able to pursue certain aims and desires, largely regardless of what those aims and desires might be.

But is choice enough for freedom? Can I have lots of choices and still not be free? It is typical, perhaps especially for Americans, to associate freedom with having lots of choices and options. We think the more possibilities we have from which to choose the freer we will be. We prize options, whether it be in the food we eat, the cars we drive, the clothes we wear, the cell phones we purchase, or even where we decide to worship. If I don't like what I hear in one church (or am taught in one religion), I can shop around for a more appealing church (or a more congenial religion). We so cherish this account of freedom that sometimes we assume that people who do not have so many choices and options cannot truly be free. What makes us free is having an abundance of things from which to choose, whether hundreds of cable or satellite television stations, scores of fast-food restaurants, or an endless array of music to download. What we choose does not matter as much as being able to choose. Too, one's freedom is lessened not by making poor choices—for when choice is all that matters, what one chooses cannot really be bad—but by having little from which to choose. Richard Gula calls this "smorgasbord freedom," and means by it the capacity to choose from among a variety of objects, each of which is morally neutral.[7] It is the freedom of the happy consumer walking down the aisles of a supermarket or department store, selecting whatever strikes her fancy.

And it is a very American understanding of freedom, one that depends on wealth and abundance to be sustained. If freedom is measured by the choices wealth makes available to us, then the poor and the struggling can never be as free as the rich. This is not a freedom much of the rest of the world can enjoy, but neither is it a freedom we can risk sharing with them because possessing it depends on hoarding the wealth and the resources that make so many choices and options possible. Greed and possessiveness, ordinarily considered to be vices, are necessary to bolster this kind of freedom, but sharing and generosity, ordinarily seen to be virtues, threaten it and expose the injustice on which it depends. We may go to war to defend this freedom, but that does not mean we are willing to share it. When freedom is rooted in scarce resources instead of God's economy of grace, it cannot be equally available to all.

Besides, is it always true that the more options and choices we have, the freer we become? Sometimes being confronted with multiple options is paralyzing because it is hard for us to know what, from among so many possibilities, we should finally choose. The more options we have, the more time it takes to investigate what might be our best choice. This is true whether we are considering what kind of car to buy, how to decorate our homes, or even what type of hamburger to order. Is this the best use of our time? Is its freedom's real purpose? In a culture of consumerism, instead of investing our freedom in relationships, in worthy projects, or in faithful love, we are encouraged to shop, purchase, and consume. No wonder we can be surrounded by comfort but still find ourselves lonely and depressed. Moreover, this consumerist view trivializes freedom because it suggests that most of the choices we make are morally neutral, matters of indifference that are nothing more than expressions of preference. It fails to take into account that many of the choices we make, particularly involving how we spend our money or what we do with our time, have repercussions on others and thus are morally significant. Seeing freedom through the lens of consumerism blurs the connection between freedom and justice. When freedom functions only to serve the ever-changing interests and desires of the individual, injustice is bound to result because our obligations to others will be overlooked and forgotten.

Closely related to the consumerist approach to freedom, today many of us identify freedom with the pursuit of self-interest. The purpose of freedom is "self-realization, self-aggrandizement, self-interest, self-fulfillment, self-enrichment, self-promotion"[8] through the satisfaction of our own self-chosen desires. The nature of these desires does not matter. What does matter is that they are ours and that we have freedom to pursue and satisfy them. This view of freedom plays off an important truth about human beings: To be human is to desire. But it neglects a second equally important truth, namely that some desires are worthy of us but other desires are beneath us. Some desires bring life to ourselves and others, but other desires diminish us and hurt others. Our desires represent what we love, and our loves make us who we are and signal the impact we will have on others. If I love and desire wrongly, I will use my freedom in ways that are destructive of self and others. This is why Christianity teaches that it is important for us to order our loves and scrutinize our desires. It is fine to enjoy nice things, but it is not fine to desire wealth more than justice. It is fine to enjoy pleasures from sex, but not apart from the faithful commitment that makes those desires an expression of love rather than selfishness. It is fine to desire power, but not for the sake of self-aggrandizement instead of for doing good. As Reinhard Hütter notes, "Without desire we would cease to be human; without God as desire's ultimate end, we cease to be humane."[9]

Freedom at the service of misdirected desires will make us inhumane. If I am dominated by a desire for pleasure, wealth, or power, my ambition for each of those things will make me careless about the effect of my actions on others. If I am obsessed with manipulation and control and make that the object of my freedom, I not only will "cease to be humane," but will diminish the humanity of those I harm. Hütter's point is that it is only when we desire God more than any other good, and devote our freedom to seeking God, that we learn how rightly to desire anything else, and thus remain free. In Christianity, freedom is connected to the fulfillment of desire, but only when our sovereign desire is for God.

Desires are dangerous. They are meant to be life-giving, but they can be morally and spiritually fatal, and sometimes, sadly, physically fatal. We see the cost of destructive desires in obsessions and addictions. We see how destructive desires can enslave, how they can make freedom disappear. When freedom is reduced to the pursuit of desires without any examination of the substance of those desires, it quickly becomes destructive. We see this in people who covet, people who do not care whom they hurt as long as they have what they desire, whether money, fame, power, pleasure, or another's spouse. Such people are not free because they are controlled by their desires, but in their misuse of freedom they do incredible harm. As Hütter summarizes, "Misdirected, our desires completely distort any serious notion of authentic freedom by subtly redefining freedom as the potential to fulfill whatever we desire."[10] For Christians, freedom is not "the potential to fulfill whatever we desire." For Christians, freedom is found in loving God wholeheartedly and everything else, especially other persons, in light of that love. In other words, Jesus' commandment to love God, neighbor, and self is a lesson on freedom.

A Christian View of Freedom

What makes us free? Are we as free as we think we are? This brief review of contemporary understandings of freedom is disquieting because it suggests that the freedom we so jealously guard may diminish us (and others) more than it fulfills us, may enslave us (and others) more than it liberates. What's so great about freedom? It's a good question to ask if the cumulative effect of the freedom we embrace weakens communities and relationships, leaves us isolated and lonely, and makes us more anxious and restless than satisfied. The famous Trappist monk, Thomas Merton, learned this about freedom. *The Seven Storey Mountain*, Merton's autobiography, focuses on the years of his life prior to his decision to become a Catholic and to enter the Trappist Abbey of Gethsemani in rural Kentucky. Few who knew Merton ever thought he would leave Manhattan for the silence and solitude of a monastery, but Merton found a freedom within the confines of that monastery that he never experienced as a young man in New York. It was, to be sure, a radically different kind of freedom, but precisely in its difference exposed his previous understanding of freedom as empty and false. As a young man in New York, Merton "perfected a pose of cool sophistication, smoking, drinking all night in jazz clubs, and writing novels in the style of James Joyce. He regarded himself as a true man of his age, free of any moral laws beyond his own making, ready to 'ransack and rob' the world of all its pleasures and satisfactions."[11] But plunging deep into the world of pleasure and being unrestrained in pursuing his desires did not bring Merton the freedom and satisfaction he expected; on the contrary, it left him depleted, anxious, and fearful. "What a strange thing!" Merton wrote. "In filling myself, I had emptied myself. In grasping things, I had lost everything. In devouring pleasures and joys, I had found distress and anguish and fear."[12]

Nonetheless, it is hard to break the hold that these contemporary accounts of freedom have on us because we are instructed to think of freedom in these ways. It's the message we hear from commercials, from television, sometimes from our schools, and sometimes even from our churches. If we are sad, lonely, anxious, and depressed we assume the problem is with us, not with how we have been taught to consider freedom. As Wendell Berry says, "However frustrated, disappointed, and unfulfilled it may be, the pursuit of self-liberation is still the strongest force now operating in our society."[13] But we have to break the spell that such views of freedom have cast on us because any account of freedom that is not connected to goodness will ultimately destroy us. We need to be disenchanted with, not captivated by, these prevailing approaches to freedom because they are morally and spiritually bankrupt and finally make us less free instead of more. We have to stop thinking of freedom simply as the power to choose, as if what we choose does not matter, and realize that freedom is the power to choose and to do not just anything, but the good.

This is the Christian understanding of freedom. The freest person is the good person, the person who knows, loves, seeks, and serves the good. In Christianity, freedom does not exist for its own sake; rather, freedom exists for the sake of doing good in all the ways good can be done. Freedom is for the sake of justice and love, for the sake of mercy and compassion. Freedom is given us so that we can be generous, patient, and faithful. For Christians, we do not deserve our freedom as much as we are entrusted with it. Freedom is a gift, a sacred trust, but it is a "gift for the good,"[14] and this means we grow in freedom and are fulfilled in freedom to the degree that we honor the purpose of freedom. When Paul writes in his letter to the Christian community at Galatia that every follower of Christ has been called to live in freedom (Gal. 5:13), he suggests that the Christian vocation is a vocation to freedom. Christ calls us to freedom, not slavery. But Paul immediately adds that this is "not a freedom that gives free rein to the flesh," indicating that the freedom Christ wins for us is a freedom meant for seeking God and serving others. That Christ has set us free, Paul says, for the sake of such freedom indicates, too, that we are neither naturally free nor immediately free. Freedom is a grace won for us by Christ, but the freedom we have been entrusted with is misplaced, weakened, and even destroyed if we use it in ways that violate its purpose. In Christianity, freedom hinges on loving and desiring the good. Freedom is for excellence.[15] And this means the perfection of freedom is found not in the person of power and wealth, but in the virtuous person, in the saint. As Servais Pinckaers writes, "In the human person the perfection of the good coincides with the fullness of freedom."[16]

Why is it that freedom is not indifferent in its purpose, but connected to goodness and fulfilled in goodness? Why is freedom properly a power not to do whatever we want, but to love and serve the good? It is first because as creatures fashioned in the image of God, our freedom is to be modeled on God's freedom and should strive to conform to God's freedom. God's freedom is always freedom for the good—freedom for excellence—because God, who is the source and perfection of all goodness, unfailingly acts on behalf of the good. In God, freedom and goodness are one and indivisible. God is perfectly free because God is perfectly good. God is perfectly free because everything about God bespeaks the good and is devoted to the good. As God's images, we find freedom through love and devotion to the good.

A second reason that freedom is inseparable from goodness and fulfilled in goodness is that God has made us so that we are naturally, if imperfectly, inclined to the good. Nonetheless, there is a tendency to picture freedom as situated at the exact midpoint between good and evil, which suggests not only that we are not naturally disposed to the good, but also that we would not truly be free if we were. In this view, freedom consists in the power to choose *either* good or evil, but would be lessened if we were naturally inclined to either of them. Here freedom resides "in the power of the will to choose between contraries," Servais Pinckaers writes, "to opt for the *yes* or the *no*," but to be no more disposed to one than the other. This is the freedom of "radical indifference," a neutral freedom that is "essentially the power to move in two opposite directions,"[17] but is not inherently attracted to either of them. To be innately disposed to goodness, such a view suggests, would restrict freedom, not direct it. The free person is the woman or man who chooses without being influenced by any natural attraction to the good.

Christian theology offers a different account of freedom because it roots freedom in a natural inclination for the true and the good. We have minds to seek the truth and wills to do the good; this is what freedom is for and in what it is fulfilled. Freedom is the power not to do just anything, as if we were fundamentally uninterested in goodness; rather, it is the power to choose the good, a power that arises from and expresses our natural attraction to the good.[18] We may misuse our freedom by becoming indifferent to the truth and neglectful of the good, but doing so contradicts the fundamental inclinations of our nature. The freedom of "radical indifference" overlooks the fact that even if we misjudge what is true and good, we cannot help but love and desire them.[19] Freedom should articulate, deepen, and fulfill our mind's natural desire for truth and our will's natural desire for the good.[20] When it does so, our freedom increases. On the other hand, embracing what is false and evil is a corruption and lessening of freedom, not a healthy manifestation of it.

Forming a Capacity for Freedom into the Virtue of Freedom

Still, being inclined to choose the good is not the same as actually choosing it. It may be true that freedom's purpose is excellence in goodness, not mischief, and that the freest person is the virtuous person. But none of us is born excelling in goodness. We struggle at being good, we work at doing what is right, but we often fail. And sometimes we simply do not care about doing what is right. We enjoy spreading gossip, taking refuge in a lie, and delighting in a little revenge. A large part of our lives can be spent using our freedom to do harm. The truth is we have wounded wills, wills that are torn and divided by conflicting possibilities. We're lured by the good, yet tempted by corruption. We know we ought to care about others, but it's always nice to put ourselves first. We promise to be faithful to our commitments, but think we'll find freedom in betraying them. If there's anything in the Bible that rings true for all of us, it's Paul's famous lament about the wrenching contradictions in the depths of his heart: "What I do, I do not understand. For I do not do what I want, but I do what I hate" (Rom. 7:15).

We are all potentially free, but none of us is perfectly free. And whether or not we actually become free depends on us forming that initial inclination to the good into a steady and enduring choice for the good. We have a capacity for freedom, but true freedom occurs when we live in such a way that our *capacity* for freedom has become a real *virtue* of freedom. This means we do not possess freedom, but grow into it. It means not that we are free, but that we become free, and becoming free requires the ongoing conversion of ourselves in the good. It is not common to speak of freedom as a virtue because we think freedom is something we naturally possess, not a skill and habit we need to develop. But if freedom is not simply for choosing, but for choosing excellence, then as with any virtue it requires taking an inclination for excellence and developing it into a habit for excellence. As we saw in chapter 3, a virtue is a habit, and we have a "habit" or true expertise for freedom when we regularly use our freedom on behalf of the good—and are happy in doing so! We may all occasionally find happiness in doing what is right, and therefore have moments of real freedom; but genuine and lasting freedom—virtuous freedom—comes only when we consistently delight in the good. We journey toward freedom and hopefully come to possess it more completely. But our hold on freedom can be fragile because there is much in us that resists the freedom that is found in goodness, and much in our world that is threatened by it. Our freedom has to be won, struggled for every day, because there are so many ways it can be lost. As the French philosopher Gabriel Marcel noted, "freedom is a conquest—always partial, always precarious, always challenged."[21]

Freedom unfolds in us the more we consistently love and seek the good. By contrast, it shrivels the more we turn away from the good. This is why Pope John Paul II, in *Veritatis Splendor*, his 1993 document on the Christian moral life, said that when we are born we are given the "seed" of freedom, the beginnings of freedom, but are hardly in full possession of freedom. We can become free, but our freedom is not guaranteed. Like anything planted and needing time to grow, it has to be watched over and cared for if it is to be brought fully to life.[22] Freedom is "bestowed in embryo at the beginning of the moral life; it must be developed through education and exercised, with discipline, through successive stages," Servais Pinckaers writes. "Growth is essential to freedom."[23] As with happiness, if freedom is to grow it requires that we take up ways of life that are conducive of genuine freedom. If we are not naturally free any more than we are naturally happy, we have to be trained in freedom just as we need training in happiness. We do this in ways of life where people teach one another what it means to be free and help one another with all that keeps us from being free.

Jesus—The "Great Event" of Freedom

Many things diminish freedom. Our freedom can be lessened by elements in our upbringing, by past relationships, by our social and cultural environment, by our temperament, and especially by our past conduct and decisions. There are multiple impediments to freedom. This is why none of us is perfectly free and why none of us can gain freedom by ourselves. We need others who help us see and overcome whatever hinders freedom in us, and who help us grow in the real purpose of freedom. And since we live in societies that often promote misguided notions of freedom, we cannot be free "without the support of the true community of the good,"[24] communities where people support one another in loving and pursuing what is best. Such communities ought to be found in churches. Christian communities should be places where people learn what it means to be free and help one another be free. They should be places where people strive for and witness freedom for excellence.

Christians learn from Jesus what it means to be free. In the Christian life Jesus is freedom's exemplary teacher because his entire way of life shows us the path to true freedom. Jesus himself is "the great event" of freedom—the very revelation of freedom—because in his attitudes and actions he embodies God's freedom in the world.[25] Jesus unwraps the freedom of God and shows us that true freedom is found not in self-promotion or excessive self-concern, much less in the unhindered pursuit of unexamined desires, but in humility, service, compassion, and especially in love. The life, death, and resurrection of Jesus testify that God is the "infinite freedom of infinite love."[26] Thus, as disciples of Jesus, Christians discover that true liberty comes not when we are sovereigns of our own lives, carefully calculating everything we do, but when we give of ourselves for the sake of others. Following the way of Jesus, Christians learn that freedom comes not when we are beholden to no one, but when we are servants of the good, people who expend themselves generously and often sacrificially on behalf of others.[27]

Jesus tutors us in a different understanding of freedom. In the Christian life, disciples learn that the deepest and most prolonged freedom is secured through obedience to the ways of God revealed to us in Jesus. Freedom is secured in a life of discipleship, a life of learning from, imitating, and embodying the attitudes and actions of Jesus. Jesus shows us that worship, service, faithfulness, and even suffering love are paths to freedom. Jesus shows us too that freedom is found in forgiveness, in mercy, in costly generosity, and even in reaching out to our enemies. These are not practices we normally associate with freedom. In fact, because each of them signifies limitation, restraint, renunciation, and even submission, we consider them freedom's opposite, not its finest expression. We think we are most free not when we are obliged to others, but when we are answerable to no one. We do not associate freedom with serving others and being faithful to them, and certainly not with obedience to a way of life whose practices not only contradict some of our most ingrained desires, but also require that they be purified and transformed. Learning the freedom that comes from Christ initially shocks us because it counters so much that we think freedom to be and demands that we unlearn much that we have previously been taught about freedom. We cannot get over the scandal of Christian freedom until we relinquish the idea that freedom means we must be masters of our lives.

Stages of Growth on the Way to Freedom

Growing in freedom is the project of a lifetime because only gradually do we acquire the virtues of Christ constitutive of freedom. I am not consistently fair, truthful, faithful, or courageous. In fact, at any moment I am more likely to be unjust, dishonest, unfaithful, and cowardly, which means I am much more skilled at things that keep me from being free than I am in the virtues that will make me free. This is why the freedom that comes from growing in the goodness of God not only has to be learned, but is also acquired only with difficulty. Servais Pinckaers divides the Christian's education in freedom into three stages, each of which parallels three stages of life: childhood, adolescence, and adulthood. Just as there are normal stages of growth in our personal lives, there are stages of growth in the life of freedom. And just as we can go backward instead of forward in our emotional lives, reverting to adolescence or childhood in our attitudes and actions even though we may chronologically be adults, so too we can go backward on the path to freedom. Pinckaers associates the first stage of education in freedom with our childhood and names it the "stage of discipline." He links the second stage of freedom with adolescence and calls it "the stage of progress" or development. The final stage in the development of freedom represents the maturity or perfection of freedom and is associated with becoming an adult.[28] These distinctions are illuminating because they indicate that if our potential for freedom is to be realized, it must be disciplined, nurtured, and refined over time.

In the Christian life, one's education in freedom begins with an honest scrutiny of whatever might keep us from being free and a disciplined endeavor to overcome it. As noted above, there are multiple impediments to freedom. Fear can weaken freedom if it controls us to the degree that we are no longer able, because of pressure, anxiety, fear of failure, or the need to conform, to do what is right. This is one reason courage is a necessary element in the discipline of freedom.[29] Similarly, as noted above, our freedom can be diminished by events from our past (especially events that were hurtful or harmful), by our family upbringing, by the history of our relationships, by our social and cultural environments, and by our own choices and actions. None of us can take up the path to freedom without first addressing whatever might stand in the way of our freedom. This means we cannot be afraid to ask, "What keeps me from being free?" Am I controlled by a hurt of the past? By something unforgiven? By anger and bitterness? By an addiction? By an unhealthy relationship? Part of our training in freedom lies in identifying what thwarts freedom in us, including our own illusions about what freedom is.

But nothing diminishes freedom more than sin, a topic we will examine more fully in the next chapter. We cannot move beyond childhood in freedom unless we reckon with habits of sinfulness that hold us captive. This is difficult because we regularly see certain harmful actions as good. But if, as Christianity teaches, freedom is given for the good and found only in seeking and doing good, then acts or habits that turn us away from the good spell the demise of freedom, not its exaltation. When we sin, we lose our freedom in the very exercise of our freedom.[30] As Bernard Häring wrote, "If practiced only in the failure which is sin," freedom is "progressively reduced to impotence for the good and ultimately impotence for true freedom altogether."[31] Häring suggests the more polished we become with sinful, destructive behavior, the less free we will be. And if we truly excel in wickedness we can lose our freedom altogether because we will have become enslaved to ways of being and acting that draw us further away from the good, and thus lessen our ability to know and choose it. We cannot move beyond infancy in our possession of freedom unless we recognize that freedom "can be gravely endangered, deeply distorted, and ultimately destroyed by particular kinds of acts."[32]

But sometimes we never learn to walk in the way of freedom because we avoid the hard work involved in learning to be free. It is hard to change bad habits into good ones, hard to change vices into virtues, precisely because we have grown comfortable with them. We cling to them (or, perhaps better, they cling to us) because, as with any habit, we settle into them and make them our own. Even when they are bad for us it is hard to renounce them because they have become second nature to us, true expressions of ourselves. When the habits we cultivate are sins, we grow skilled at weaving our own captivity because we have practiced those habits with such regularity that we no longer recognize their destructiveness. The habitual liar does not see that nobody trusts him, or that he deceives himself much more than he fools others. The chronically angry person does not recognize how unhealthy her persistent bitterness is because it's her normal way of engaging life.

It is also true that some people prefer not to be free. Christianity teaches that freedom comes with goodness, but the effort required to "turn away from evil and do good" can frighten us. Freedom is hard work—it is the hard work of ongoing conversion—because to move along the path of freedom from childhood through adolescence and into adulthood asks nothing less than the remaking of ourselves in the goodness of God. The more we abide in the goodness of God the freer we will be, but for that very reason growth in freedom demands the discipline (*ascesis*) of ongoing transformation. It is hard to consent to a Christian understanding of freedom because it says in order to know freedom we first have to change. We cannot stay the way we are and be free. In the language of Christian baptism, our training in freedom begins when we die to one way of being a self and, as a disciple, commit ourselves to following the way of Christ.

We cannot learn what it means to follow the ways of Christ without being instructed in the laws and commands of God, particularly the Ten Commandments. This is contrary to our intuitions because so much of our contemporary philosophy of freedom is built on the principle "*less law, more freedom; no law, all freedom*."[33] We think law and freedom are opposed because laws by their very nature restrict us. Freedom and law are opposed if freedom means nothing more than being able to do whatever we wish. But if freedom is understood as "the movement of the human toward good," then far from undermining freedom, laws can shape and direct our freedom to find its true meaning and perfection in God.[34] "God's law does not reduce, much less do away with human freedom; rather, it protects and promotes that freedom," Pope John Paul II wrote in *Veritatis Splendor*.[35] God's laws and commandments enable us to take our first feeble steps in the ways of freedom because they delineate what frustrates and threatens freedom, as well as what protects it.

If we take the Ten Commandments to be a kind of grammar in freedom, we learn that freedom is lost when we forget that we are creatures, when we deny or neglect our obligations to others, when we succumb to violence, injustice, lying, or covetous desires. More positively, the Ten Commandments teach us that freedom is found in the praise and honor of God, in love of our neighbors (parents, family, friends, and strangers), in cultivating truthfulness, and in justice and respect toward others. The laws and commandments of God tutor us in the ways of freedom by articulating how our attitudes, desires, and dispositions must be trained and directed if the seed of freedom entrusted to us is to grow.[36] Just as parents have rules that help their children take their first steps in being responsible, so the Ten Commandments are "the *first necessary step on the journey towards freedom*, its starting-point."[37] As Augustine wrote, "The beginning of freedom is to be free from crimes . . . such as murder, adultery, fornication, theft, fraud, sacrilege and so forth. When once one is without these crimes (and every Christian should be without them), one begins to lift up one's head towards freedom. But this is only the beginning of freedom, not perfect freedom."[38]

In the second stage of one's formation in freedom (adolescence), the focus shifts from confronting the things that hinder or diminish freedom to cultivating the virtues through which freedom is most perfectly expressed. If freedom means excellence in goodness, then freedom grows as we learn to do the good not from fear of punishment and not even because it is what we ought to do; rather, our freedom deepens as we learn to do the good from love.[39] This is the mark of virtuous persons. Their hold on freedom is greater because they possess more completely the goodness in which freedom is found. They are truly free because goodness is second nature to them, not sporadic or accidental. They are free not occasionally but characteristically, because they regularly do the good with skill, ease, and delight. If we think of our training in freedom as an apprenticeship, in the first stage of this apprenticeship we work to unlearn the bad habits that, unless corrected, will keep us from excelling in freedom. Even the most promising athlete has first to correct any habits that will prevent her from becoming as good in the sport as she possibly can be. But once we have corrected anything that might prevent our growth in freedom, we must then nurture the habits and skills that will enable us to excel in what it means to be free, and that is what the virtues do. We move from being clumsy apprentices in freedom to becoming skilled experts in freedom as our attraction to the good increases. The more deeply we possess the goodness of the virtues, the greater our hold on freedom becomes because we are increasingly less interested in behavior that threatens or contradicts it.

A life of virtue is a life of freedom. An act of justice is not something other than freedom, but the way freedom is embodied and expressed in our relationships with others. Compassion is not something other than freedom, but how freedom is displayed in the face of another's suffering. Throughout the years of a marriage, faithfulness is not the opposite of freedom, but the form freedom takes in order to sustain love over time. Similarly, patience and perseverance do not restrict freedom but protect it because they guard us from bitterness and resentment, both of which diminish freedom. We may be accustomed to think that the virtues limit freedom because we often assume freedom is the capacity to do anything. We think our freedom has to be indeterminate; thus, the virtues would seem to restrict freedom because they make it harder for us not to choose and do the good. But that is what freedom means. Freedom does not consist in endless possibilities of doing just anything; rather, freedom means faithfulness to the good. A person who "learns to carry out a task with care, to practice justice, act honestly, seek the truth, and love sincerely, even though such actions may require sacrifice or be unnoticed by others,"[40] is the person who is free.

The final stage in the apprenticeship of freedom (adulthood) comes when all of one's actions are directed to a higher end, an end or purpose that calls us out of ourselves in service to others. We earlier asked, "Who is the freest person you know?" and "What is it that makes that person free?" In a Christian theology of freedom, the freest people are the women and men who have wholeheartedly devoted their lives to a project that calls them forth in service and love. Freedom reaches maturity not when our choices are unlimited and our responsibilities few, but when we put our freedom in service to a cause that is greater than ourselves. Marriage is an ordinary but compelling example of a way of life that directs our freedom to the care and love of others. Parenting certainly is too. A commitment to justice, witnessed so powerfully in people like the Catholic social activist Dorothy Day or the Protestant minister Dr. Martin Luther King Jr. expresses this highest level of freedom as well. Anytime we use the gifts, talents, and opportunities of our lives to increase goodness through committed devotion to causes and projects that call us out of ourselves in love and service to others, we exemplify the perfection of freedom. Freedom is fulfilled in devotion to purposes that are worthy of the gift of our lives and bring love, justice, and goodness more fully to life in our world. As Servais Pinckaers explains, "The perfection of moral freedom is shown by the response to a vocation, by devotion to a great cause, however humble it may appear to be, or the accomplishment of important tasks in the service of one's community, family, city, or Church."[41]

Ultimately, if God is "the freedom to love, to create, to redeem,"[42] then human beings, as God's images, find their greatest freedom in contributing to the creative and redemptive work of God. As suggested in the previous chapter, we are to use our freedom in partnership with the freedom of God. We are to work with God for the ongoing redemption of the world. This is freedom's grandest work and its greatest dignity. No matter what our particular situation in life might be, no matter what our gifts and talents may be, we can use our freedom in service of God's ongoing work of creation and redemption. As Bernard Häring notes, God "wants us to be co-creators, co-artists, and not just spiritless executors of his will."[43] In the Christian life, freedom is meant for faithful and creative obedience to the plans and purposes of God. And faithful and creative obedience means using our freedom thoughtfully and imaginatively to advance God's love and justice in the world. As Häring comments, "In and through his own creativity, God has shown us that he does not want mechanical applications of his laws or weary, stereotyped responses."[44] What God wants is the creative, energetic freedom that is born from love.

Conclusion

For freedom Christ has set us free. In this chapter we have explored a Christian theology of freedom, suggesting that freedom is a gift, a sacred trust that is to be used for doing good. What's so great about freedom? The greatness of freedom lies in the summons to use our freedom to share in and contribute to the creative and redemptive work of God. In Christianity, the freest persons are the man and woman whose foremost desire is to leave behind a legacy of love and goodness in the world. They are the ones who take the seed of freedom entrusted to them and nurture it to fullness. If the Christian life is training in happiness, then it must also include training in freedom because happiness requires using the gift of freedom for excellence in love, service, and goodness.

But freedom is a dangerous topic because separated from goodness it becomes a power for destruction, not life. Each of our lives, as well as the history of our world, is riddled with examples of the destructive work of freedom. Unconnected to goodness, the harvest of freedom is hurt, harm, and diminishment. Unconnected to goodness, freedom kills morally and spiritually, but often also physically. This is what happens when freedom walks not in the path of goodness, but in the path of sin. Unconnected to goodness, freedom destroys itself. The language of sin may be quaint, but the reality certainly is not. Sin is freedom's opposite, and it is what we will explore in chapter 6.

Some Questions for Reflection and Discussion

1. What makes freedom a dangerous topic?
2. Who is the freest person you know? What makes that person free? How have you been taught to think about freedom?
3. What do you think is the purpose of freedom? Can we have lots of choices and still not be free?
4. How would you explain a Christian understanding of freedom? Does it make sense to you?

5. Has another person ever helped you be free? Have you ever helped another person be free?
6. Do you agree that freedom, like any other virtue, has to be learned, but can also be lost?

Notes

1. Reinhard Hütter, *Bound to Be Free: Evangelical Catholic Engagements in Ecclesiology, Ethics, and Ecumenism* (Grand Rapids, MI: William B. Eerdmans Publishing Co., 2004), 6.

2. Hütter, *Bound to Be Free*, 112.

3. Kenneth R. Melchin, *Living with Other People: An Introduction to Christian Ethics Based on Bernard Lonergan* (Collegeville, MN: The Liturgical Press, 1998), 73.

4. James P. Hanigan, *As I Have Loved You: The Challenge of Christian Ethics* (New York: Paulist Press, 1986), 57.

5. Hanigan, *As I Have Loved You*, 59.

6. Hanigan, *As I Have Loved You*, 59.

7. Richard M. Gula, SS, *Reason Informed by Faith: Foundations of Catholic Morality* (New York: Paulist Press, 1989), 77.

8. Wendell Berry, *Sex, Economy, Freedom and Community* (New York: Pantheon Books, 1992), 149.

9. Hütter, *Bound to Be Free*, 160.

10. Hütter, *Bound to Be Free*, 160.

11. Robert Ellsberg, *The Saints' Guide to Happiness* (New York: North Point Press, 2003), 14.

12. Cited in Ellsberg, *The Saints' Guide to Happiness*, 14.

13. Berry, *Sex, Economy, Freedom and Community*, 152.

14. Bernard Häring, *Free and Faithful in Christ: Moral Theology for Clergy and Laity*, Vol. 1 (New York: The Seabury Press, 1978), 114.

15. Servais Pinckaers, OP, *The Sources of Christian Ethics*, trans. Sr. Mary Thomas Noble, OP (Washington, DC: The Catholic University of America Press, 1995), 389.

16. Pinckaers, *The Sources of Christian Ethics*, 412.

17. Pinckaers, *The Sources of Christian Ethics*, 332.

18. Bernard Häring, *The Law of Christ*, Vol. 1, trans. Edwin G. Kaiser (Westminster, MD: The Newman Press, 1963), 99.

19. Pinckaers, *The Sources of Christian Ethics*, 410.

20. Pinckaers, *The Sources of Christian Ethics*, 381.

21. Gabriel Marcel, *The Existential Background of Human Dignity* (Cambridge, MA: Harvard University Press, 1963), 146.

22. John Paul II, *Veritatis Splendor*, appendix to *Considering Veritatis Splendor*, ed. John Wilkins (Cleveland: The Pilgrim Press, 1994), #86.

23. Pinckaers, *The Sources of Christian Ethics*, 375.
24. Häring, *The Law of Christ*, 113.
25. Häring, *Free and Faithful in Christ*, 114.
26. Häring, *Free and Faithful in Christ*, 104.
27. John Paul II, *Veritatis Splendor*, #87.
28. Pinckaers, *The Sources of Christian Ethics*, 359.
29. Pinckaers, *The Sources of Christian Ethics*, 356.
30. Häring, *Free and Faithful in Christ*, 70.
31. Häring, *The Law of Christ*, 102.
32. Hütter, *Bound to Be Free*, 133.
33. Hütter, *Bound to Be Free*, 135.
34. Hütter, *Bound to Be Free*, 145.
35. John Paul II, *Veritatis Splendor*, #35.
36. Hütter, *Bound to Be Free*, 130.
37. John Paul II, *Veritatis Splendor*, #13.
38. John Paul II, *Veritatis Splendor*, #13.
39. Pinckaers, *The Sources of Christian Ethics*, 363.
40. Pinckaers, *The Sources of Christian Ethics*, 363.
41. Pinckaers, *The Sources of Christian Ethics*, 366.
42. Häring, *Free and Faithful in Christ*, 68.
43. Häring, *Free and Faithful in Christ*, 68.
44. Häring, *Free and Faithful in Christ*, 69.

CHAPTER SIX

~

False Steps on the Path to Happiness

Losing Our Way and Finding It Back

We are made for happiness, fashioned for bliss.

But we sure know how to make a mess of things. In the book of Genesis, the story of creation ends with God's emphatic judgment that everything God created is stunningly good. Nothing is lacking, nothing amiss, nothing less than perfect in this paradise fashioned from love. The world is a garden of delights, an Eden of beauty and goodness that God designed for the first human couple—and all who would come after them—to enjoy. There is no hint of evil in a universe carefully brought into being by God, no trace of imperfection. It is a gift expressly fashioned to bring joy. Everything is designed for the first couple's happiness, but strangely happiness is not enough for them; at least not the happiness God entrusted to them. There is no reason for them to be discontent because in a world that could not be better they have everything they could possibly need.

But paradise is not enough. Instead of being grateful for the gift, they resent the Gift-giver. More than happiness, they want power, especially the power that comes from being not creatures but gods. And so when the serpent, "the most cunning of all the animals" (Gen. 3:1), tells them that if they eat the forbidden fruit they will not die, as God declared, but "will be like gods" (Gen. 3:5), they succumb. In that one act of defiance paradise is lost, evil and death enter the world, and the long, bloody saga begins. Through a single act of disobedience everything that had begun so well was turned upside down, and solidarity, trust, and love were replaced by alienation, envy, and fear. The man blames the woman, the woman blames the serpent, and the first of their offspring, filled with resentment, kills his brother. Sin goes from being a stranger in paradise to "a demon lurking at the door" (Gen. 4:7). In their quest to be like gods, these first human beings unleash a force they are powerless to stop. Without divine intervention, the process of de-creation begun by them cannot be reversed.

When men and women play at being gods, the results are always catastrophic. Evil is our creation, not God's. It is the handiwork of our freedom when instead of surrendering ourselves to God we, in a declaration of independence, assert ourselves against God. Humanity's first false step on the path to happiness was taken when, in an act of rebellion, our forebears attempted to throw off their dependence on God. Deceived by the serpent's lie, they began to live a lie, the lie that is the heart of every sin; the lie that suggests we are not needy, dependent creatures who cannot live apart from God, but sovereign deities who have no need for God. It is tempting to blame the mess of the world on the foolish pride of the first human couple, but we cannot distance ourselves from them, because their original sin gets replayed in our lives. All sin is a kind of deception about happiness, and there is no greater deception (and surely none more common) than to think things will go better for us apart from God. No one likes to think that self-realization and fulfillment come by loving and serving and worshiping something greater than ourselves. This is why the first couple's temptation remains *the* human temptation. Like them, we think being dependent on God hinders us. We think being creatures instead of the Creator is unfair, and we suspect, as the serpent suggested, that God wants to hold us back, not perfect us. Thus, like our ancestors in waywardness, we rebel. Instead of learning from their mistake, we repeat it across the ages in equally uncreative ways. Against our better judgment but of our own free will, we replay the story of the Fall and make our own contribution to humanity's work of de-creation.

There are certain truths about ourselves that we cannot afford to forget. Christianity teaches that we are God's very images fashioned from love and called to fellowship with God and one another. It teaches that there is a beauty and dignity and honor to every one of us, and that we can use our intelligence and freedom to cooperate with God in fulfilling the most promising meaning of our lives. But it also teaches that we can live in ways that contradict and violate that meaning; we can of our own free will live in ways that move us further and further from the God who is our happiness. Sin never makes sense—there is an inescapable craziness to sin—because to sin is to become an agent of our own destruction. As Josef Pieper asks, "How could a human being possibly and with full deliberateness undertake an act of resistance to the very meaning of his own existence?"[1] But we do it all the time and often quite skillfully; in fact, the real danger of sin is to grow so comfortable with it that we no longer recognize the destructiveness of our actions. Just as goodness and virtue can become second nature to us, so too can vice and wickedness. We can grow blissfully unaware of the harm we do to ourselves, to other human beings, to other species and the earth, and to our relationship with God by sin. Thus, we cannot afford to forget that we are fallen creatures who need to be rescued from ourselves.

The Christian life can rightly be understood as a rescue operation. It is what we mean when we speak of salvation and redemption, of grace, pardon, and deliverance. The story of the Fall indicates not only that there is a sizable gap between what the world is and what it should be, but also that there is something wrong with us that needs to be put right, but we cannot do it ourselves. If there is any hope for the world, the calamitous story that began with Adam and Eve's rebellion needs to be reversed. The history of sin must become a salvation history, a narrative of rescue and redemption. In this chapter we shall explore what makes that rescue operation necessary by first examining the nature of sin, focusing on it as a rejection of our true identity and as a way of being that distances us further from happiness. We shall then consider the Christian teaching of original sin, a doctrine that offers a sobering but realistic assessment of ourselves that must be considered if we are to appreciate both the necessity and sheer giftedness of redemption. Finally, we will conclude by asking how those who are lost and fallen find their way back to happiness. How do we reverse the false steps we have taken? What we shall discover is that the Christian life is an ongoing convalescence, a never-finished healing and rehabilitation through which we are reconnected to the good we initially rejected, the good we thought we could live without. This gives a different slant to thinking about the Christian life as a quest for happiness. It suggests that we will never understand, much less reach, true happiness unless we claim our identity as recovering sinners. The Christian life is a life for recovering sinners. We are always in recovery, and it is only when we recognize this that we come to understand what real and lasting happiness is.

Sin—Pursuing a Case of Mistaken Identity

In the Bible sin is described in a variety of ways. Sin is an act that "misses the mark" (*hamartia*) in the way that an archer's misguided arrow misses the target or our own efforts to love are misdirected by selfishness. It is an act of injustice (*adikia*) that comes from failing to fulfill one's duties and obligations to others, such as occurs when we break a promise or are unfaithful in a relationship, or when we lie, cheat, and steal. Sin is lawlessness (*anomia*) and rebellion. It is any act that threatens the harmony of a community; violence would be an obvious example, especially the typically unrestrained violence of war.[2] Each of these suggests that to sin is "to go wrong" by falling short of or turning away from the good, or by neglecting our responsibilities and obligations to others. But the Bible also speaks of sin not only as an external transgression, but also as a debilitating quality of soul or a perverse quality of character. A sinner is someone of "hard heart and a stiff neck," someone who is spiritually blind and deaf.[3] Sinners "walk in darkness" and persist in iniquity. They "wander from the path," and their deeds leave them "twisted, crooked or bent."[4] Both as an act and as a quality of character, sin alienates a person from God, from other persons, and even from him or herself.

Besides presenting sin as an act and as a description of a person's character, the Bible also depicts sin "as a universal human condition, a pervasive and tragic fact of our creaturely existence"[5] that weakens our orientation to the good and leaves us flawed, misspent, and broken. We are born into sin and cannot by ourselves escape its powers. This is captured most poignantly in Psalm 51 when the psalmist, pleading for mercy and healing from God, confesses, "True, I was born guilty, / a sinner, even as my mother conceived me" (51:7). Finally, the Bible depicts sin as a hostile, malevolent power seeking dominion over us and our world. Sin is in us, but it is also bigger and more powerful than we are. A force for death, sin is a demonic power of darkness that viciously opposes God and works to undo creation. Its aim is to master our hearts and rule the world. It allures with promises of freedom, but always results in captivity.

Sin may be depressingly familiar, but it is never normal or healthy or wise because it represents a way of being that frustrates, and ultimately prevents, our fulfillment as persons. Sin can never be embraced as a truly life-giving option or creative alternative because it contradicts and rejects the most fundamental truth of our nature: We are inherently religious creatures who ultimately can find happiness and fulfillment only in God. Sin doesn't affirm, it denies; and it is only in light of what sin denies that it can be rightly understood. The primary affirmation Christianity makes about human beings is that we are creatures fashioned from the love of God who live only from the love of God and are fulfilled only in the love of God. Sin asserts otherwise. Every sin echoes Adam and Eve's original sin because every sin in some way contends that we are independent creatures who can thrive and flourish apart from God. Sin doesn't give, it takes, and it takes by robbing us of our only true identity as persons called to friendship and communion with God. We live solely from the creative generosity and goodness of God. As creatures, we live only by participating in the life and love of God, by receiving our being from God's being. In more biblical language, we are "covenant creatures" who have life by abiding in faithful communion with God. This is why to enter a life of sin is to step outside of the very relationship that gives us life—it is to move from light into darkness, from love into nothingness. As C. S. Lewis put it, if God "is the fuel our spirits were designed to burn," then to turn to sin is not to turn to an alternative life source (because there is none), but to nothing. "God cannot give us a happiness and peace apart from Himself," Lewis explains, "because it is not there. There is no such thing."[6]

Christian theology commonly speaks of sin as violating the covenant relationship we have with God. As exemplified in Israel's covenant with Yahweh, to live in a covenant with God means not only that we are known and identified by that relationship, but also that we cannot have life apart from it. Israel found life only by remembering that they were God's people. Whenever their infidelity led them away from God they discovered that life outside of the covenant was not an alternative kind of existence, but death. Sin did not bring them prosperity, but dissolution. It is no different for us. Sin begins as an attempt to liberate the self from its relationship with God—to strike out on one's own, as it were—but it always results in the loss of the self. Sin is a case of mistaken identity (or perhaps *misplaced* identity) because to sin is to misunderstand who we really are: persons whose being and identity come from God and cannot be found apart from God. Sin is notoriously *self*-destructive because it attempts to make us into something we cannot possibly be, persons who thrive without God.

The metaphor of covenant suggests that sin is best understood as a religious concept, not a juridical or even a moral one. Even when our sin targets another human being, it is principally an act against God, to whom we are bonded in love. To lie is to treat our neighbor unjustly, but it is a sin against God, whose covenant life calls us to truthfulness. Murder is a horrendous crime against another human being, but it is a sin against the God who makes all life sacred. Sin is a betrayal of love and responsibility, rooted in ingratitude, to a God who is always faithful to us. Like infidelity in the covenant of marriage, sin is less the breaking of a law and more the betrayal of a relationship.[7] Perhaps the reason many of us have a diminished sense of sin is that we no longer think of our lives in this way. We see a relationship with God as an option, not as a requirement of our nature. We may turn to God or we may not, but even if we do God is more a lifestyle choice than the single source of life. God is one more item among countless other items to choose, and whether we choose God or not is a matter of preference, not necessity. In a culture of individualistic consumerism where the self is sovereign, not indebted, the concept of sin is unintelligible. Sin makes sense only when there is an unsurpassable Being of love we can offend, but apart from whom we cannot live.

Sin—Pondering Truly Unnatural Acts

Apart from a religious understanding of life, we cannot make sense of sin. Apart from a religious understanding of life, sin has no meaning. We may fall short, make mistakes, and even do terrible harm, but we cannot sin. Sin only makes sense when we envision ourselves as creatures incontestably oriented to God and fulfilled in God. Sin makes sense only when we believe we are bonded in love to a God apart from whom we cannot live and to whom we are accountable. Once we embrace this understanding of ourselves, the language of sin is not only intelligible, but also absolutely crucial because it calls our attention to ways of being that are dangerously contrary to our nature as creatures who begin in, always depend on, and are perfected in God. Christianity has traditionally spoken of sin as any act or way of life that is "contrary to nature" (*contra naturam*). As human beings we are naturally inclined to life with God as the perfection of ourselves. This desire for God is not something we create; rather, it is like a "hidden gravitational pull" within us that draws us to God as the supreme good of our lives.[8] No matter how commonplace or predictable, sin is utterly unnatural because it is starkly at odds with the deepest impulse of our being to be drawn to and conformed to the beautiful and the good, the fullness of which is God. This is why sin never brings contentment and peace, but only turmoil and restlessness. It is why, Josef Pieper suggests, "we can never sin with the unreserved power of our will, never without an inner reservation, never with one's whole heart."[9] It is hard to put ourselves completely behind sin—to sin wholeheartedly—because every sin distances us from what we most need and, despite ourselves, desire. Sin, in the most complete sense of the term, is a thoroughly "unnatural act" because it alienates us from the good that is the perfection of our being. In a most dangerous and damaging way, it "misses the mark" by turning us away from the good that is happiness.

Similarly, Christian theology frequently speaks of sin as "contrary to reason" (*contra rationem*) because it is irrational to live and act in ways that turn us away from the most fitting end for human beings and that leave both our lives and our world disordered. Sin never makes sense. There is an abiding absurdity to sin because with every sin we consent to an act that goes against our good. There may be pleasure in sin—even seductive delight in sin—but there is never logic or happiness because with sin we freely and deliberately undermine our own well-being. How can we do this? How can we assent to ways of being that are essentially self-defeating? How can we invest ourselves in behavior that can only bring sadness and pain? Sin is always against our better knowledge. The thief knows this before he steals, the plagiarist before she cheats, the adulterer before he betrays. The only way we can proceed down paths of ruin against our better judgment is by convincing ourselves that what we know isn't right or good is, at least for us in these circumstances, fitting. At the heart of every sin is self-deception because the only way that we can "do evil and not wince"[10] is by allowing ourselves to be fooled. In this respect, we do not sin with "full knowledge"; rather, we sin with deliberately distorted knowledge, a knowledge that blurs and obscures, because the only way we can endorse self-defeating behavior is by not allowing ourselves to see clearly what we are doing.

There is a scene in John Steinbeck's novel *East of Eden* where Samuel Hamilton visits Adam Trask. Adam is sitting in a room with his wife, Cathy. "It was almost pitch-black inside," Steinbeck writes, "for not only were the shades down but blankets were tacked over the windows." When Samuel asks Adam, "Why are you sitting in the dark?" Adam replies, "She doesn't want the light. It hurts her eyes."[11] When it comes to sin, the same is true with us. Like Cathy, we don't want the light—it hurts our eyes—because if we allowed ourselves to see clearly what sin involves, we could not carry through with it. The man who cheats on his wife does not see it as adultery, but as having his needs met. The woman who cheats on her income taxes does not see it as dishonesty, but something everybody does. Shunning the light, we find ways not to see lest we glimpse clearly what our actions involve. Sin presupposes blindness because the only way we can endorse it is by not allowing its full reality to be illuminated. It is no accident that so many of Jesus' miracles involve restoring sight to the blind—teaching people to see—and no wonder that Paul calls Christians to renounce the darkness of sin in order to "walk in the light." To sin is to take refuge in darkness, to refuse to see lest the light that "hurts our eyes" expose the destructiveness of the behavior we have come to enjoy. In *People of the Truth*, Robert Webber and Rodney Clapp say "because of the Fall people can no longer see what is real,"[12] a striking phrase that suggests the natural human condition is one of illusion and unreality, not clarity of vision. We can be so blinded by the fantasies and illusions we weave to justify our actions that we no longer recognize the beauty of the good, much less the light that is God (2 Cor. 4:4). With eyes adjusted to the darkness, we continue down paths that terminate in sadness.

To persevere in darkness brings death to the soul. Christian theology speaks of "mortal" or "deadly" sins to call our attention to acts and ways of being whose cumulative effects are so morally and spiritually corrupting that they can permanently separate us from our true good and turn us toward evil as if it were our good. Seven vices, traditionally known as the "seven deadly sins," are considered to be especially toxic. Their names are pride, envy, anger, sloth, greed, gluttony, and lust. Christians are warned not to embrace these vices because they are morally and spiritually deadly.[13] If we embody them, they will ruin us. The seven deadly sins name vices to which all of us are susceptible, but that must be wrestled with lest in conquering us they disfigure us in evil. At its most extreme, to settle into a state of deadly sin is to be so habitually given over to evil that it is difficult for us not to do what is wrong. It is not that we have then completely lost our freedom, but that we have so continually misused it that we cannot, without grace, redirect it to the good. To speak of mortal or deadly sin is to recognize that we can live "contrary to nature" for so long that from the innermost center of our lives we regularly choose evil over good. In describing the effects of sinning mortally, Vincent MacNamara says, "We must be talking then about someone who is attached to wrongness in the depths of the heart, who has, so to speak, settled for it."[14]

Such sinning unto death leaves people radically alienated from God. They are, in a very real sense, in hell; however, it is not God who put them there but themselves. With every sin, they endorsed ways of being that moved them further away from their good and shut them off from life. They are in hell, but their hell, Josef Pieper notes, "should not be thought of as a dungeon inside which one has been forcibly locked up against one's will. The bolt on the door that seals off the way into the open air is not located outside, but inside, the person."[15] As Pieper suggests, hell is not so much a place, but a condition into which we place ourselves by a lifetime of choices so corrupting that we no longer realize the destructiveness they perpetuate. There is something final and irreparable about deadly sin inasmuch as the sinner, thoroughly deceived, has no awareness of his or her catastrophic condition and, despite the absurdity, knows only how to reaffirm it. Such persons replicate their errors listlessly and joylessly because they are, even in their destructiveness, the only things they have learned to do well. André Gide called hell "sinning on and on, against one's better knowledge and without any real desire to do so."[16] It's a good description of despair and captures well the fate of one who "misses the mark" for a lifetime.

Original Sin—Why We Are Easily Pulled Off Center

Too many false steps to happiness can leave us so lost that we never find our way back. Why does this happen? Given that sin is totally at odds with our flourishing—given its craziness—why do we embrace it? Why do we settle into habits and practices guaranteed to prevent our fulfillment as persons? C. S. Lewis captured this contradiction at the heart of every person when he said there are two indisputable truths about human beings. "First, that human beings all over the earth, have this curious idea that they ought to behave in a certain way, and cannot really get rid of it. Secondly, that they do not in fact behave in that way. They know the Law of Nature; they break it. These two facts are the foundation of all clear thinking about ourselves and the universe we live in."[17]

What Lewis articulated Christianity calls original sin. Its purpose is not to lead to a gloomy, pessimistic assessment of ourselves, but to help us "make sense out of the actual world in which we find ourselves."[18] First, the teaching affirms that we are born into a world already wounded and broken by sin, a fallen and disordered world. Every infant comes to consciousness in a world weakened by sin. Evil surrounds us before we open our eyes. It is part of the air we breathe, part of the fabric of life. Original sin means evil precedes us and awaits us, but does not originate with us. When we sin we add to what is already there. "When we commit a sin, we do not present evil for the first time to a previously innocent world," Ted Peters explains. "Sin was here before we arrived."[19] I may get caught up in evil, I may contribute to it and increase it, but I do not begin it any more than I can single-handedly defeat it. "The story of Adam and Eve awakens us to the truth that 'I do not begin evil; I continue it.'"[20]

This first dimension of original sin affirms that God's creation remains indisputably good, but it is not perfect. Like ourselves, the world needs to be healed and restored; it too awaits redemption (Rom. 8:19–22). The doctrine of original sin means that nothing in the world is quite as it should be. Structures and institutions that should serve the plans and purposes of God become "demonically subverted"[21] into powerful instruments for doing harm. They ought to sustain life and serve the well-being of persons, but instead become twisted and perverse. Economic policies that should work for an equitable distribution of wealth and resources commonly favor the privileged few over the many. Marriages that should be partnerships of intimacy and love sadly deteriorate into abusive, destructive relationships. Families that ought to be centers of affirmation and acceptance sometimes become households of death. Political parties that mouth the ideals of justice and liberty can become pathetically self-serving and cynically corrupt. Churches become "beds of corruption and ruin"[22] when they stray from the teachings of Christ, distort and conceal, and become more concerned about power than service. Such is what it means to live after the Fall. At birth we enter a world that may be blessed but is sometimes more darkness than light. It is a world that undeniably bears the scars of sin.

Theologians often refer to this evil that precedes us and shapes us, and is greater than any one of us can be responsible for, as *social sin*. Social sin points to "a surplus of evil beyond what can be ascribed to individuals."[23] It is the evil embedded in the laws, structures, institutions, and practices of societies when instead of serving the requirements of justice, they increase the disorder of injustice. We see social sin at work in tax policies that favor the already too wealthy over the struggling poor. We see its presence in practices designed to protect the interests of the powerful and in institutions that violate human rights and victimize the oppressed. And we see it in the greed and carelessness that destroy the environment and endanger the earth. Social sin captures how the cancer of evil, particularly manifested in injustice, infests society's structures and institutions, often becoming legally enshrined in them. It expresses how we are surrounded and influenced by an evil we did not create, but often protect and increase. The reality of social sin affects us even if we are barely aware of it. Since it saturates the world we are born into, we easily take it for granted, especially if its injustice benefits us. Those who glory in wealth and power are much less likely to have their eyes opened to the reality of social sin than those who are crushed by it. Those who plan and profit from wars are normally much less disturbed by it than those who are asked to fight those wars.

And so even if social sin is something we discover, not something we initiate, we nonetheless contribute to it and too often remain untroubled by it. Social sin may be bigger than all of us, but it is a work of human hands, ours usually among them. We add to this surplus of evil when we cooperate with sinful structures, work to sustain them, or fail to speak out against them. We are morally culpable for social sin because even though none of us singlehandedly creates the world's injustice, we often work to increase it in our societies, in the workplace, in our churches, and even in our homes. Even though no one of us is solely accountable for the evil of the world, we are nonetheless, to some degree, responsible for it either through actions that reenforce it (sins of commission) or through the silent indifference that fails to challenge it (sins of omission). We may be born into a world already deformed by sinful structures and institutions, but we are implicated in that evil whenever we accommodate it, profit from it, or do nothing to address it. As Russell Connors and Patrick McCormick observe, "these injustices, embedded as they are in our world and our hearts, could not continue to exist without some help from us."[24] This social manifestation of original sin witnesses the tight connection between our personal actions and the seemingly impersonal reality of social sin. Unjust social institutions and structures are the work of human hands, but after years of one generation after another contributing to them, they become so vast and pervasive that they seem virtually indomitable. We who created them now seem to be ruled by them and have little idea how to change them. This is why the stranglehold of injustice is so hard to break.

Probing Our Bent to Disorder

The second dimension of original sin calls our attention to the evil that lives not in our world, but in our hearts. We may be living, breathing images of the love and beauty and goodness of God, but we live after the Fall, and this means the image of God in us is tarnished and obscured. Original sin refers to all those dimensions of ourselves that work against goodness. It is why we who are summoned to grow in the good scamper off in other directions. We love and we fail to love. We are faithful and we betray. We are just, but we are also greedy, truthful but often deceitful. Original sin means all is not well with us; before we do anything, we are already broken. Even though human beings are good in important ways, we are also wayward creatures whose misdeeds wreak incredible harm. A theology of original sin claims there is much about us that is not quite right, not quite in order, and this disorder bred in our bones asserts itself in all the confounding ways we go wrong. There is a deep division in our hearts that is felt every time we fail to do what we know we ought to do. We flirt with temptations we know we are too weak to avoid. We surrender to thoughts, words, and deeds we know will lead us astray and likely hurt others. We let anger get the best of us, resentments master us, and past hurts control us. We take all these false steps to happiness against our better judgment because there lives in us a "bent towards disorder"[25] that impacts everything about us. Original sin is a disorder of the heart that results in the disorder of the world. No matter how much we want to find happiness through love and goodness, there is a force in us that pulls in another direction. The opposite of the energy of grace, the energy of original sin works on our woundedness, weakening and diminishing our capacity to do good.[26] It leaves us living off balance, always inclined for a fall.

When I was growing up in Louisville, Kentucky, there was an amusement park in the west end of the city called Fontaine Ferry Park. It was one of those dusty old amusement parks, filled with the smell of cotton candy and the sounds of summer, that were magic to a child. One of the attractions of Fontaine Ferry Park was Hilarity Hall, a large, ramshackle room filled with all sorts of wonders. There were mazes, slides, and constantly trotting wooden horses inside Hilarity Hall, and there was the Wheel of Joy. The

Wheel of Joy was a large polished disk in the center of that wacky room that was a magnet for kids. You'd crowd into the center of the Wheel of Joy with nothing to hold on to but each other. Then it would begin to spin, not so fast at first, but with increasing velocity. The idea was to stay on the Wheel of Joy as long as possible, but that was the problem. It was not possible to stay on the Wheel of Joy. No matter how hard you tried, you could not remain in its center. The man in the control booth (who always seemed to have a mischievous smirk) would set it spinning faster and faster so there would be kids flying off in all directions, tumbling over each other as they bade farewell to the Wheel of Joy. No matter how strong your resolve, the Wheel of Joy always won.

Years later it struck me that the Wheel of Joy is a perfect metaphor for original sin. No matter how hard we try, we cannot stay centered on the good because there are forces in us and in our world that pull us in all sorts of misguided directions. We are pulled off center by temptation, by our own self-deception, by cultural and social forces whose messages bewitch us, and by the prompting of others who play on our weaknesses. We are pulled off center when unwieldy ambition leads to dishonesty, when our wounded pride has us plotting revenge, when our lust for pleasure drives us to use and manipulate another. If there are patterns of destructiveness alive in our world, they are also alive in our hearts.

One of the best analyses of original sin comes from Thomas Aquinas. In talking about original sin, Aquinas draws an analogy between physical health and illness, and spiritual health and illness. Prior to the Fall, in that paradisiacal state of harmony and innocence, the first human couple were completely healthy and whole. Nothing was awry in them or in their world. Aquinas calls this the state of "original justice," suggesting that before sin entered the world everything was exactly as it should be. But with sin everything was thrown out of order, not destroyed but damaged. Sin is a disintegrating force that weakens everything. It's a toxic force that tries to undo God's creation. Aquinas speaks of the personal effect of original sin principally in terms of a congenital defect that is every individual's inheritance; it is a kind of malignancy of the soul.[27] We are not completely corrupted by original sin, but we are unmistakably infirm. For Aquinas there is nothing slight or superficial about the impact of original sin on our nature; rather, its disabling effects infect every dimension of our being. In assessing the damage of original sin on us, Aquinas uses the metaphor of wounds. We are wounded in our minds (the wound of ignorance), wounded in our hearts (the wound of malice), wounded in our ability to withstand temptation (the wound of weakness of will), and wounded in our ability to love things in the right way (the wound of concupiscence or disordered desire). These wounds of original sin depict how our natural orientation to the good is weakened.[28]

For instance, the wound of ignorance describes how sin affects our desire for truth and our ability to know it. Too, we can choose to be ignorant if we do not want to know what is true lest that knowledge challenge us to live and act differently. The wound of malice represents "our proclivity to evil" and how repeatedly acting on that inclination can leave us "hardened against the true good."[29] The wound of weakness of will speaks to our frequent inability to withstand temptations in order to do what is right. We experience this wound when we know what we ought to do but do not do it on account of weakness or fear or pressure or the need to conform. And concupiscence, the wound of disordered desire, burns within us when we cannot "temper the pleasurable,"[30] whether it be our desire for the pleasures of food and drink, the pleasures of power, wealth, and possessions, the pleasures of fame and celebrity, or the pleasures of sex. At the root of concupiscence is love, but it is an immoderate and ultimately unreasonable love that leaves us being controlled by goods that do not deserve such excessive attention. We know the wound of concupiscence when we prefer "the things that are lower" over "the things that are higher,"[31] whether it be typically choosing entertainment over study, alcohol over prayer, possessions over friendships, or casual sex over true intimacy.

If wounds are not to become fatal, they need to be healed. This discussion of original sin casts the Christian moral life as a quest for happiness in a different light. It suggests not only that we are easily confused about where real happiness lies and frequently sidetracked in our pursuit of it; but also, more importantly, that a healing must occur for us to rightly understand and enjoy happiness at all. If happiness is found in goodness, then we can be truly and completely happy only when all the inclinations to evil in us are overcome. And if the perfection of happiness consists in loving communion with God, such happiness can be enjoyed only when our restless and conflicted hearts learn to love God most of all, that is, only when we are no longer afflicted by the disorder of the heart that is sin. We begin the Christian life wounded and weak. We begin darkened by ignorance, perverted by malice, stymied by weakness of will, and perplexed by concupiscence. This is who we are as we take up the journey and, to some extent, it is who we remain. These wounds have to be treated if we are not to remain permanently impaired, creatures who can never enjoy the happiness for which they are made.

Anyone who is ill must undergo a regimen of healing so that her health can be restored. It is no different in the Christian life. In light of the effects of original sin, our training in happiness must include a process for uprooting everything in us that turns us away from God. It is fitting to picture the Christian moral life as an ongoing convalescence or rehabilitation in which we who are born wounded and infirm gradually regain our health. We are "patients" who need to be healed and restored, but we cannot heal ourselves. The recovery from sin that is necessary for happiness is the work of a lifetime, but it is primarily God's work more than our own. The remaking of ourselves that happiness requires principally occurs through grace, Christ, the sacraments, and the Spirit. It is what Christians mean by justification (being made right by God) and sanctification (being made holy by God).

How the Sick Get Sicker—the Danger of Habitual Sin

Nonetheless, even if we cannot heal those wounds ourselves, we can certainly deepen them. Like anyone who is sick, we can live in ways that make us worse instead of better, and this is what happens when we choose to persist in sin. The real peril of sin is ordinarily not found in isolated acts of wrongdoing, but in repeated patterns of wrongdoing that lead to greater evil. The ordinarily faithful husband does not suddenly decide to commit adultery; rather, adultery is commonly the result of smaller acts of unfaithfulness that, extended over time, make the infidelity of adultery seem not only acceptable, but inevitable. Similarly, it is not the single then quickly repented lie that is worrisome, but persistent failures in truthfulness that make lying a habit in us, not an occasional and regretted failure. "Small, untidy failings often enough grow and flourish, becoming major and destructive forces in our lives," Patrick McCormick writes. "Little choices tend to set the groundwork for more disastrous and malicious decisions."[32] If we choose to reenforce the wounds of original sin by cultivating habits of sinfulness, our occasional waywardness soon becomes a customary way of being. Our sins are no longer isolated and rare, but commonplace and predictable. Destructive behavior becomes second nature to us—we're accomplished at it—because instead of resisting the disordered forces of our hearts, we continually affirm them. At this point, the "small, untidy failings" of our lives have transmogrified into large, destructive forces that master us. It's what the Bible means when it speaks of living under the dominion of sin.

But what makes habits of sinfulness especially dangerous is that because they have become second nature to us, we no longer realize their destructive effects. The woman consumed by envy fails to see how her resentment of others' gifts and successes prevents her from enjoying friendships with them. The promiscuous lover has no sense of the loneliness that will be his future. There is no more dangerous predicament than to have become so accomplished in sin that we no longer realize what we are doing to ourselves. A passage in the *Catechism of the Catholic Church* captures this peril when it speaks of sin creating a "proclivity to sin," of sin tending "to reproduce itself and reinforce itself" in ways that "cloud conscience and corrupt the concrete judgment of good and evil."[33] Unless broken by repentance and contrition, and countered by the development of virtue, the sin that keeps reproducing itself becomes a fatal addiction, an ongoing conversion unto death.

Habits of sinfulness lock us into self-destructive ways of being. Habits of sinfulness, which are what the vices are, work the wrong kind of transfiguration in us. Instead of cultivating our inclinations to love and goodness and holiness, they make us accomplished in the very things that bring sadness and dissolution: greed and self-centeredness, pride and resentment, jealousy and anger, meanness and maliciousness. Human beings are creatures of habits. We "choose readily those things which habit has made congenial."[34] Virtues are habits that make goodness congenial to us, but vices are habits that make us comfortable with evil. If sin becomes habitual in us—truly second nature for us—we come to find pleasing the very things we should disdain. The utmost peril of habitual sinning is to begin to find wickedness, in all its many manifestations, more agreeable and attractive than goodness. This may be unnatural, but it is not rare. There are countless persons so bewitched by wealth that they are blind to the dangers of greed. There are people who delight in demeaning and ridiculing others. There are many who take pleasure in destroying another's reputation. And all of us know people who never let anything get in the way of their pleasure. In each case some sin has so completely mastered these people that they have come to love what will ultimately destroy them. We choose according to our tastes. Habitual sinners are resolved to do evil because they've acquired a taste for it. Instead of abhorring cruelty, dishonesty, ruthlessness, or bitterness, they have grown to enjoy them. As Aquinas notes, they "choose what is spiritually evil" in order to satisfy their "newly acquired taste."[35] If sin's hold on them is to be broken, they must once again find bitter what they have learned to find sweet.

Finding Our Way Back Home—Rescue and Recovery

So here's the Christian story. The first of our kind entered a world that could not have been better, a garden of delights that was splendidly and perfectly good. Like all who have come after them, they were creatures fashioned for happiness. But they took a wrong turn. Instead of trusting the bliss God's love had made for them, they fell for the lie. Taking the serpent's trickery for truth, they rebelled. They resented their status as creatures—albeit perfectly happy creatures—and thought they could do better on their own. But in their attempt to seek a better paradise, they lost the only one the world has ever known. That first false step to happiness begot the Fall, a disordering of ourselves and our world so deep that we cannot, by ourselves, put things right.

But that's okay. If there's anything Christianity insists on it is that everything is from first to last a gift. Our fall from goodness and grace is a key element of the story (and one we cannot afford to forget), but it is hardly the whole story. Like any good drama, there are plenty of twists and turns and surprises in the Christian story, but the briefest possible synopsis goes like this: The God we reject and betray loves us all the same. God wants our good; that's the central theme of the Christian story, and it is why, despite our persistent chronicles of sin, it has always been called a salvation story, a story of grace and hope, not a narrative of defeat and despair. It would be a tragedy if sin ultimately conquered, but sin doesn't conquer, love does. It would be a tragedy if sin were the last word in the story, but in the lexicon of Christianity grace, love, and forgiveness are spoken much more often, much more eloquently, and much more powerfully than the language of sin. Sin is real, it is virulent and it is toxic, but it pales before the liberating power of grace and the healing power of forgiveness.

In the gospels, "it is never sin, but always grace, the proclamation of God's mercy, that predominates,"[36] and that is why even amid our failures we can live in hope. Gospel means "good news," news truly worthy of our attention, and it would hardly be good news if the stranglehold of sin and death could not be broken. The New Testament tells the story of a world-changing victory, the victory of God's goodness and love over the demonic energies of evil. Sin may be a pervasive reality and a fearfully destructive one, but it is neither the first nor the last word about life. That belongs to the language of love, the language of grace and forgiveness, and it is why hope should be the natural disposition of a Christian.

Sin does not have the final word in the Christian story because God is gracious to us. Christians worship a God not of wrath and vindictiveness, but of loving-kindness and mercy. Like a forgiving friend, God does not hold our wrongs against us. The gracious person "needs to have the ability to love even an enemy."[37] Sometimes we are the enemies of God, but God refuses to let our enmity prevail. Like a friend who won't give up on us, God works to free us from our destructive inclinations through the creative ingenuity of love. There are many ways to speak of the absolute prevalence of God's love over the ravaging powers of sin, but the most common way in the Christian tradition is in the language of grace. "Grace is perhaps the most salient character trait of God," God's most distinguishable attribute, and grace is "God's loving disposition toward his creatures. The God of grace is a God who loves—loves even sinners."[38] This is why sin is real, but does not prevail.

Nothing demonstrates more eloquently and convincingly that God is lovingly disposed to us than the life, death, and resurrection of Jesus. Jesus embodies God's gracious love. Everything about his teachings and actions testifies that God does not hold our wrongs against us. But nothing bespeaks this more powerfully than the forgiveness spoken by Jesus on the cross. The sufferings and death of Jesus poignantly witness that God is able to love an enemy and to extend mercy powerful enough to reverse the story of destruction and death inaugurated by the Fall. With the forgiveness offered by the crucified Christ, the story of sin becomes a narrative of hope and redemption. In this respect, our journey to happiness begins at the foot of Jesus' cross because without God's forgiveness the journey would not be possible. Without forgiveness we would be mired in the muck of sin, unable to free ourselves. This is why an essential ingredient to happiness is learning to live a forgiven and forgiving life.[39] Remembering that we are forgiven, continually beholden to grace, points us on the way to happiness.

The Christian life can rightly be understood as an ongoing recovery from sin—and every Christian "in recovery"—because only gradually do we unlearn the habits and practices of sin and grow in the new life of grace and forgiveness. We never completely lose our identity as "recovering sinners" because "recovery from sin is a process, a lifelong process."[40] Think of how hard it is to replace jealousy with graciousness, vindictiveness with reconciliation, arrogance with genuine humility. Our convalescence from the weakness and infirmity of sin to the health and wholeness of the life of grace is the project of a lifetime because the wounds of sin run deep. The pardoning grace of God's forgiveness begins this healing and rehabilitation, but it must be deepened and sustained through all the practices that comprise the Christian life so that we can be wholly remade in Christ. Being remade in Christ involves taking on an entirely new identity, a change so complete that we speak of it as dying to one kind of life and rising into another. This is no piecemeal transformation, and it explains why this remaking of the self from sinner to saint is never, short of death, complete.

Baptism begins the gradual rehabilitation of the self by inserting us into the story of Jesus and calling us to make that story our own. But baptism is rightly called a sacrament of initiation because it only begins a life of ongoing conversion and reconciliation whose ultimate effect is to make us a "new creation" in Christ (2 Cor. 5:17). The new life begun in baptism grows through the Eucharist because the Eucharist teaches what it means to leave the unpromising life of sin behind for the liberating life of Christ. Through the Eucharist we learn how to be real students of Christ, disciples who take to heart the teaching and example of Christ. Through the Eucharist we help one another break free from the unpromising paths of sin in order to grow together in the love and life of God and, therefore, know happiness. But at no point are we completely free from the fear and anxiety that make us vulnerable to sin and leave us falling back into behavior we thought we had escaped. No matter how far along we are in the Christian life, we feel traces of things that once held us captive. Even those closest to God sometimes fall all over again, taking false steps they thought they would never repeat. In our journey to the happiness that is found in God, we remain "holy penitents," persons growing in goodness but still struggling with, and repenting, sin.[41]

The Christian moral life is one of ongoing conversion, the continuous turning of oneself from the waywardness of sin to discipleship with Christ. But we who have such difficulty in losing weight, quitting smoking, or gossiping less can hardly make ourselves a "new creation." The conversion of the self that happiness requires is foremost the work of God, not our own achievement. Our analysis of sin has shown that we can find all sorts of ways to be agents of our own unhappiness, but are much less adept at accomplishing bliss. Happiness is God's gift to us. The same holds true for the transformation of the self that genuine conversion achieves. It is from first to last the work of God who in Christ overcomes the alienation and animosity harvested by sin (Col. 1:19–20). Sin separates us from happiness, but we cannot overcome that separation on our own. Only God can bring us back to our real place of belonging, the place where our true good is found. The Christian life is a lifelong reclamation project, for just as at creation when God brought life out of nothingness, so too do the grace, compassion, and mercy of God rescue the dying from the nothingness of sin. The initiative is always with God, a God who "accepts us and comes to meet us where we are in order to lead us to where he wants us to go: to his kingdom of love and justice."[42]

In *Unlikely Ways Home*, Edward Beck tells the story of David and Debbie, parents who never gave up on their son, Cary, despite years of suffering from his belligerence, abusive selfishness, and incredible thoughtlessness. Struggling to understand their faithful love for an absolutely ungrateful son, a love that Beck thought "unwarranted, foolish, and maybe even detrimental," he concludes that the best word to describe such love is "unconditional." "Not surprisingly," he writes, "it's the same word some use to describe the way God loves us—unconditionally, no prerequisite, no payback necessary. Free gift."[43] It's the love exemplified in a God who remains ever present to us despite our persistent transgressions and faithlessness. "In the Scriptures conversion never happens as a result of abandonment," Beck notes, "but rather by the steadfastness of people (and God) who stand with the sinner even in destructive life choices. People turn their lives around because others believe in them enough to walk with them until they find their way home again."[44] Conversion means turning our lives around. But, as Beck says, that we can move from sin back to life is only because God, despite our legacy of destructive choices, never abandons us. We can, even amid our sins, live in hope, because God (like Cary's parents) never stops believing in us, walks with us, and helps us find our way back home.

Conclusion

Sometimes when we look back on our lives we see the beauty of what could have been. We wonder what would have been different if we had loved better, been kinder and more generous, or let go of a hurt and taken a chance with forgiveness. We mourn the false steps and wish we had walked a different path. But no matter how many false steps we take in our quest for happiness, they need not define us. With God's grace, we can always find our way back. With God's grace, we can break free of narratives of diminishment and death and begin to live lives of remarkable joyfulness and hope. It's what the apostle Paul meant when he called Christians to walk in newness of life (Rom. 6:4). We take our first frail steps in this new life when we "put on Christ" at baptism and promise to make Christ's story the model for our own. We discover then that happiness is not an idea, but a distinctive way of life that Jesus embodied for all who choose to follow as his disciples. What it might mean to tell the story of our lives this way will be the subject of chapter 7.

Some Questions for Reflection and Discussion

1. Why do you think we seldom hear the language of sin? People commonly speak of mistakes, regrets, and errors, but not of sin? Why is this?
2. Why is sin essentially self-destructive? A case of mistaken identity?
3. When you look at the list of seven deadly sins, do you think any of those vices can honestly be so morally dangerous? Has anyone ever told you to be extremely wary of pride, envy, anger, sloth, greed, gluttony, or lust?
4. What makes overcoming social sin so difficult?
5. What is the danger of habitual sin? What do we risk if sin becomes second nature to us?

6. Despite Christianity's dogged honesty about sin, why is it really a story of hope?

Notes

1. Josef Pieper, *The Concept of Sin*, trans. Edward T. Oakes, SJ (South Bend, IN: St. Augustine's Press, 2001), 33.

2. Ted Peters, *Sin: Radical Evil in Soul and Society* (Grand Rapids, MI: William B. Eerdmans Publishing Co., 1994), 7.

3. Cornelius Plantinga Jr., *Not the Way It's Supposed to Be: A Breviary of Sin* (Grand Rapids, MI: William B. Eerdmans Publishing Co., 1995), 5.

4. Patrick McCormick, *Sin as Addiction* (New York: Paulist Press, 1989), 16.

5. Russell B. Connors Jr. and Patrick T. McCormick, *Character, Choices and Community: The Three Faces of Christian Ethics* (New York: Paulist Press, 1998), 206.

6. C. S. Lewis, *Mere Christianity* (New York: Macmillan Publishing Co., 1952), 54.

7. Richard M. Gula, SS, *Reason Informed by Faith: Foundations of Catholic Morality* (New York: Paulist Press, 1989), 91.

8. Pieper, *The Concept of Sin*, 37.

9. Pieper, *The Concept of Sin*, 38.

10. Dennis P. Hollinger, *Choosing the Good: Christian Ethics in a Complex World* (Grand Rapids, MI: Baker Academic, 2002), 77.

11. John Steinbeck, *East of Eden* (New York: Bantam Books, 1955), 219.

12. Robert E. Webber and Rodney Clapp, *People of the Truth: A Christian Challenge to Contemporary Culture* (Harrisburg, PA: Morehouse Publishing, 1988), 23.

13. Henry Fairlie, *The Seven Deadly Sins Today* (Notre Dame, IN: University of Notre Dame Press, 1979), 3–36.

14. Vincent MacNamara, *Love, Law and Christian Life: Basic Attitudes of Christian Morality* (Wilmington, DE: Michael Glazier, 1988), 177.

15. Pieper, *The Concept of Sin*, 90.

16. Cited in Pieper, *The Concept of Sin*, 90.

17. Lewis, *Mere Christianity*, 21.

18. Peters, *Sin*, 31.

19. Peters, *Sin*, 24.

20. Peters, *Sin*, 25.

21. Webber and Clapp, *People of the Truth*, 26.

22. Webber and Clapp, *People of the Truth*, 26.

23. Kenneth R. Melchin, *Living with Other People: An Introduction to Christian Ethics Based on Bernard Lonergan* (Collegeville, MN: The Liturgical Press, 1998), 94.

24. Connors and McCormick, *Character, Choices and Community*, 220.

25. Thomas Aquinas, *Summa Theologiae* (New York: McGraw-Hill, 1966), I-II, 82,1.

26. Gula, *Reason Informed by Faith*, 107.
27. Aquinas, *ST*, I-II, 82,1,2.
28. Aquinas, *ST*, I-II, 85,3.
29. Aquinas, *ST*, I-II, 85,3.
30. Aquinas, *ST*, I-II, 85,3.
31. Peters, *Sin*, 126.
32. McCormick, *Sin as Addiction*, 103.
33. *Catechism of the Catholic Church* (Liguori, MO: Liguori Publication, 1994), #1865.
34. Aquinas, *ST*, I-II, 78,2.
35. Aquinas, *ST*, I-II, 78,2.
36. Servais Pinckaers, *The Sources of Christian Ethics*, trans. Sr. Mary Thomas Noble, OP (Washington, DC: The Catholic University of America Press, 1995), 41.
37. Peters, *Sin*, 268.
38. Peters, *Sin*, 269.
39. L. Gregory Jones, *Embodying Forgiveness: A Theological Analysis* (Grand Rapids, MI: William B. Eerdmans Publishing Co., 1995), 163–239.
40. McCormick, *Sin as Addiction*, 182.
41. Bernard Häring, *Free and Faithful in Christ: Moral Theology for Clergy and Laity*, Vol. 1 (New York: The Seabury Press, 1978), 429.
42. Häring, *Free and Faithful in Christ*, 422.
43. Edward L. Beck, *Unlikely Ways Home: Real-Life Spiritual Detours* (New York: Doubleday, 2004), 147.
44. Beck, *Unlikely Ways Home*, 147.

CHAPTER SEVEN

~

Finding a Story Worth Handing On

Narrative and the Moral Life

The night before my Uncle Bill died he gave a party I will never forget. It was Saturday, August 16, 1969, and Uncle Bill had invited fifteen to twenty people—family members and close friends—to the basement of his home in Louisville. He loved the card game pinochle, and that night we were going to have a pinochle tournament. Uncle Bill told us that whoever won that night in Louisville would be going to San Diego the following weekend for the national championship. Of course this wasn't true, but it made for a much more interesting evening. Before we got down to the serious business of playing cards, Uncle Bill fed us. It was a memorable feast. Spread across a table were all the foods Uncle Bill loved: lots of rye bread and purple cabbage, all kinds of sandwich meat, limburger cheese (his favorite), plenty of potato salad, and sauerkraut. Behind the table and next to the washing machine sat Uncle Bill's little record player on which he had stacked a half dozen albums of German polka music to soothe us while we ate.

Then the pinochle playing began. Uncle Bill orchestrated the evening as only he could. He was constantly changing our partners to be sure that during the night we would be paired with everyone else at least once. He kept score, so none of us ever really knew how we were doing. The party went on for hours, but at the end of the evening, to no one's surprise, Uncle Bill declared himself the winner and announced that he would be going on to San Diego the next weekend. Still, those of us who lost couldn't feel too bad because Uncle Bill had prizes for everybody: a fifth of Early Times bourbon for the adults, and for me, only eighteen at the time, a box of Russell Stover candy.

The next evening Uncle Bill came to our home for dinner and did everything for which he was known and loved. He teased my sisters and brothers. He caused all kinds of commotion. And he got into a wild poker game with my parents and some of my great aunts and uncles. But when it came time for everyone to leave, I noticed something different. Uncle Bill would always drive, but this night he didn't. He asked one of my other uncles if he would drive and then climbed into the backseat. For some reason I lingered in the driveway as they were pulling away and Uncle Bill turned and looked at me. I'll never forget the look on his face. He looked stricken, almost ghostly. Five minutes later we received a call saying he had suffered a heart attack less than a mile from our house and died.

Looking back on that weekend in August 1969, it has always seemed to me that Uncle Bill's pinochle party was his Last Supper. On the night before he died, he gathered together some of his family and friends and did everything for which he is so fondly remembered. He fed us, he celebrated with us, he made us laugh, and he let us know how good it is to be together. Uncle Bill had suffered with a poor heart for years and I suspect he knew he was coming to the end of his life. In a sense, he was saying to us that evening, "If my life is about to end, how have I done? What have I made of the life I have been given? Have I told the story well?" Everything he did that evening said something about the story he had tried to write with his life and how he wanted to be remembered. He wanted us to remember him as a man whose life had honored God. He wanted us to remember him as someone who was good, kind, honest, generous, and dependable. He was telling us to enjoy life, to be good to one another, and for heaven's sake not to take ourselves too seriously. On the night before he died he turned the story of his life over to us and asked, "How have I done? Has it been a good story? Is it a story worth handing on and remembering?"

Christians believe that in Jesus they have found a story worth handing on and remembering. It is a story that says joy and confidence are more in step with reality than depression and despair, that goodness is the power that sustains the world, and that love offered to anybody, even an enemy, is always the right way to go. It's a story that gives us freedom to fail because the God who brought us to life in the beginning will do so again and again.

In this chapter we will explore why for Christians a life of happiness requires being initiated into the story of God that comes to us in Jesus and becoming part of the community that promises to make that story its own. But first we will consider why the language of story or narrative has emerged as a fitting way to speak about morality, particularly Christian morality. Second, we will look at the story of God that entered the world in Jesus, why that story was seen to mark the beginning of a "new age" with new possibilities, and what it might mean to become part of that story. Third, if Christians are called to "walk in newness of life," what does this new life look like? What kind of community does the story of Jesus create? We will conclude then by noting some of the distinctive characteristics of the story that Christians are called to bring to life in the world.

Narrative and the Moral Life

Everybody loves a good story. That's not surprising since every human life takes the form of a story—or really several stories. Some of those stories we inherit and some we choose. We are born into a story as soon as we enter the world and become part of a family. Our family narratives shape us for life. They contribute to our sense of ourselves and our sense of the world. Where we are born makes a difference too. If you were born in Kentucky, like I was, your story will be different from someone born in Texas, California, or Manhattan, and very different from someone born in Latin America, India, or Africa. When we are born makes a difference as well. People who grew up during the Depression, like my parents did, will write a story quite different from someone growing up forty or fifty years later. Anyone with firsthand experience of war will tell a very different story from someone who has never known those horrors. Think of black South Africans growing up under apartheid. Think of anyone living in the Middle East today. The narratives of our lives reflect our social, political, economic, and cultural contexts. They reflect our histories, the pivotal events of our lives and our most formative experiences. That is why even though every person is a story, no two stories are ever exactly the same.

We not only are stories, but we also need stories to help us make sense of things. Stories hold our lives together. They help us stitch together the different episodes and dimensions of our lives so that we can say, "This is who I am, this is what my life is about, and it is for this that I am living." Stories give unity, intelligibility, and coherence to our lives. They give purpose and direction to our lives. Without a story to give a framework to our lives, they become fragmented and scattered; indeed, without a story to guide us, our lives become incoherent. It is hard to know who we are or what might be the meaning of our lives apart from narratives that give us goals and purposes worthy of ourselves.

The narratives of our lives also shape our view of the world, our sense of reality and history, and our expectations for the future. Years ago the theologian H. Richard Niebuhr captured this by saying all of our actions are responses to the story we think is being told around us. Our actions are *reactions* to the story we have come to know. This is why it is difficult to know a person or understand his or her behavior without knowing something about the stories that have shaped him or her. As Niebuhr wrote, "we attempt to answer the question: 'What shall I do?' by raising as the prior question: 'What is going on?' or 'What is being done to me?'"[1] A person who has been badly hurt, manipulated, or abused, will likely answer those questions quite differently from someone who has known love, respect, and appreciation. Someone who has been diminished by the cruelty and ridicule of others will have a different answer to "What is going on?" than someone who has been lifted up by kindness and affirmation. This does not mean that those well acquainted with misfortune cannot move beyond it and begin to tell their story another way, but it does mean that their sense of life will be colored by the stories they have lived. If the painful elements of our stories are not to master us, we need to find narratives and communities that help us reinterpret our pasts both truthfully and hopefully.

Why Theologians Started Talking about Stories

That story or narrative might be a helpful way of understanding Christian morality emerged in reaction to approaches to ethics that failed to take into account the unique features of people's lives. Beginning with the Enlightenment of the seventeenth and eighteenth centuries, and particularly under the influence of the German philosopher Immanuel Kant, there was a growing conviction that a good morality was one that was true for anyone and everyone, regardless of the distinctive features of their lives. Kant's aim was to develop a universal morality whose truthfulness not only in no way depended on cultural customs and communal traditions, religious beliefs and practices, personal cares and commitments, but also transcended them. It was to be an ethic of "pure reason," one whose truthfulness was secured by being untainted by all the messy particularities of our lives. Moral truth did not hinge on one being Christian or Buddhist, theist or atheist, Asian or African, capitalist or socialist. The true and the good were determined by enlightened human reason, and reason produced principles and rules that were applicable to all human beings regardless of their religious beliefs, cultural contexts, or social locations. Kant's goal was a noble one. He recognized how hard it is to arrive at any consensus in morality in a world divided by so many conflicting understandings of what constitutes the true and the good. Moreover, he was keenly aware of how different moral beliefs can threaten the peace and stability of society, a fact depressingly confirmed today when we consider the often shrill debates on fundamental moral questions such as abortion, war, capital punishment, stem cell research, or euthanasia. Therefore, he wanted to achieve harmony in moral matters by severing any connection between the true and the good and the distinctive convictions, customs, and traditions of our lives.

But is that really possible? Do we arrive at the true and the good by stepping outside all the things that make us who we are: our histories, our relationships, our beliefs and convictions, our traditions and practices, our loyalties and loves? We might wish that stripping away all the distinctive elements of our lives would lead us to the truth, but it is more likely to make us disappear—or at least wonder why we believe what we do about anything.[2] Our deepest moral convictions are formed by the relationships that shape us, the experiences and practices that define us, the traditions that have formed us, and the communities with which we have aligned our lives. For example, if you believe deeply in the importance of faithfulness and loyalty, did this conviction come by memorizing moral principles or by learning lessons in faithfulness through family and friends? If you grasp the importance of courage for life, did your appreciation for this virtue come from mere reflection or from suffering the adversity that cannot be survived without courage? This is not to deny the importance of study and reflection in ethics, but it is to say that what any of us thinks and feels about morality is primarily informed by the communities, traditions, practices, cares, and convictions that have comprised the story of our lives.

It is impossible to establish a universal morality in the way Kant attempted because every ethical system (Kant's included) is rooted in and shaped by a tradition. That philosophers and theologians have increasingly turned to story and narrative for understanding the moral life reflects a growing awareness that we arrive at the true and the good not by distancing ourselves from the communities, practices, and traditions that make up our lives, but by finding ones that help us understand better what the true and the good might be. As Stanley Hauerwas, one of the first theologians to appreciate the importance of narrative for Christian ethics, noted, "every ethic requires a qualifier"[3] because in order to know who we should be as well as what we ought to do, we must first know the story or stories that have most defined our lives. For each of us, what the "qualifiers" of our lives might be and how they affect our understanding of morality will vary, but we must attend to them in order to understand why we think, feel, act, and judge the way we do. Our moral beliefs, values, and practices will be qualified for better or worse by our history and experiences, by our religious beliefs, by our temperament, our culture, our relationships, our social and economic status, our gender, our sexual orientation, and many other factors. Hauerwas himself wrote a now famous essay on what it was like to be both a Christian and a Texan, musing about how each of those formidable qualifiers might relate to one another in his life and wondering if they were always compatible.[4] His point was to draw our attention to the multiple narratives that comprise our lives, how they shape our identity and our view of the world, and why we must eventually choose one over others to guide us through life. In short, Hauerwas suggested that choosing to give normative authority to the narratives of Christianity, rather than the stories and traditions of his beloved Texas, made all the difference in how he understood both happiness and goodness.

Why the Story We Choose Matters

Where are our stories taking us? What are they making of us? Are they forming us into persons capable of goodness and happiness? We need to ask these questions because ultimately what becomes of us as persons depends on the story we grant utmost authority to in our lives. Stories offer accounts of what it means to be human, accounts of what we should aspire to as persons, accounts of how we should understand happiness, meaning, and success in life. Stories are arguments about life and what is worth pursuing in life, arguments about what counts as excellence and fulfillment in life. This is why each of us has to reflect on the stories of our lives, how they are forming us, and where they are leading us. Is what they teach about happiness, success, and meaning really true? If we embrace a particular story to guide us through life, at the end of our life will people be able to say of us, "That person really lived!"

It is important to reflect on the stories we live because the narratives with which we most identify our lives not only shape our self but also, more fundamentally, give us a self. Our self is *story-formed*. We do not first have a "self" and then take on a story; rather, whatever self we have is a reflection of the stories we have lived—and of the stories we have rejected. This is obviously true for our family narratives. So much of our self and identity grows from our family history. Similarly, the most significant relationships of our lives (friendship, marriage, within communities) can also be seen as narratives that bequeath us with a sense of self. And it is especially true of the story we choose to be the "master narrative" of our life, the one that governs our sense of identity, meaning, and purpose in life. Stories create a world for us to inhabit. We enter into the world of a story and make it our own. The longer we are at home in the world of a story, the more it shapes our understanding of ourselves and what matters most to us. This is why our identity as persons does not come separate from the stories we have lived or made our own, but only in and through them. As Hauerwas commented, "I am not suggesting just that we require stories to understand who we are, though we certainly do. . . . But rather I am suggesting that the mysterious thing we call a self is best understood exactly as a story."[5]

The story we choose to be sovereign in our lives makes all the difference. Some narratives are rich in wisdom about what it means to be human. But others are at best grossly superficial and at worst corrupting. Think of the "stories" television, movies, and advertising often urge us to embrace. If we enter into them, where will they take us? What will they make of us? They are not worthy of the gift of our lives not only because they cannot deliver the happiness, meaning, and contentment they promise, but also because they misconstrue what it means to be a person. It is no secret that many people today are living stories that are lies because those stories deceive us about what it means to be human, about what counts for flourishing and success, and about what ultimately will complete us. If we embrace these narratives of deception, will people be able to say of us, "That person really lived"?

All of us are formed by multiple stories. We are born into families, societies, and cultures we do not choose, but in which we simply find ourselves. We are formed in narratives of marriage, friendships, professional relationships, narratives of colleges and universities, of businesses and corporations, and also of religion. Some of those stories help bring us more fully to life, but they can also mislead and harm us. We have to find a story that can show us what a good human life looks like and how we must live in order to achieve it. We need to become part of a story that can teach us to live truthfully and hopefully. We need a story capable of educating us in happiness.

What Makes a Story Worth Living?

What would such a story look like? With so many rival accounts of life, how can we tell the difference between stories "that distort the real meaning of what it is to be human"[6] and stories that help us achieve our distinctive excellence? How do we distinguish between stories that can be seductively alluring but will leave us with lives we ultimately regret, and stories productive of genuine goodness? What are the marks of a good story? There are many, and perhaps no list is exhaustive, but eight seem especially important.

First, a good story should teach us to recognize, respect, and respond to the full humanity of all persons regardless of their social, economic, cultural, religious, or racial background.[7] There is a tendency in all of us to narrow our vision so that we recognize only a few as being truly human and, therefore, worthy of consideration. Most often those we are willing to acknowledge are the ones who most resemble ourselves. And it is not unusual to quietly think that the rich, the powerful, the famous, and the attractive are more fully human than the poor, the marginal, the disabled, the elderly, and the infirm. Any story that does not teach us how to recognize, respect, and respond to the full humanity of all persons is not a good story because it is unable to see that all human beings—and indeed the whole of creation—matter.

Second, a good story should help us see the full truth of who we are. So many narratives offer partial accounts of our humanity, illuminating some aspects of ourselves but overlooking others. Too, they tend to flatter and reassure where they should challenge and critique. In order to grow in happiness, we need to know the "full story" of our nature. We are creatures made for fellowship and friendship with God and with one another, but we are also beset with weaknesses and flaws that lead us away from God, and sometimes leave us with more breakdowns than accomplishments in love. A story cannot present a distorted portrait of ourselves. If it is to tutor us in the distinctive promise and excellence of human beings, it must help us see ourselves truthfully and completely, illuminating both our tremendous potential for love and goodness, but also our unsettling potential for mischief and corruption.

A third characteristic of a good story is that it ought to make genuine community possible; that is, it should teach us how to live together in peace. Human beings are created for community and fulfilled in the love that sustains community, whether that is in families, in friendships, in marriage, in churches, or in the larger society. But there are many things that threaten the relationships and communities on which our flourishing depends. A good story trains us in the skills necessary for dealing with all that imperils the unity and peace necessary for authentic communal existence. Therefore, it must teach us how to deal with conflict, how to address and overcome divisions, and how to achieve and maintain peace without having to resort to violence. In other words, a good story trains us in the virtues of justice, patience, fraternal correction, forgiveness, and reconciliation.

Fourth, a good story helps us work against our tendencies toward rationalization and self-deception so that we can see the world, other people, and ourselves justly and truthfully. One of the reasons relationships break down, communities fragment, and nations go to war is because of our deeply ingrained inclinations, both personally and collectively, to illusion and deceit, especially regarding our own goodness, our importance, and the priority of our preferences and needs. It is easy to develop the self-aggrandizing vision that twists reality so that the world and everything in it exists for our sake instead of the well-being of all. This is true whether we are talking about individuals, institutions, or whole societies. All of us are vulnerable to the "blinding self-centered aims and images"[8] that seem so reasonable and sensible to us, but wreak harm on others, as well as the whole of creation. Thus, a good story ought to nurture the kind of reverent, humble, and benevolent vision necessary for justice. To do so, it must teach us to see the world as a gift.

Fifth, we cannot flourish together as human beings without hospitality and openness to others, especially those whose differences might initially disturb or even threaten us. All of us are easily rattled by what we perceive as "other," whether what makes another "different" is a matter of culture, religion, politics, gender, race, sexual orientation, or physical or mental ability. We avoid, dismiss, and find all sorts of ways to exclude persons and communities whose differences we judge unacceptable. But any narrative that allows us to establish our own identity by denying the identity of another cannot be good because it makes injustice and violence inevitable. A good story must open us to the narratives and experiences of other persons, communities, and traditions, especially those we are most likely to overlook or dismiss.[9] This would particularly include the stories of the poor, the stories of the victims of society, the stories of those who are never allowed to count, the stories of those whose voices are seldom heard, and even the stories of those we take to be our enemies. Likewise, even though Christians believe that the fullest account of what it means to be human is revealed in the story of Jesus, we can learn from, and be enriched and challenged by, the narratives of other religious traditions. Something of God is revealed in Islam, Hinduism, Buddhism, Judaism, Native American religions, or any other religious tradition. Indeed, something of God can be revealed to us in the stories of those who have nothing to do with religion and deny there is a God at all. A good story teaches us how to honor and respect other stories. Even if we never claim them as the authoritative story for our own lives, all of them can give us a richer and more insightful understanding of what it means to be human.

A sixth mark of a good story is justice. If the aim of a good story is to create the kind of world where all persons can flourish and be fulfilled, this is impossible without just persons who create just communities. Too many narratives are driven by ideologies of privilege and exclusion. Too many encourage us to secure our interests by disregarding the interests of others, to prosper at the expense of others, and to live in ways that makes it hard for others to live at all. Too many stories counsel self-promotion and self-interest in ways that make it comfortable for us to ignore the needs and well-being of others. Any account of life that results in injustice toward others cannot be good for any of us. Consequently, a good story forms us into the kinds of persons who stand in solidarity with the poor and the oppressed, with the overlooked and forgotten of the world, and who work for justice on their behalf.

Seventh, a story that promises happiness must not deny the disappointment, suffering, and misfortune that is part of life, but teach us how to deal with it in hope. Any view of the moral life that envisions it as an ongoing quest for happiness has to be realistic about suffering and adversity. No matter how well we plan our lives, sometimes things simply do not work out. Parents disappoint children and children disappoint parents. The friends we thought we could trust betray us. We don't get the jobs we think we deserve and we lose jobs we thought we would always have. The people we cannot imagine life without die suddenly and unexpectedly, leaving us bereft. No life is immune to sorrow, no life is a stranger to grief. A good story teaches us how to deal with sorrow, suffering, losses, and grief without being undone by them. A good story helps us persevere through suffering not only in hope, but also without abandoning joy.

Finally, a good story is a story of freedom and life. Too many stories promise life, but offer more death-in-life than life. Too many stories promise happiness, pleasure, and success, but are little more than death disguised. Our fundamental moral obligation is to renounce "death" in all its wily manifestations and to choose life. A good story offers us life and teaches us how to choose it over death. This does not mean that it does not challenge us, ask much of us, and change us in startling ways; but it does mean that we experience real freedom and real life as we live it.[10]

Rising to New Life—Beginning to Tell the Story of God

And so where do we find a good story?

Christians believe they have found a good story in Jesus. They believe the life of Jesus, and especially his death and resurrection, permanently changed the world. For Christians, the life, death, and resurrection of Jesus give birth to an astonishing confidence and a resilient hope, to a deep, enduring joy, and to a peace that not even the threat of death can shake. The first Christians believed that the death and resurrection of Jesus began a new age with new possibilities.[11] It was history's decisive moment because in raising Jesus from the dead, and vindicating everything Jesus' life was about, God declared that the powers that move the world are not wealth, violence, animosity, and death, but generosity, justice, love, forgiveness, and peace. With Jesus' resurrection "the great reversal"[12] took place because the dominion of death was broken, and with its defeat an old and unpromising story was brought to an end, and a new story begun. Jesus' whole life showed that people do not have to be governed by fear and mistrust, by calculated self-interest, by defensiveness or insecurity. Rather, they can afford to be generous, to risk the vulnerability of love, and not feel foolish when forgiving because the resurrection of Jesus testified that God's love rules the world and will triumph over all attempts to defeat it. What God had done in Christ invited radical reconsideration of what it meant to be human, radical reevaluation of our life together in the world, and radical rethinking of the attitudes and practices that lead to life. Jesus' life, death, and resurrection brought something absolutely new into being, something so remarkably different that the apostle Paul could say, "So whoever is in Christ is a new creation: the old things have passed away; behold, new things have come" (2 Cor. 5:17).

The only reason to take up the new story to which Jesus invites his disciples is if it is better than the old story they would leave behind. If what Jesus invites us to is only "more of the same," why be part of it? But as the Sermon on the Mount in Matthew 5 and The Great Discourse of Luke 6:17–38 illustrate, to take up the story of God that comes to us in Jesus is to enter a dramatically different world. Jesus notes the striking contrast between the way the world's story is usually told and what it would mean to live this new story of God. In the story of God Jesus preached, taught, and witnessed, enemies are loved, not hated; those who curse us are blessed and prayed for, not despised; and compassion and mercy bring us much closer to God than judgment. Too, unlike most stories, Jesus' story results in a way of life (which he calls the reign of God) where everyone is welcome and everyone can belong.

Baptism—Crossing a Boundary into a New Way of Life

To take up a new story is to take on a new life. This is how the first Christians understood baptism, the sacrament through which they entered the story of Jesus and became part of the community that promised to make that story their own. Baptism ritually symbolized their response to Jesus' call to discipleship because through it they broke with one way of life in order to "put on Christ" and to make Christ's life the rule for their own. Everything about the sacrament indicated that the changes brought about by baptism were drastic and profound. The exorcism that was part of the ritual, the renunciation of evil, the disrobing and immersion, the being clothed in a new garment, all dramatically indicated the sharp rupture between one's past life and the new life one was entering.[13] A boundary had been crossed and a lifelong conversion begun. To be baptized was to follow a distinctively different path; in Paul's words it was to "live in newness of life" (Rom. 6:4).

But this demanded dying to a past way of life—burying that life for good—in order to be raised up with Christ into the liberating new life of grace. Baptismal immersion symbolized a genuine rebirth; a drowning that signified death to one way of life, and then being lifted up into new life. To be baptized, as every fresh Christian was told, was to become "a new creation" (2 Cor. 5:17). As Wayne Meeks notes, "Baptism represents a dying and rising, and the rising entails a new life. The ritual of initiation dramatized as sharply as possible the discontinuity between the old and the new, between the world the convert was leaving and the world he or she now entered, between the 'old human' and the new."[14] Today the radical implications of baptism are easily missed because we often reduce the significance of the sacrament to the ceremony alone. But the first Christians could not fail to grasp that to be baptized is to be given a new identity, to become part of a new community, and to learn a new way of ordering our lives together.[15]

Indeed, the relocation of one's life entailed by baptism was understood to be so far reaching that some early Christian writers compared it to leaving one's native land behind and traveling to a new homeland whose culture and traditions presented a very different understanding of life. Baptism was a transfer of allegiance, a change of citizenship, that marked "the separation from one life and one society and the joining of another, leaving the family of birth and the culture of residence and becoming a sister or brother of those who are God's children."[16] Too, becoming a citizen of "the reign of God" required unlearning the "culture" and "traditions" of one's past life in order to be resocialized into the culture and traditions of the new Christian community. For the early Christians, baptism clearly did not mean "more of the same." To be baptized was to begin a lifelong process of moral reeducation whereby one "took off" the vices of a past life and "put on" the virtues of Christ.[17] If at one time the newly birthed Christian was clothed in habits of anger, resentment, jealousy, and vindictiveness, now, as one of "God's chosen ones," he or she was to be clothed with "heartfelt compassion, kindness, humility, gentleness, and patience" (Col. 3:12). The resocialization begun in baptism meant "bearing with one another and forgiving one another, if one has a grievance against another; as the Lord has forgiven you, so must you also do" (Col. 3:13). It meant letting Christ's peace govern one's heart; being animated by love, instructing, and helping; and when necessary, admonishing one another. Above all, it meant giving thanks to God in all things (Col. 3:14–17).

To be baptized is to begin to tell a new story. Stories are arguments about life, arguments about what is good for human beings and what will bring them to fulfillment. In Jesus, we as Christians not only believe that we have found a good story, but we are indeed convinced that in Jesus we encounter *God's story for us*. We have already discussed some elements of this story in our examination of the role of friendship in the Christian life; the importance of virtues such as magnanimity, courage, and compassion; our analysis of freedom; and our explication of sin and restoration. In subsequent chapters we will look at other features of this story, particularly the foundational virtues of love and justice. For now, however, it might be helpful to look at three preeminent characteristics of a community that strives to live the story of God that comes to us in Jesus: *confidence* and *joy*, *reconciliation* and *peace*, and *the capacity to suffer in hope*. Other characteristics could be considered, but these are essential because any community that would lack these qualities would be living at odds with the story of Jesus. If they are faithful to the story of Jesus, Christians will be people of confidence and joy, people of reconciliation and peace, and people who can suffer in hope.

Living God's Story for Us

Being a People of Confidence and Joy

Without Easter there would be no story to tell, at least not a story worth passing on and remembering. Without Easter, death wins. The heart of the Easter message is that death may be real, but love is stronger. Death is real, and so are suffering, loss, and failure, but none of them finally triumphs because in the death and resurrection of Jesus God conquered all the things that assail hope. This is why we can live in confidence and joy. Easter shows that in God we do not encounter a love that tries its best but ultimately fails; rather, Easter shows that in God we find a love powerful, faithful, and resilient enough to bring things to life not just once, but again and again. This is why no one is beyond hope.[18]

The resurrection of Jesus affirms a portrait of God first sketched in the creation accounts of Genesis. If God called things into being at the dawn of creation and delighted in that creation, Easter shows that God calls us into being again and again because not even death will undo what God's creative love began. We should abide in joy and confidence and hope, never in fear, anxiety, or despair, because Easter means we live in and from a love that all the forces of evil and death could not overcome. Anything that denies us life—anything that says to us "do not be"—cannot be from God. A message of Easter is that every human being, as well as all of creation, is rejoiced in by God. Any person who finds his or her identity in this truth can live with joy and confidence and hope. Put differently, to live the story of Jesus is to live continuously from the knowledge of being loved and believed in by God.[19]

Living with joy and confidence and hope requires a certain kind of community and a certain way of being together. Saying that God calls us to life means little if we are stuck in communities, families, and relationships doing their best to make us die. We will hardly be marked by confidence and joy if what we encounter in life is more hostility than affirmation, more indifference than care, or more belittlement than respect. We need an environment where joy and confidence about life are made credible by how people attend to one another and even challenge one another. We need an environment in which it is not difficult to believe that there is a God who rejoices in us, who is glad that we are, and who is committed to our well-being.

The first Christians had a joy and confidence about life because their belief in the resurrection empowered them to live together in a different way. Gerhard Lohfink described the life of the first Christian communities as a "praxis of 'togetherness,'" and meant by this the particular attitudes and behaviors Christians were to have toward one another in their everyday lives. They were to honor one another (Rom. 12:10), live in harmony with one another (Rom. 12:16), welcome one another (Rom. 15:7), and care for one another (1 Cor. 12:25). In their life together they were to serve one another (Gal. 5:13), comfort one another (1 Thess. 5:11), be kind and compassionate to each other (Eph. 4:32), and forgive one another (Col. 3:13).[20] Each of these practices concretely illustrated what it meant to be resocialized into the story of Jesus. They indicated that even though joy and confidence and hope are gifts and graces from God, they also require a certain form of life in order to be sustained. Joy and confidence come to life in communities where people are responsible for one another, build up and encourage one another, are patient with one another, and console one another. And they abide where people are committed to do for one another what God did for Jesus at Easter: raise one another up, bring one another to life.[21]

Living God's Story for Us—Being a People of Reconciliation and Peace

Second, living the story of God that comes to us in Jesus means being a people of reconciliation and peace. We sometimes think peace is little more than the absence of conflict, or else the sort of fragile truce that results when we leave one another alone, tolerate our divisions, and simply let things be. But such an approach does little to address the animosity, misunderstanding, or fears that engender suspicion and foster alienation; in fact, such peace is often little more than hostility disguised or delayed. The peace that comes in Christ is far richer and much more challenging. And just as there are certain attitudes and behaviors that imperil peace, likewise there are attitudes and behaviors that constitute the "way of peace," a metaphor frequently used in the Bible (Isa. 59:8; Luke 1:79; Rom. 3:17).[22] Like joy and confidence, peace may be a gift of God's grace and an expression of God's Spirit, but it calls for a distinctive way of life in order to be sustained.

The New Testament presents the peace of Christ as God's ongoing work to overcome all the hostility, conflict, and divisions that leave us estranged from one another and threatened by one another. Christ's peace is the work of reconciliation and forgiveness. It is a peace that heals, a peace that overcomes barriers, and a peace that creates community where community was never thought possible before. Consider the famous passage in the New Testament's letter to the Ephesians where the author celebrates how Gentiles and Jews, assumed to be permanently alienated from one another, were made one through the reconciling work of Christ. Gentiles were considered the true outsiders, the absolutely excluded ones who could never be part of the people of God. Not included in God's covenant with Israel, their lot was to remain strangers to God, people with neither life nor hope. As the author of Ephesians says about the Gentiles, at one time you were "strangers to the covenants of promise, without hope and without God in the world" (2:12). But it was precisely the reconciling peace of Christ that overcame this catastrophic chasm. Through the death and resurrection of Jesus all division, alienation, and exclusion were done away with so that those "who once were far off" were now part of the people of God (2:13). Speaking to the Jewish and Gentile Christians at Ephesus, the writer of Ephesians says Christ "made both one and broke down the dividing wall of enmity, through his flesh, . . . that he might create in himself one new person in place of the two, thus establishing peace, and might reconcile both with God, in one body, through the cross, putting that enmity to death by it" (2:14–17). In the peace of Christ, there are "no longer strangers and sojourners" because all are "fellow citizens with the holy ones and members of the household of God" (2:19).

Seen from a distance of nearly two thousand years, this declaration of the community born from the reconciling peace of Christ can lose its explosive power. But for the Jewish and Gentile Christians of the church at Ephesus, its impact could hardly be missed. Baptized into the one Christ, these former enemies were summoned to see themselves in a new way. For them to "walk in newness of life" meant envisioning one another neither as strangers nor enemies, but as brothers and sisters living together in peace as members of the one body of Christ. If they were to "put on" the story of Jesus, they had to accept what they had previously considered impossible. They had to recognize that they who could never envision themselves together had been made one by the cross of Christ. As Philip Kenneson summarizes, "Whatever hostility had existed before was now abolished in the very body of Christ, which brought them together to form a new and culturally revolutionary dwelling place for God. Out of two peoples whose hostility toward each other was legendary, God had established one new humanity."[23]

The peace of Christ works to dismantle all structures that exclude, all attitudes and practices that divide and allow one people to gain its identity by dismissing another people. This is abundantly clear in the teaching and ministry of Jesus. Jesus scandalized those in power because he challenged them to find their identity in God's love for them, not by lording it over others. In his table fellowship with tax collectors, sinners, and prostitutes, in his welcoming outreach to women and children, Jesus strove to create a new and unified humanity, a community to which everyone could belong, Jew and Gentile, male and female, slave and free (Gal. 3:28). In Christ not only do those old divisions no longer matter, they are absolutely overcome because they frustrate God's desire that human beings grow and flourish together. "It was characteristic of Jesus that he constantly *established community*—precisely for those who were denied community at that time, or who were judged inferior in respect to religion," Gerhard Lohfink writes. "Jesus made clear through his word and even more through his concrete conduct that he did not recognize religious-social exclusion and discrimination."[24] As Lohfink suggests, being resocialized into the story of Jesus means coming to see that peace can never be built on injustice.

Peace was Jesus' gift to his disciples (John 14:27), but that gift would live only if those trying to tell his story actively cultivated the attitudes and practices conducive to the way of peace. Christ's peace was to reign in their hearts (Col. 3:15), but if that peace was to flourish among them and characterize their relationship with the world, their life together had to be guided by certain commitments. First, they had to reject violence and revenge as strategies for justice because both are starkly incompatible with the teaching and example of Jesus. In the Sermon on the Mount Jesus declares peacemakers to be the true children of God (Matt. 5:9). He instructs his followers to surpass the traditional law of retaliation ("an eye for an eye and a tooth for a tooth") with the command to "offer no resistance to one who is evil. When someone strikes you on [your] right cheek, turn the other one to him as well" (Matt. 5:39). Too, they are to love their enemies and persecutors instead of seeking revenge against them (Matt. 5:44). Even more, Jesus' death on the cross poignantly demonstrates that God does not rule by violence but by patient, suffering love. Throughout the gospels Jesus works to differentiate the politics of the reign of God from the politics of the world, and nowhere is the difference more striking (and perhaps more alarming) than in Jesus' renunciation of violence. Violence and vindictiveness have no place in the new social order that is the reign of God. In fact, it is precisely Jesus' rejection of violence that makes his teaching offensive because we assume the necessity of threat, violence, and retaliation in order to achieve an imperfect peace in a demonstrably fallen world where loving one's enemies seems an imprudent risk, not a path to life.

The gospels are full of surprises, and there is probably no more unsettling surprise in the story of Jesus than the revelation that God's rule will come by the cross and not by the sword.[25] Jesus' kingdom truly "does not belong to this world" (John 18:36) because unlike most political and social orders, the "politics of God" are founded on love, justice, forgiveness, and peace.[26] This can sound hopelessly utopian in a world that is no stranger to war and bloodshed. But the purpose of Jesus' teaching is not to create an unreal world, but a reconciled and redeemed world where people, instead of diminishing one another, help bring one another to life. As long as the necessity of violence and retaliation are assumed, nothing really changes. Put more strongly, if the world must be governed by the rule of violence and not by the rule of Christ's peace, then the Easter message that love is stronger than death is a lie, not the innermost truth of reality. Because of Easter, Christians witness a different story, a story in which renouncing violence is not foolishness, but key to the world's re-creation. This is why they submit to a way of life through which they are pried away from practices of violence and learn instead to embrace practices of peace. As Richard Hays puts it, "Instead of wielding the power of violence, the community of Jesus' disciples is to be meek, merciful, pure, devoted to peacemaking, and willing to suffer persecution—and blessed precisely in its faithfulness to this paradoxical vision."[27]

Second, in addition to a renunciation of violence and revenge, living according to the peace of Christ requires a commitment to patience. Patience may not be a popular virtue, and it certainly is not one easily acquired, but there is no way that human beings can live together in peace without becoming skilled in patience.[28] In fact, peace is the handiwork of patience because without patience all the things that imperil peace ultimately shatter peace. Patience means "to suffer" or "to endure," and it is the shape love must take when we are confronted with challenging, unpleasant, or frustrating individuals, institutions, or situations, all of which wear us down and none of which can be easily changed. Patience is steadfast love because with this virtue instead of giving up on a spouse, a son or daughter, a friend or a community, or even an enemy, we bear with them, work through difficulties along with them, and sometimes suffer on account of them. This does not mean that patience requires putting up with everything, particularly longstanding patterns of abuse, malice, cruelty, or violence. But it does mean that our first response to the ways others mistreat us is not to abandon them or to retaliate against them, but to bear with them in love. Patience is the willingness to listen to the views of those with whom we disagree. It demands "learning to yield" to another inasmuch as we do not "insist that we are always right" and admit that we have often been wrong.[29] As hard as it is to practice, patience is essential for living together in the peace of Christ. Christians, like everybody else, are no strangers to conflicts, divisions, hurts, and misunderstandings. But if they are faithful to the story of Jesus, they will work to overcome these things rather than allow them to prevail. Patience may be a difficult virtue to acquire, but without it we can lose the things we love, whether a spouse, a friend, or a community, and know enmity and bitterness far more than we know peace.

Third, walking in the way of Christ's peace demands communities where people are willing to speak the truth to one another and, when necessary, correct one another. One reason friendships, communities, and even churches fall apart is that people are increasingly unable to be truthful with one another about attitudes and behavior that weaken relationships, cause conflict, or simply fall short of what we are called to be. Often this is because we intuitively know the friendships and communities are not strong enough to bear the truth. We ignore one another's faults because we fear addressing them will destroy an already fragile relationship. But we also "let one another be" because we tend to view our behavior as nobody else's business. This, however, guarantees weak relationships and makes life together impossible because no one holds anyone accountable and behavior detrimental to relationships or communities goes unquestioned. Whatever "peace" exists is more the result of negligence, apathy, and acquiescence than truthfulness and mutual accountability. The only way for friendships, marriages, families, communities, and churches to flourish is when people are committed enough to be truthful with one another about the misunderstandings and conflicts that sometimes divide us, and care enough about each other to address them.

This is what distinguishes the peace of Christ. Christ's peace characterizes relationships and communities where people prosper together not because they always get along, but because they refuse to let hurts, misunderstandings, disagreements, and divisions fester and abide. Such a peace is based on the recognition that my behavior is never simply "my own" because everything I do in some way affects somebody else. The good I do builds up my relationships and strengthens community, but the bad I do weakens them. Bad behavior cannot be overlooked if the goodness, life, and happiness that can only be found in partnerships with others can continue to be ours. Without the courage to speak the truth to one another in love, and the courage to allow others to speak truthfully to us, we inevitably grow distant and apart. When we ignore behavior that weakens relationships and community life, we become strangers to one another, disconnected individuals rather than friends, spouses, or community members. Consequently, we lose touch with the most promising goods of our lives, particularly the love, support, and happiness we need for authentically good lives, but which we can only receive from others. Thus, part of what it means to be faithful to one another, whether in marriages, friendships, or churches, is to care enough about one another to be truthful with each other. The only way Christians can tell the story of Jesus well is if they have "the courage to help each other discern where and how we continue to fall short of God's desires for us."[30]

Living the peace of Christ is a complex reality. Far more than an interior quality of soul, it constitutes a whole way of life that must be worked at and attended to if it is not to be undermined by all that threatens it. This is why speaking the truth to one another in love sometimes must take the form of fraternal correction or admonishment.[31] In Matthew 18:15–18 Jesus outlined a process for fraternal correction by instructing his followers not to be reluctant in addressing one another's faults and transgressions, but always to do so in ways that lead to reconciliation and the restoration of peace. In other words, Jesus knew correction would result in reconciliation only if it was truly *fraternal*. Similarly, in Romans 15:14 Paul praises the community not only because they are "full of goodness" and "filled with all knowledge," but also because they are "able to admonish one another." And in Galatians 6:1 Paul tells the Christians of that community that if they see a sister or brother sinning, they "should correct that one in a gentle spirit" and do their best not to fall into the sin themselves. Like Jesus, Paul saw fraternal correction not as a sign that the community was in trouble; rather, he saw it as testimony of the depth of their love for one another, and as something absolutely necessary if they were to continue to grow together in the peace of Christ. Living the peace of Christ requires that each member of the community watch after one another. This is the hard work of love without which friendships, marriages, and communities fall apart. Like the renunciation of violence and revenge, like the practice of patience and truthfulness, fraternal correction is one of the ways Christians keep one another on the path of peace and live the story of Jesus. As Lohfink observed, "in a truly fraternal community conflicts absolutely must be resolved, not suppressed or artificially concealed. The courage to admonish others fraternally and the humility to let oneself be corrected are among the most certain signs of the presence of authentic community and of consciousness of community."[32]

Finally, if living the Christian story entails walking in the way of Christ's peace, this cannot be done without people willing to forgive one another. Forgiveness is difficult, sometimes even scary, because we do not always know what it will ask of us or where it might take us. But forgiveness has to be learned (and risked) because it is the power to renew, re-create, heal, and restore relationships and communities that otherwise remain broken or dead. It is hard to live at peace with one another; friends know this, spouses and their children surely do, and communities and congregations know it too. We are often more skilled at nursing hurts than offering forgiveness, more skilled at plotting revenge than risking reconciliation. And many of us believe when we have been hurt by another the only way to restore the balance is by hurting them in return. But where does it stop? And where does it take us? Far from restoring relationships, such strategies only perpetuate situations where hurts and grievances are multiplied, not overcome. The only way to change such bleak scenarios is for people to be willing to "turn their energies from the power to destroy to the power to build up."[33] This is what forgiveness does. Forgiveness does not let hurts, betrayals, divisions, and disappointments have the final word. It insists there is a love powerful enough to overcome all of these things if we open ourselves to receive it and commit ourselves to practicing it. The heart of the Christian story is that in God we find a love that is stronger than death, and that the God who once called us into life calls us to life again and again. This is the power of forgiveness. It is the love by which we call one another to life again and again. Christians learn from the story of Jesus, especially his death on the Cross, that sometimes the only way love can conquer death and restore us to life is by taking the form of forgiveness.

To tell the story of Jesus is to live a forgiven and forgiving life, for without forgiveness everything is just "more of the same"—more broken relationships, more lingering hurt and bitterness, more vengeance and revenge. Peace grows from the hard work of forgiveness and reconciliation because peace is possible only when people decide not to hold the sins and failures of others against them any more than God holds our sins and failures against us. Peace is impossible without forgiveness, and Christians risk forgiving one another because in the crucified Christ God risked forgiving us. Through the life, ministry, death, and resurrection of Jesus God says, "I desire mercy, not sacrifice" (Matt. 9:13), and so in imitation of God Christians choose mercy and forgiveness over bitterness and revenge. They forgive because they have been forgiven. But they also forgive because, having been gifted with God's forgiveness, they are free to practice something much more creative, innovative, and life-giving than revenge and retaliation. They know from the example of Jesus that forgiveness, however costly, works and is ultimately much more effective than retaliation. They know that forgiveness, however difficult, liberates, while anger, resentment, and vindictiveness only enslave. Forgiveness is an essential practice for living in and from the peace of Christ because forgiveness enables us to redeem the past in hope and, therefore, move unburdened into the future.[34] Put differently, nothing jeopardizes growing together in the happiness of God more than anger, resentment, and retaliation, and nothing safeguards it more than forgiveness. This is why anyone who tells the story of Jesus today must see herself as having been entrusted with the mission of carrying on God's ministry of reconciliation in the world (2 Cor. 5:18–19).

The Peace of Christ and Just War

Given Jesus' renunciation of violence and the centrality of reconciliation and peace, not only in the gospels but also throughout the New Testament, it is not surprising that most early Christians rejected the practice of killing in warfare and saw pacifism as a requirement of discipleship. But in the fourth century things began to change. Not long after Emperor Constantine's victory at the battle of the Milvian Bridge in October 312—a victory he attributed to the God of the Christians—he ended the persecution of the Christians by the Roman Empire. He later made Christianity the official religion of the empire, and by the end of the fourth century it was "the only legal religion in the empire." Thus, "within one century, the Christian church had moved from the status of a minority, persecuted sect to that of the only legally sanctioned religion in the Roman Empire."[35] Christians were no longer a persecuted minority whose beliefs and practices were threatening to the rulers of society, but had themselves begun to rule society. And once they assumed positions of power, they were prompted to ask if in order to ensure the safety and security of a society, war might ever be justified.

The most influential answer to this question came from Augustine, the primary architect of what became known as the *just war doctrine*. Augustine argued that war, even for Christians, could not only be just, but also a moral duty. Augustine taught that going to war could be a requirement of Christian love if it was the only way to protect one's neighbor from unjust harm. War might be brutal and barbaric, but it could also be just if there was no other way to insure the stability and peace of society. Augustine did not deny Jesus' call to nonviolence, but reasoned that in a fallen and imperfect world war may sometimes be the only way to restore order and maintain peace.

But even then the moral priority of nonviolence remained. The principal assumption of the just war doctrine is that wars are not just. The doctrine of just war did not overturn the long-standing Christian position in favor of nonviolence and against war; indeed, it is crucial to remember that pacifism came first in the Christian teaching on war and that the just war doctrine developed out of a commitment to pacifism. Consequently, the just war doctrine assumes the priority of pacifism and is built on the principle that war should always be the *exception*, never the normal way of settling conflicts. The teaching is designed to limit and restrict the waging of war, not legitimize it. It is meant to restrain the impulse to go to war, not endorse it. This is why within the just war doctrine the burden of proof is stringent and falls on the person arguing in favor of war. He or she must show that a situation is so dire that the ordinary prohibition against war must be overridden.

The just war doctrine is built around seven criteria for determining when waging war might be justified.[36] Because the teaching aims to challenge and restrain those who argue in favor of war, it has to be shown that each of the seven criteria has been satisfied before a war can be declared just and, therefore, *not sinful*. The first criterion is *just cause*. Traditionally, three reasons have been seen to justify war: protecting people from unjust attack, restoring rights that have been unjustly taken away, and defending or restoring a just political order. This first criterion indicates that not every reason for going to war can be justified. Wars cannot be justified for reasons of national aggrandizement, to increase a country's wealth, to expand its possessions, or to ensure its access to natural resources.

Second, in order to be a just war, it must be declared by a *competent authority*. Ordinarily this refers to those entrusted with safeguarding the peace and well-being of the community, particularly the executive leaders and legislative bodies of a society. For example, in the United States the approval of Congress is required for a declaration of war. Today, however, many argue that how this second requirement of the just war doctrine is commonly understood must be reconsidered. Are presidents and legislatures customarily prudent and wise in making decisions about war? One does not have to be a cynic to suggest that government leaders have often used the just war doctrine to support decisions to go to war that have already been made. This is why "competence" in making such decisions ought to be extended to include voices of dissent and the wisdom and insight of a variety of communities.

Third, war should always be a *last resort*, never a first response. The principle of last resort insists that war can be justified *only* when all peaceful alternatives have genuinely been attempted and have truly failed. The fourth criterion of the just war doctrine is *comparative justice*. Comparative justice means no side in a dispute is ever perfectly just. There may be comparatively greater justice on one side, but there is never absolute justice. The principle of comparative justice argues against moral self-righteousness and challenges a nation to examine its own role in contributing to a conflict.

The fifth criterion is *proportionality*. Even if there is just cause for going to war, a war cannot be justified if the evil caused by it (e.g., the number of deaths, the extent of destruction, environmental devastation) significantly outweighs whatever good might be gained. Will the good to be gained by going to war (protecting human rights, restoring justice and peace) clearly outweigh the costs, risks, and evil of war? The principle of proportionality is a sobering reminder that war always involves great evil. There is no truly "good" war because of the terrible costs every war entails, even for the victors. It cannot be presumed that the costs of war, even when sustained in pursuit of a just cause, are justified. Because of the almost uncontrollable damage unleashed by war, many people today argue that whatever good war might achieve, it is glaringly disproportionate to the death and destruction that accompany war.

The final two criteria for determining a just war are *right intention* and *probability of success*. To speak of a right intention for going to war means that if a nation's decision to go to war is motivated by vindictiveness, hatred for an enemy, or national pride, it will not be a just war. A country's intentions for going to war must be carefully and honestly examined because they often conceal a variety of motives, many of which have little to do with securing justice and peace. And probability of success means that even when there are valid reasons for going to war, it cannot be justified if there is little reason to believe that an aggrieved nation can overcome an aggressor. Too, what does it mean to have a successful war? Is a war successful if it results in the deaths of thousands of civilians? If it destroys entire cities? If it guarantees more violence in the future? Today many people question if any war can truly be won, particularly when wars do little more than sow seeds of future discontent.

In addition to these seven guidelines that must be reviewed prior to going to war (*jus ad bellum*), the just war tradition adds an eighth criterion meant to ensure right conduct in war (*jus in bello*): *proportionate means* and *discrimination*. Both are meant to temper the viciousness and destructiveness of wars, especially their tendency to spiral out of control. Proportionate means are those that aim to limit the destructiveness of wars by insisting that no more force can be used than absolutely necessary for restoring peace. The principle of discrimination is meant to protect noncombatants in wars. It not only forbids the direct attack of civilians in war, but also says that before attacking any target of war serious efforts must be made to avoid injuring or killing innocent people. Although these principles for guiding the conduct of war are important, many persons increasingly question how any war today could be fought in a way that would not violate them. Wars today, despite promises to the contrary, are commonly indiscriminate in their destructiveness, which is the very thing the just war tradition aimed to avoid.

The just war doctrine is an important part of the Christian moral tradition. Nonetheless, a major difficulty has been that instead of employing it to restrain decisions to go to war—which is the doctrine's intent—it has often been used to give justification for wars that have already begun or that a government has already decided to undertake. As the theologian Lee Camp argues, Christians have been "morally lazy" and often less than honest when working with the just war tradition. We have too frequently used it, Camp insists, to provide "*rationalization* for Christians killing their alleged enemies. When governments tell Christians to wage war, Christians wage war. When governments tell Christians to pledge their allegiance, Christians pledge allegiance. When governments tell Christians to prepare for the mass slaughter of millions of innocent lives through nuclear warfare, Christians give both their consent and their support." Contrary to Jesus' teaching and example, "rather than loving our alleged enemies," Camp concludes, "we prepare to kill them—and when called to kill them, we do so. Moral laziness does not take the criteria of the just war tradition seriously."[37] Camp's critique stings. But it is important to take it seriously because it underscores how easily we forsake Jesus' renunciation of violence because we believe that sometimes the only way to make things right is for us to be willing to kill the enemies Jesus calls us to love. When that happens we begin to live and tell a story other than the one Jesus entrusted to us.

Living God's Story for Us—Learning to Suffer in Hope

Finally, the story of God that comes to us in Jesus is a story worth handing on and remembering because it teaches us how to suffer in hope. It is odd to speak of suffering in hope because one of the most unsettling aspects of suffering is its power to undermine our confidence in life and our hope about the future. Suffering seems much more likely to attack hope than strengthen it because suffering upends the normal order and stability of our lives. As we mentioned in chapter 3, nobody wants to suffer because suffering threatens our sense of ourselves and our trust in the meaning and purpose of our lives. Anyone struggling with a serious illness, the unexpected loss of a job, the death of a loved one, or the end of a relationship knows this to be true. Suffering is an unwelcome intrusion into our lives because it undermines basic human goods such as health, financial security, relationships, and our capacity to plan for the future.[38] We would rather flee suffering than embrace it because more often than not suffering stands as an obstacle between us and the plans and purposes we have made for our lives.[39] Suffering renders certain hopes and dreams unattainable, forcing us to readjust our lives in ways we never would have chosen and can often resent.

Nobody goes looking for suffering, but doesn't it seem that suffering often goes looking for us, and that no matter how hard we try to hide from suffering, it inevitably finds us? Suffering finds students in the painful awareness that they might not have the talents necessary for the careers they have always desired. Suffering finds parents when the behavior and decisions of their children violate their deepest beliefs and go against everything they had taught them. Suffering finds the forty-year-old woman who ate the right foods, exercised regularly, and watched over her health, but is told the fatigue she's been struggling with lately might signal the presence of a serious disease. A story worth living must be able to address the troublesome reality of suffering because sooner or later it is part of every person's life. Suffering is an unwelcome visitor, but unless we learn how to greet it and what to do with it, suffering will defeat us.

Knowing how to respond to suffering is especially essential in an account of the moral life that envisions it as a quest for happiness. If suffering, as many people believe, is inherently incompatible with happiness—something that renders happiness unattainable—then any attempt to shape the moral life in terms of happiness seems at best quite questionable and at worst totally misguided.[40] Suffering presents an unanswerable challenge to this understanding of the moral life unless there is a way that suffering, for all its undesirability, need not destroy the goods on which happiness depends.

And this is what Christians believe. Through the story of Jesus they learn not that suffering is good, but that suffering need not separate us from the God who is our greatest good and the source of our happiness. If happiness ultimately depends on health, financial security, power, physical or mental ability, or just having things go our way more often than not, then any appearance of suffering jeopardizes happiness. But if the essence of happiness is growing in the love and goodness of God in order to share intimately in the life of God, then suffering, far from being an obstacle to happiness, can deepen our participation in happiness, something the saints surely learned. As Robert Ellsberg notes, the saints "did not believe that suffering is 'good' but that God is good and that 'neither death nor life . . . nor height, nor depth' can deprive us of access to that good if we truly desire it. They found that there is no place that is literally 'godforsaken,' but that in every situation, even the most grim and painful, there is a door that leads to love, to fullness of life . . . to happiness."[41]

The saints are the people who learned and lived the story of Jesus best, and what they discovered is that if "we define joy or happiness as the *absence* of something undesirable, such as pain, suffering or disappointment,"[42] then no one can finally be happy. Suffering is part of the fabric of life, an unchosen and unwelcome part for sure, but nonetheless something we all eventually encounter. If the only way to secure happiness is by arranging our lives to minimize suffering, then happiness becomes more a matter of avoiding something evil than pursuing something good. What Christianity teaches, however, is that happiness is essentially defined not by the absence of something undesirable, but by "the *presence* of something desirable: God."[43] And if, as Paul says (Rom. 8:35–39), no suffering, however terrible, is powerful enough to rob us of God, then suffering need not be the enemy of happiness; and all of us, even in the darkest moments of our lives, can suffer in hope. This is something all persons need to learn if they are not to be undone by the sorrows and afflictions of life, and any story that teaches us how to do this is a good story, a story worth handing on and remembering.

Conclusion

Where are our stories taking us? What are they making of us? In this chapter we have explored what it means to see our lives through the lens of narrative and story. Every human life is a story—really a variety of stories—and each of those stories shapes us in some way. Ultimately, we choose a story to be the one we live by, a story that tells us what life means for us and what our fundamental purposes and goals will be. The story we choose makes all the difference for how we see the world, for how we understand what it is to be human, and for what happiness, success, and goodness mean for us. Every story is an argument about life, an argument about what it is to be a person, about excellence and fulfillment, about what is worth pursuing, and about what might be worth dying for.

The night before my Uncle Bill died he gave us a glimpse of the story he had tried to tell with his life. A Christian, he saw himself as having been entrusted with the story of Jesus and as having been given the vocation of bringing Jesus' story to life in the world. This does not mean duplicating Jesus' life, as if being a Christian means slavishly imitating everything Jesus did, which would be both impossible and presumptuous. None of us can retreat to first-century Palestine, chase moneylenders out of temples, or be crucified by Roman soldiers! But it does mean re-presenting the story of Jesus in our world today in our own unique and inimitable ways, with originality and insight, with creativity and grace, all of which Uncle Bill did the night of his infamous pinochle party in Louisville. He had found in the life of Jesus a story worth handing on and remembering. Living it faithfully, growing into it each day, and being changed by it made him a person rich in goodness and happiness. It was easy to say about him, "That person really lived!"

The moral life is a matter of taking a good story to heart. Christians believe they have found such a story in Jesus. They take that story to heart not only because they believe by growing into it they will share more fully in the goodness and happiness that is God, but also because they are convinced it is a story the world needs to hear and needs to see. It may not be an easy story to tell in a world suspicious of hope and often confused about happiness, but it surely is a story worth handing on and remembering.

Some Questions for Reflection and Discussion

1. Why is it helpful to think of the moral life as a story or narrative? What are the advantages of this approach? What might be some possible disadvantages?
2. How have the different narratives of your life shaped you and your outlook on life?
3. What for you would be the qualities or characteristics of a "good story"? A story worth living? Where would you find such a story?
4. What about the life of the first Christian communities appeals to you? What would you find difficult or unappealing?
5. Do you think Jesus, in his call to renounce retaliation and violence, asks too much of us? Why or why not? Is it possible to follow his "way of peace" in the world today?
6. How would you evaluate the just war doctrine? Do you believe it is possible to fight a just war today? Do you think the just war doctrine helps or hurts Christians?
7. Have you ever known a community whose members practiced fraternal correction? Why would many of us find this a difficult thing to do for one another? What would be the point of practicing it?

Notes

1. H. Richard Niebuhr, *The Responsible Self: An Essay in Christian Moral Philosophy* (San Francisco: Harper & Row Publishers, 1963), 63.
2. Stanley Hauerwas, *The Peaceable Kingdom: A Primer in Christian Ethics* (Notre Dame, IN: University of Notre Dame Press, 1983), 17–18.
3. Hauerwas, *The Peaceable Kingdom*, 17.
4. Stanley Hauerwas, *Christian Existence Today: Essays on Church, World and Living in Between* (Durham, NC: The Labyrinth Press, 1988), 25–45.
5. Stanley Hauerwas, *Truthfulness and Tragedy: Further Investigations into Christian Ethics* (Notre Dame, IN: University of Notre Dame Press, 1977), 78.

6. Russell B. Connors Jr. and Patrick T. McCormick, *Character, Choices and Community: The Three Faces of Christian Ethics* (New York: Paulist Press, 1998), 87.

7. Connors and McCormick, *Character, Choices and Community*, 88.

8. Iris Murdoch, *The Sovereignty of Good* (London: Routledge & Kegan Paul, 1970), 67.

9. Connors and McCormick, *Character, Choices and Community*, 88–89.

10. Paul J. Wadell, *The Moral of the Story: Learning from Literature about Human and Divine Love* (New York: The Crossroad Publishing Co., 2002), 7–39.

11. Richard B. Hays, *The Moral Vision of the New Testament: A Contemporary Introduction to New Testament Ethics* (San Francisco: Harper, 1996), 19.

12. Allen Verhey, *The Great Reversal: Ethics and the New Testament* (Vancouver, BC: Regent College Publishing, 1984), 15.

13. Wayne A. Meeks, *The Origins of Christian Morality: The First Two Centuries* (New Haven, CT: Yale University Press, 1993), 32–33.

14. Meeks, *The Origins of Christian Morality*, 94–95.

15. Philip D. Kenneson, *Life on the Vine: Cultivating the Fruit of the Spirit in Christian Community* (Downers Grove, IL: InterVarsity Press, 1999), 98.

16. Meeks, *The Origins of Christian Morality*, 12.

17. Meeks, *The Origins of Christian Morality*, 67.

18. Charles R. Pinches, *A Gathering of Memories: Family, Nation, and Church in a Forgetful World* (Grand Rapids, MI: Brazos Press, 2006), 154.

19. James Alison, *On Being Liked* (New York: The Crossroad Publishing Co., 2003), 133.

20. Gerhard Lohfink, *Jesus and Community*, trans. John P. Galvin (Philadelphia: Fortress Press, 1984), 99–100.

21. Lohfink, *Jesus and Community*, 101.

22. Kenneson, *Life on the Vine*, 83.

23. Kenneson, *Life on the Vine*, 85.

24. Lohfink, *Jesus and Community*, 88.

25. John Howard Yoder, *The Politics of Jesus: Vincit Agnus Noster* (Grand Rapids, MI: William B. Eerdmans, 1972), 115–34. See also John H. Yoder, *The Original Revolution: Essays on Christian Pacifism* (Scottdale, PA: Herald Press, 1971), 34–52.

26. Allen Verhey, *Remembering Jesus: Christian Community, Scripture, and the Moral Life* (Grand Rapids, MI: William B. Eerdmans Publishing Co., 2002), 415.

27. Hays, *The Moral Vision of the New Testament*, 322.

28. Kenneson, *Life on the Vine*, 108–14.

29. Kenneson, *Life on the Vine*, 214.

30. Kenneson, *Life on the Vine*, 193.

31. Paul J. Wadell, "Sharing Peace: Discipline and Trust," in *The Blackwell Companion to Christian Ethics*, ed. Stanley Hauerwas and Samuel Wells (Oxford: Blackwell Publishing, 2004), 299–300.

32. Lohfink, *Jesus and Community*, 106.

33. Robert E. Webber and Rodney Clapp, *People of the Truth: A Christian Challenge to Contemporary Culture* (Harrisburg, PA: Morehouse Publishing, 1988), 62.

34. Paul J. Wadell, *Becoming Friends: Worship, Justice, and the Practice of Christian Friendship* (Grand Rapids, MI: Brazos Press, 2002), 159–80.

35. Lee C. Camp, *Mere Discipleship: Racial Christianity in a Rebellious World* (Grand Rapids, MI: Brazos Press, 2003), 22.

36. Much of the material in this section is taken from my *What Does the Church Teach about Just War?* (Liguori, MO: Liguori Publications, 2005), 8–21.

37. Camp, *Mere Discipleship*, 129.

38. Sebastian K. MacDonald, *Moral Theology and Suffering* (New York: Peter Lang Publishing, Inc., 1995), 2–3.

39. James F. Keenan, SJ, *Moral Wisdom: Lessons and Texts from the Catholic Tradition* (Lanham, MD: Rowman & Littlefield Publishers, Inc., 2004), 68.

40. Robert Ellsberg, *The Saints' Guide to Happiness* (New York: North Point Press, 2003), 115. As Ellsberg writes, "It is a serious error to imagine that suffering in itself is ever 'good.' But it can be productive. If our definition of happiness requires the absolute avoidance of suffering, then any pain or frustration is an obstacle to our goal."

41. Ellsberg, *The Saints' Guide to Happiness*, 104.

42. Kenneson, *Life on the Vine*, 62.

43. Kenneson, *Life on the Vine*, 62.

CHAPTER EIGHT

~

Doing What the Good Requires

Conscience and Prudence in the Moral Life

To live well is to act well.[1] But it is hard to act well because it is easy to overlook something upon which an act's goodness depends. Take something that at first glance seems simple: telling the truth. A fundamental moral principle is that we should always tell the truth. But how we tell the truth and when we tell the truth—as well as why we tell the truth—makes all the difference. Consider the case of whistleblowers. In response to injustices others refuse to address, they feel compelled to speak the truth. But if their telling of the truth is to be not only right but also good, they must first scrutinize their motives, be sure their assessment of the situation is correct, and consider the least harmful way to rectify the injustice. There is nothing simple about doing what the good requires. It is hard work that demands a variety of skills, something we discover when we find ourselves repeatedly saying about the mistakes of our lives, "I meant well."

A good life requires a history of making good decisions. And yet, it is hard to create such a promising legacy for ourselves not only because it is often not clear what doing the good requires, but also because it is far easier to get things wrong than right. It is harder to do the good than we usually think, because for an act to be truly good everything about it has to fall into place.[2] A good act is a careful blend of right intention, a keen appreciation of circumstances, foresight about the act's possible consequences, a consideration of alternatives, and wisdom about the most fitting means for achieving the good. This is why true goodness is never mechanically done. Just as "painting by numbers" is easier than being a true artist, but hardly creates a work of beauty, bringing a good act to life is not the result of rote adherence to rules, but of insight, perception, skill, and astuteness. There is an artistry and style to goodness that results from a history of doing the good insightfully. None of us naturally has such insight about goodness, but we do need to acquire it because if happiness consists in excellence in goodness, it demands learning how to do what is right and good consistently and wisely.

We began our investigation of the Christian moral life contending that it is best to start a study of Christian ethics not by focusing on decisions, but by envisioning the moral life as an ongoing quest for happiness. But this does not mean the decisions we make are unimportant. They are crucially important not only because they reveal what we think happiness is and where we think we will find it, but also because the only way to move toward happiness is through the everyday choices and decisions of our lives. And if happiness is a matter of growing in goodness, we will hardly be happy if we regularly misfire in our desire to do what is right and good. What is truly good here? What is the right thing to do? We ask these questions every day, but we need to know how to answer them if we are not to be stalled or misdirected in our quest for happiness, especially a happiness that is found in imitating and sharing in the goodness of God.

Answering such questions is the work of conscience, and prudence, its primary virtue. It is through conscience that we recognize, respect, and respond to the good, through conscience that we decide and act on behalf of the good. But conscience is intimately related to prudence because prudence helps us determine how the good is best achieved in all the diverse situations that comprise our lives.[3] To be of good conscience involves sensitivity to values, empathy for others, and a basic awareness of moral principles and traditions. But it also requires being skilled in prudence because ultimately the purpose of a good conscience is not only to make us sensitive to the good, but wise and astute in doing it, which is exactly the contribution of prudence. Conscience is completed in prudent action, in seeing how the moral call is best responded to in the situation before us. Prudence is integral to conscience because prudence gives insight and ingenuity to our desire to do the good.

In this chapter we shall look first at what it means to speak of conscience—what conscience is and what it isn't—and the various elements that comprise conscience. Second, we will consider what it means to be responsible for one's conscience and how one might develop a well-formed conscience; but we will also examine the various ways we can fail to be responsible for our conscience. Third, we will analyze prudence, the virtue that puts a good conscience to work. We'll explore why it is impossible to lead a good life without prudence, and investigate some of the components of prudence that must be developed if we are to bring God's goodness to life with insight, wisdom, and verve.

Conscience

Bringing Our Best Self Forward

Conscience. It is probably the most well-worn word in our moral vocabulary. We speak of people of good conscience and people of bad conscience. We talk of a troubled conscience and of a peaceful conscience, of a certain conscience and of a doubtful conscience. One of the first lessons in our moral education told us how important it is to listen to our conscience and to follow our conscience. We are instructed always to respect another person's conscience and never to act against our own conscience. A document of the Catholic Church speaks of conscience as a sacred possession, "the most secret core and sanctuary" of a person, where he or she is "alone with God" and where God's law is revealed.[4] We know stories of people who felt compelled by their conscience to risk their lives for what they believed was right. But we also know stories of such viciousness and depravity that we wonder if some people have a conscience at all. Were they born without moral awareness? Could they never tell the difference between right and wrong? Did it even matter to them?

We talk frequently about conscience, but what exactly is it? It is popular to speak of conscience as "a special faculty or piece of equipment which we possess,"[5] or as a "moral switch" that is turned on whenever we feel the tug of responsibility or the pangs of guilt, but that is otherwise inactive. We think of conscience as some nagging "inner voice" coaxing us to do some good or to avoid some evil. But the trouble with such understandings of conscience is that they suggest conscience works the same way in everybody, and that is clearly not true. Some people are obviously more conscientious than others. There are people with very mature and well-developed consciences, but there are also people who seem to have no conscience. There are people with very alert and sensitive consciences, but others who seem to have let their consciences die. Most of us have selective consciences. We are attuned to the moral call in some areas of our lives, but tone-deaf in other respects. We may grieve the destructiveness of war, but not think twice about what we do with the money we make. We may rightly care about the environment, but not worry much about cheating on an exam or fudging on our taxes.

And so it is better, following Vincent MacNamara, to say, "It is not so much that I have a conscience—a special piece of equipment—as that I am a conscience."[6] MacNamara's point is that *we are our conscience.* At the most basic level, conscience registers a person's awareness that good is to be done and evil is to be avoided, that certain behavior is right, but other behavior is wrong and, therefore, inhuman. Conscience describes the basic moral awareness we have about right and wrong, about good and evil, and about our obligations and responsibilities to others as well as ourselves. Conscience measures our awareness that life is a moral matter and that to be human is to be accountable and responsible. A person of good conscience hears the "moral call" that is present in certain situations, while those of poor conscience may not hear it at all. A person of good conscience feels the tug of responsibility and obligation, particularly toward other persons, while a person whose conscience has been repressed, silenced, or abandoned feels nothing. A person of strong and healthy conscience is deeply attracted to what is true, right, and good. Such a person feels compelled by the true, the right, and the good because he or she has learned to love them.[7] But others, of course, feel compelled by nothing more than their own interests, pleasure, and satisfaction. They have a keen sense of what they think is good for them, but rarely think about what might be good for others. Their conscience is seldom stirred, pricked, or troubled, because they are hardly aware of any reality greater than themselves.

Bringing Our Whole Self Forward

Our conscience is a reflection of our character, a reflection of the unique moral identity we have fashioned for ourselves as a result of our most consistent attitudes, intentions, feelings, perceptions, convictions, and actions. As an expression of our character, our conscience is not some tiny part of us, but the whole moral self we bring to every situation. Far from being some independent little voice that whispers to us, our conscience is our entire moral personality. It is the whole self, for better or worse, with which we engage life. We may not be accustomed to thinking of conscience in this way because we tend to locate conscience exclusively in our mind and to see it as a mental faculty and nothing more. But our conscience, while obviously including our intellect and our reason, involves much more. Conscience captures not only how we think or reason, but also how we intuit, feel, and perceive. It involves our intellects, but also our feelings and emotions, our convictions and beliefs, our freedom and our will. It is our whole self at work honoring and responding to what is right and good. Thus, even though the ultimate work of conscience is to move us to decide and to act, those decisions and actions are the result of a variety of capacities, each of which makes an important contribution to our living and acting in "good conscience."

Some people are uneasy about incorporating the emotions into the work of conscience. They fear that the emotions, precisely because of their intensity, will frustrate the work of reason, obscure our perception of the good, and lead us to be careless and impetuous. At best, they think, the emotions are irrelevant to the work of conscience; at worst, they are positively dangerous and must be suppressed. Suspicion of the emotions can be traced as far back as Plato and characterizes a view of human beings that sees reason and intelligence to be the highest and most noble thing about us and assigns the emotions to the unruly and rebellious parts of our nature. In this tradition, reason is supreme and its sovereignty must be maintained. By contrast, the passions, affections, and emotions are inherently unstable and untrustworthy. They mislead and deceive. They keep us from thinking clearly, from being rational and impartial. They are reason's nemesis, not its ally, and therefore must remain subordinate to reason and constantly held in check by it. In summarizing this view Sidney Callahan says, "When sentiment is allowed to reign, we will be led astray by moral decisions marred by the unreliable personal caprice of subjective feelings. For this reason, the primary task of a moral person when making a moral decision should be to suppress emotion in order to be able to follow the light of reason and make more objective, more correct moral decisions. The first goal of a moral decision maker is to achieve a nonemotional state of detachment."[8]

One response to this argument is that the last thing we want to be when pursuing what is right and good is utterly detached. Total detachment and complete impartiality sound more like apathy and indifference, and hardly supply the commitment necessary for doing what is right. But isn't it also true that our emotions, far from distracting us and leading us astray, often call our attention to what truly matters and sometimes lead us straight to the heart of what needs to be done? And even though we sometimes are "blinded by emotions," are we not also, and hopefully more often, enlightened by them? The danger of making reason sovereign in the workings of conscience is not only that it places far too much confidence in human reason to be objective and unbiased, but also that it shortchanges and neglects other dimensions of ourselves that are important sources for moral insight and awareness. Obviously, reason and intelligence are indispensable for helping us discern the true and the good, but they are hardly sufficient. A well-formed and reliable conscience is a synthesis of reason, emotions, perceptions, convictions, and intuitions, each of them working together, guiding, illuminating, and critiquing one another, to help us see clearly what ought to be done.

Take, for example, the fundamental emotion of love. What role does love play in the work of conscience? For one thing, we desire, are attracted to, and pay attention to what we love. Every lover knows this. Love focuses us. In the moral life, cultivating a love for the true and the good is absolutely crucial because the more we love what is true and good, the more we desire them, seek them, care about them, and attend to them. So much of the moral life comes down to paying attention, to being focused on some things rather than others. Love focuses our attention on what matters most to us.[9] This is true whether we are talking about God, another person, our favorite sports team, or a piece of chocolate cake. In people who have learned to love what is truly good, love can be an indispensable source of moral wisdom and insight because genuine love helps us see things more keenly and perceptively, and because lovers see things more detached observers overlook. This does not mean that the insights of love are always reliable or that they do not need to be assessed, but it does mean they can never be ignored if our judgments of conscience are to be sound.

Moreover, love sends us signals from the heart that ought not to be suppressed. Sometimes we know in our hearts what is right and ought to be done long before we can offer a detailed rational argument for why this might be true. And haven't we all been in situations where our heads told us one thing, but our hearts told us something else, and we sensed that the messages of the heart were closer to the truth? And haven't there also been times when we might have been able to offer a very cogent argument for a proposed moral action, but nonetheless felt troubled in our hearts? Despite the logic of our argument, something held us back. These discordant feelings that flow from a troubled heart are morally important in the work of conscience. They let us know we are not yet ready to make a decision or commit ourselves to an action. But they also signal that there may be something important to the situation—some essential good or value—that we have yet to consider.

Finally, the passions and emotions give us the energy and motivation necessary to do the good and to attack evil. We always fight harder for something we love because we care more about it. We are more invested in and committed to what we love. For example, anger, which ought to be an aspect of love, has an important role in the working of conscience because it energizes us to address immoral situations. We ought to be angry when something we love (including ourselves) comes under attack. Anger focuses our attention on evil and rouses us to overcome it. This is true whether the target of our anger is another person, an institution, or society. Righteous anger provokes the moral indignation that rivets our conscience on situations of injustice and empowers us to address them. Too, as part of the work of love, anger awakens us to evils we might otherwise miss and guards against the complacency that keeps us from confronting them.[10]

Why Some People Are More Conscientious Than Others

In light of this analysis we can, following Sidney Callahan, define conscience as "a personal, self-conscious activity, integrating reason, emotion, and will in self-committed decisions about right and wrong, good and evil."[11] Callahan's definition helps us understand why some people have better consciences than others. Some people are decidedly more aware of, responsive to, and committed to what is right and good than others. Some people think clearly and reason well. They work hard not to be misled by bias, self-interest, or prejudice. They are self-critical, thoughtful, and open to the insight and correction of others. They also have "virtuous passions," emotions, and affections that are trustworthy guides to what is right and good.[12] But other people are hardly reflective at all. They seldom think hard about anything because they are overly confident about their grasp of reality and too often mistake ideology and prejudice for the truth. Their commitment to the good is weak, and it disappears entirely whenever honoring it is costly. Their passions are not "virtuous" but dangerous because they have never developed a strong love for the good. Conscience does not work the same way in everyone, because our conscience, for better or worse, reflects our intellectual, emotional, and moral maturity. Not everyone will exhibit the same capacity to recognize and respond to the true and the good. Not everyone will be able to see clearly what ought to be done, much less care about doing it. Some people remain morally infantile because they are incapable of appreciating anything that does not serve their needs, whereas others, even when young, act from a genuine love for the good.

Our conscience is a living thing, and like all living things it can grow and flourish, but it can also stagnate, weaken, and die. We cannot take our conscience for granted. As any living thing, it must be watched over, cared for, and developed. Everyone may be born with a *capacity* for conscience—a capacity for moral awareness, sensitivity, and responsibility—but that capacity has to be nurtured, honed, and developed into a *habit* or *virtue* of moral awareness, sensitivity, and responsibility. A person of good conscience is characteristically attentive to the moral dimension of life. He or she regularly exhibits a keen sense of obligation and responsibility, and an abiding passion for the true and the good. On the other hand, persons of weak or indifferent conscience may occasionally notice the moral dimension of life and occasionally exhibit a sense of responsibility, but they certainly cannot be counted on to do so, and they definitely will ignore their conscience whenever following it is inconvenient for them. And then there are people who seem to have no conscience. They have ignored the moral call of life for so long that their consciences are dead.

In many respects, our conscience is our own creation. This is why we are responsible not only *to* our conscience, but also *for* our conscience.[13] If we had no role in the making of our conscience, we might be responsible to it, but we could hardly be held responsible for it. But that is not the case. What becomes of our conscience is largely up to us. At birth we are given the materials necessary for conscience (free will, intelligence and imagination, moral awareness, the capacity to reason and to feel), but it is up to us (and our communities) to fashion the raw materials of conscience into an astute, trustworthy, and resolute moral guide. Rather than inheriting a conscience, we craft our conscience through the choices we make, through the virtues we develop or fail to develop, through the perceptions and feelings we endorse, through the company we keep or choose not to keep, and through the behavior we adopt or else deliberately avoid. Our conscience is our own handiwork insofar as it reflects what we have made and each day are making of ourselves morally and spiritually. As Vincent MacNamara says, "A genuine personal conscience is not presented to us by life as a gift and is not by any means an automatic attainment. It has to be forged in the smithy of the individual's soul."[14]

Nonetheless, there is much that has shaped our souls before we take up the work of crafting our consciences. We bring to the formation of conscience our upbringing; the history of our relationships; the social, economic, and cultural environments we have known; our religious training or lack of it; the expectations of others; our personality and temperament; and even genetic influences. These facts of our lives are not inert. They are integral parts of who we are and influence how we see the world and respond to it. Some of these elements of ourselves and our histories facilitate the development of conscience. But others—to borrow a term from Catholic moral theology—are genuine moral impediments because they weaken our capacity to recognize and respond to the moral dimension of life. All things considered, it is easier to develop a sensitive, astute, and responsible conscience when we have known love, care, and affirmation in our lives, when we have been surrounded by goodness, when we have been blessed with wise and trustworthy mentors, and when we have been taught to care about right and wrong.

But not everyone is so fortunate. There are people who have never known love, who from the earliest age have learned not to trust, and whose world has hardly been inhabited by goodness. Can we expect the same of them? When they fail, how should we judge them? As MacNamara writes, "Others have had cruel luck. They have been born into structures that crush their sense of significance and self-esteem. They had known no kindness. They have lived in suspicion. They have learned not to trust life or others or the future. They have known only tawdry pleasure. They have no sense of participation, no stake in things, no sense of identity."[15] Moreover, there are some who have been "so remarkably deprived that they can hardly be said to inhabit the world of morality at all. Moral considerations make no impact. They do not ring true or compelling. They exercise no fascination."[16] How would we tell them to craft their consciences? Where should they begin? This is not to suggest that any of us is completely determined by the past, for indeed one mark of a mature and responsible conscience is our ability to recognize and gradually overcome what hinders our moral development. But it is to affirm that we are conditioned, and sometimes limited by, our past, as well as by aspects of our temperament and personality, and must reckon with this not only in the development of our own consciences, but also when assessing what we can rightly expect of others. Sometimes we have to temper our assessment of what a person's conscience may be capable of seeing and understanding, and what we can reasonably expect of him. We cannot have the same moral expectations of everyone because we come to the moral life with varying capacities for knowing and responding to the good. This does not excuse immorality, but it does explain why being responsible for our conscience will mean something different for all of us.

Taking Responsibility for Our Conscience

Cultivating an Attraction for the Good

Whatever the details of our past or the "givens" of our lives might be, each of us is entrusted with the responsibility of developing our conscience. No one is perfectly equipped for fashioning his or her conscience because all of us struggle with dimensions of our history and our character that stymie our moral development. But if we surrender to those elements instead of addressing them, we never become true moral agents who take responsibility for our lives. A conscience is a call to grow to moral adulthood,[17] not a summons for complacency, much less for surrendering to those aspects of ourselves and our pasts that frustrate our moral development. Too, no matter how healthy our moral upbringing might have been, our conscience remains a "work in progress" because there is no point at which our ability to recognize, care about, and respond to the good is perfect, no point at which it cannot deepen and increase. We may be disposed to seeing and doing the good, but that disposition has to be developed into an enduring quality of character. If our conscience is a living thing that can grow and be strengthened, but that can also be neglected and weakened, what might it mean to take responsibility for our conscience? What can we do to ensure that our love for the good and our commitment to what is right become resilient and abiding parts of who we are, and not things whose disappearance we might hardly notice but some day mourn?

If persons of good conscience are wholeheartedly committed to what is right and good, being responsible for our conscience first requires that we cultivate in ourselves a desire for and attraction to the good. As Sidney Callahan puts it, "the overarching ideals of goodness, rightness, and truth have to be felt as magnets attracting and exerting an overriding obligatory moral force" on us.[18] We will hardly be concerned about what is right, especially when doing it is demanding, if we are halfhearted about the good. People of good conscience are wholeheartedly committed to what is right and good because they find goodness compelling, even beautiful, and have come to desire it more than anything else. They can be counted on to do what is right even at great cost to themselves because goodness captivates them. What dominates their lives is not personal gratification or convenience, but an abiding love for goodness. Through the choices they have made, the practices that have guided their lives, and the virtues they have acquired, they have grown enchanted by goodness and repulsed by evil. They have taken our natural appetite for the good and developed it into an abiding hunger for the good. For them, to be attentive to what is right and good is not an onerous duty, but an obligation of love. A central task in the formation of conscience must be to foster in ourselves an abiding love for and attraction to the good, because without it we will not be steadfast in doing it. As Richard Gula notes, "We can give all the moral instruction we want, or provide the best moral mentors we know, and create an environment where it is easy to be good, but if the person does not care about being good, nothing will happen to produce a morally good person."[19]

Too, without a strong, passionate love for the good we will lack the strength of will needed for doing good.[20] Often we fail not because we have no desire to do what is right and good, but because at certain moments we are more powerfully attracted by other desires and too weak to resist them. We know what we ought to do, and maybe even want to do, but we are too weak to do it. At such moments our resolve to do good is temporarily overwhelmed by the counterattraction of something less than good. It is not that "we repudiate or abandon the good forever," but because our love for the good is inadequate we allow contrary desires and attractions to conquer us. Because of weakness of will we refuse to "submit to the moral obligations that we recognize," and "watch ourselves do what we know and feel is morally wrong, even as we do it."[21]

There are, of course, people who do "repudiate or abandon the good forever" because over their lifetime they have devoted themselves to fostering a love for and attraction to evil. Through their everyday behavior they effectively make "a conscious commitment . . . to harden the heart and abandon moral standards" altogether.[22] But it is more likely that we encounter people who have not explicitly embraced evil, but who are "morally tone-deaf" inasmuch as moral concerns never override their own needs or gratification, and thus become increasingly insignificant in their lives.[23] These people may do what is right when it serves their purposes and comes at no cost to themselves, but readily set aside moral considerations when attending to them would frustrate their plans and desires. "They choose evil by default," Callahan says, "because they abandon all commitment to moral values. The self's will is autistically enthroned, and moral indifference serves as a protection from outside interference or restraint."[24]

If the consciences of some people are deadened on account of the upbringing, history, and environment they have known, the consciences of these others are slowly suffocated by their own decisions and choices. By habitually choosing to ignore the demands of conscience, they eventually abandon their consciences altogether. What rules every decision they make is not a love for the good, but a love for self and its imperial interests and demands. One sign of a mature, responsible conscience is the ability to look beyond one's own comfort, interests, and gratification in order to seek what is truly good, particularly the good of others.[25] But some people, having spent a lifetime of putting themselves first, never take others into account. They have so regularly ignored the moral dimension of life that they are no longer aware that there is one. Virtuosos at doing harm, they are dangerous people who ought to be repudiated because of the misery they create. The problem, however, is that they are easily overlooked, and sometimes even admired, because they are frequently intelligent and quite successful, and because they are often in positions of power and influence. Sadly, sometimes the only way to learn that "moral concerns are meaningless to them" is to experience how callous they can be with anyone who stands in their way.[26] Dealing with such people, or seeing the effects of their behavior, reminds us of the cost that comes to ourselves and to societies when people fail to develop a love for the right and the good.

Human beings are born with a natural love for the good and a natural desire to be good, but in order for that desire to prevail it has to be strengthened. We have to attend to the nurturing of our conscience because like everything else about us that is neglected or unused (our minds, muscles, emotions), our conscience too can quickly deteriorate and eventually die.[27] It is one thing to do wrong and allow the bite of conscience to redirect us to the good, but quite another thing to regularly ignore our conscience in order to avoid the salutary uneasiness wrought by guilt. If we consistently distance ourselves from the warnings of our conscience, we eventually lose touch with it altogether. We may initially choose to avoid our conscience simply in order not to be troubled by it, but such acts of avoidance habitually repeated form us into persons with no conscience at all. To ignore, repress, or silence our conscience begins a moral decline that if left unchecked culminates in a complete moral collapse. At that point our conscience is dead inasmuch as we no longer have any idea of what the good is or why it is important. Regular neglect of our conscience transforms us into persons for whom moral concerns do not register at all.[28]

How then can we cultivate a love for and attraction to the good? There are many ways, but three seem most important. First, we learn to love what is right and good by doing what is right and good. Our attraction to the good increases the more we regularly attend to it in our everyday lives. If I seek to do what is right and good each day, my love for it will grow greater because I have strengthened my attachment to it. If I treat people thoughtfully, if I am respectful and kind, if I am honest and just, all of those actions extended over time will fortify my love for the good. Second, our love for the good can also be deepened through regular practices of prayer, whether through personal reflection, meditation on the scriptures, or the worship of a religious community. To pray is to direct our minds and hearts to God, the luminous source of all goodness, truth, and beauty. The more our lives are centered on the goodness and beauty of God, the more we will be filled by that goodness and beauty and the less likely we will be to turn away from it. So much of what and how we love is a matter of what most has our attention. To pray is to "give our attention" to God so that we may be more fully formed in the love and goodness of God. Third, our love for the good is strengthened when we see it embodied in others. This is why friends, mentors, and healthy moral communities can enhance our desire for what is right and good. We need attractive examples of goodness in our lives, people whose kindness, thoughtfulness, generosity, and compassion make goodness attractive to us. But we can also learn the attractive power of goodness by studying the biographies of good people, through works of literature, and even through the beauty of art and music. Anything that sensitizes us to the good and helps us become enchanted with it can serve the development of our conscience.

Seeking the Counsel of Others

Our conscience is too important to be guided by ourselves alone. As Richard Gula has noted, making up one's mind *for* oneself, which is a mark of a mature conscience, does not mean making up one's mind *by* oneself.[29] This is why a second requirement for taking responsibility for our conscience is regularly to seek the counsel and guidance of others. Seldom can we discover what ought to be done entirely on our own. Our experience, knowledge, insight, and awareness are too limited to always be trustworthy moral guides. Too, there are many things that blur our perception of reality. Sometimes we are so caught up in situations where decisions must be made that we cannot see things clearly and objectively. Other times, thanks to sin, we do not want to see clearly and objectively lest doing so challenges what we want to do. We avoid consulting the persons or communities whose wisdom would help us lest they draw our attention to facts we'd rather overlook. We practice what Sidney Callahan calls "motivated, culpable ignorance" because we want *not to know*.[30] Or we fail to acknowledge what we already know, conveniently choosing to forget it, because it goes against our plans. We silence intuitions and dismiss feelings that might lead us to truths whose discovery would suggest obligations we would rather escape. We make situations more complicated than they really are in order to do what we have already decided to do even if it might not be the right thing to do. We are all prone to rationalization. We can remember moments when we chose not to pay attention to the moral call of a situation, moments when we filtered out anything that might reveal the true shape of the situation and our responsibilities. As Callahan said, "Humans are clever at using partial truths and subtle but slipshod reasoning to project and avoid moral responsibility."[31]

This is why being responsible for our conscience demands not only that we develop a love for and attraction to the good, but also that we seek the counsel of others. The word conscience means "knowing together with,"[32] a fact that suggests that the education of our conscience requires the ongoing input, guidance, and even correction of others. If this is so, whose counsel do we need to consult? First, we need to consult the moral teachings and traditions of the communities of which we are a part, especially our churches. The moral teachings of Christian churches represent the collective wisdom of communities of faith about important matters of life. This is why their teachings and traditions have a privileged role in the ongoing formation of our conscience. Christians have a responsibility to know what their faith communities teach about various moral issues and an obligation to attend to these teachings when making decisions. Too, even if we initially do not see the relevance of a teaching or perhaps disagree with it, we must consider it with openness and respect, and work to understand the goods and values that the church is trying to protect through the teaching. In other words, being responsible in developing our conscience means being teachable, and to be teachable is not only learning what our faith community holds on a variety of moral issues but also, like any good student, doing our best to make that teaching our own. Thus, we do not prejudge the teaching, much less immediately dismiss it, but allow it to speak to us, enlighten us, and challenge us.

Still, even though we have an obligation to carefully attend to the moral teachings of our faith communities, those teachings cannot be the sole basis of our decisions. The teachings should play a critical role in the formation of our conscience, but they are not the only source of moral wisdom, and they are not always sufficient for revealing what doing the good requires in a particular situation. Too, after carefully studying the moral teaching of a church we may not be able to assent to it because, despite our efforts to understand the teaching, our initial questions and uncertainties remain. We do not find the arguments for the teaching compelling. We have approached the teaching with openness and respect, we have tried to make it our own, but we remain unconvinced. And it may be that the teaching doesn't resonate with the wisdom we've gained from experience. This is why knowing, respecting, and attending to the moral teachings of our Christian communities is indispensable in the development and formation of our conscience, but it is not sufficient. Our faith communities should inform our decisions of conscience, but they cannot replace them. And that is because sometimes what the true and the good require may be other than what a church's teaching strictly suggests.

Along with the teaching and traditions of our faith communities, if our conscience is to be a trustworthy moral guide, we should also seek the counsel of people whose lives exhibit wisdom, goodness, and integrity, people whose virtuous character makes them worthy sources of insight and direction. We can find such mentors in our families, in friends who want our good and sometimes know us better than we know ourselves, in teachers and pastors, in fellow church members, in colleagues, and sometimes even in strangers whose advice could not have come at a better time. We can also find them in the lives of those who have gone before us, people whose legacy constitutes a source of moral guidance and illumination. These can be revered family members, parents and grandparents, aunts and uncles, whose words and example left us with a tradition of moral wisdom we can trust. We often find ourselves remembering their advice when important and difficult decisions have to be made, and we feel more confident about our decisions when we recall what we have learned from them. And, as suggested above, we can also find helpful moral guidance in biographies of good people, in the stories of the saints of our communities, and even in works of fiction as we watch characters struggle with discerning what is right and good.

Finally, and for Christians most importantly, we need to seek the counsel of God. The last thing Christians should do is to form their consciences without conversation with God. God has to be a conversation partner in the formation of conscience because it is in dialogue with God that we grow in our ability to see what is true and good. In prayer we open ourselves to God and ask for the guidance of the Spirit. In prayer we invite God to be an active partner in our lives and to guide us in all of our actions. In prayer we do not "go it alone" in the formation of our conscience, but ask God to enlighten us so that we can see what needs to be considered and discern what needs to be done. We can seek the counsel of God through regular meditation on the scriptures, especially the prophets and psalms of the Old Testament, Jesus' teachings and parables in the gospels, and the moral reflection of the first Christian communities that we find in the Acts of the Apostles and the Epistles. But we also receive guidance from God when we participate in the worship of the church and belong to communities where people, bonded together in the love of God, help one another understand "what it means to live the story of Jesus that Christians still love to tell."[33] Christian communities are primary settings for the formation of conscience because in them we should learn what it means to choose, act, and decide in ways faithful to God.

The Courage to Be One's Own Person

Third, nurturing a mature, well-developed conscience requires the courage to be one's own person. This means we must be willing to identify with the choices we make and claim them as our own without rationalizing our decisions, blaming others, or distancing ourselves from what we have done. Furthermore, having the courage to be one's own person means taking responsibility for who we are and what we do, and never abdicating that responsibility to others. Instead of being like a child who unquestionably submits to the authority of others, a person of mature conscience freely commits herself to what she honestly discerns to be true and good. When faced with difficult choices and decisions, she does not surrender the responsibility of her conscience by asking others, especially those in authority who may be very willing to tell her what to do, to make the decision for her.

Accepting responsibility for who we are and what we do means that "no authority, no Church, no other person can take the place of one's personal conscience."[34] Despite the cost (misunderstanding, rejection, condemnation, isolation) that can come from following one's conscience, a person of mature conscience cares more about what is right and good than about what might be safest, most convenient or advantageous, or else most acceptable to others. Having achieved a certain level of self-transcendence in their lives, such persons are motivated not by a need for the acceptance and approval of others, but by a genuine love for the good.[35] Again, while it is absolutely imperative to inform our consciences with the insights and wisdom of others—especially the teachings of our moral communities—no one can make a decision of conscience for us. The difference between being infantile in the moral life and being an adult is that the morally mature person does what he or she genuinely discerns to be right and good, not just what persons in authority claim they ought to do. As Richard Gula summarizes, "It is not enough to follow what one has been told. The morally mature person must be able to perceive, choose, and identify oneself with what one does. In short, we create our character and give our lives meaning by committing our freedom, not by submitting it to someone in authority. We cannot claim to be virtuous, to have strong moral character, or to give direction to our lives if we act simply on the basis that we have been told to act that way."[36]

Freedom of Conscience—Do We Always Deserve It?

There is much talk in Christian ethics about the sovereignty of conscience and the absolute importance of freedom of conscience, but sometimes they are too quickly taken for granted, as if they can be equally endorsed for everyone. That would be a mistake. We do not begin with freedom of conscience, we work up to it. Freedom of conscience is the well-earned prerogative of those who have taken responsibility for forming their conscience and for acquiring the virtues. Freedom of conscience does not precede, but follows upon a way of life in which persons have cultivated a strong love for and commitment to what is true and good, and a way of life in which they have been formed by the teachings and traditions of moral communities. Freedom of conscience is more a privilege earned than a right to be casually assumed. It befits those who have learned to be loving and just, truthful and responsible, but it is dangerously entrusted to those whose primary commitment is to themselves. We do not hesitate to tell people who are morally responsible to follow their conscience, but are rightly uneasy to offer the same advice to those who infrequently allow moral considerations to matter at all.

For those who have regularly attended to the moral dimension of life and who are compelled by what is true and good, conscience truly is "a holy place, a sacred space . . . where the individual meets God."[37] Such persons recognize that to attend to their conscience is not to turn in on themselves, but to pursue a life in which they regularly dialogue with God about the direction of their lives, the choices they have made, and the challenges that confront them. They know what gives their conscience authority is not the fact that it is their own, but that it represents what they honestly believe God is calling them to do. And once they are convinced of this, it is more accurate to say not that they are *free* to follow their conscience, but that they are *bound* to follow their conscience.[38] The language of "freedom" could suggest that one might, in such moments, just as easily ignore his conscience as follow it. But for persons of good conscience this is never an option because conscience represents not only what they are convinced ought to be done, but also what they believe is God's objective demand to them.[39] It is to these people that Thomas Aquinas's famous claim "that we ought to die excommunicated rather than violate our conscience" properly pertains.[40]

Similarly, it is only with people of such good conscience that we can fully appreciate the cost of acting against one's conscience. For people of little conscience—people more amoral than moral—it makes no sense to speak of the cost of not following one's conscience. They are not concerned with what is right and good to begin with, much less with what might be the demand of God. It does not bother them to ignore their conscience because there is little integrity for them to betray. But for the truly conscientious it is different. There is incalculable cost for them not to follow their conscience because to do so not only would go against everything they believed to be right and compelling, but would also be unfaithful to God. For them there is a twofold betrayal at the heart of every refusal to heed the call of conscience, a betrayal of their self and their integrity, but also a betrayal of God.

Caring for Our Conscience—The Cost of Small Betrayals

We might think that we could occasionally ignore our conscience without too much cost to our integrity, but that would be a mistake. In *Faith That Dares to Speak*, Donald Cozzens refers to "The Monastery Cemetery," a poem by Kilian McDonnell. In that poem McDonnell speaks not of "grand betrayals," but of "small treasons."[41] He is not talking about dramatic acts of failure, but of small, perhaps scarcely noticed betrayals that we can embrace without recognizing what we lose when we do so. His point is that we ordinarily do not betray our conscience in one grand and singular act; rather, we do so bit by bit, a little at a time, in those small treasons that are easy to ignore. Small treasons occur when we know what conscience commands but fear, concern for acceptance and approval, or the expected reactions of others, especially those in authority, lead us to ignore it. Small treasons occur when we fail to speak out, when we allow something we know to be wrong to continue, or when we remain uninvolved because nobody else seems very concerned anyway. As isolated instances, small treasons may seem trifling. But they are dangerously corrosive because they make us comfortable with violating our conscience whenever heeding it might be costly. As Cozzens notes, ordinarily what harms us most in the moral life are not dramatic acts of failure, but "a series of small betrayals that nevertheless chips away" at our integrity.[42] "Without necessarily recognizing it," he warns, "individuals become compromised."[43]

Our integrity also suffers if we allow any person, institution, or authority to persuade us to act against our conscience. There is no higher moral authority than conscience because for Christians the authority of conscience rests not in the autonomy of the individual, but in the summons of God. This is why nothing supersedes or can override the authority of conscience, no other person or group, no society or state, no church. To make a religious leader or a religious tradition the absolute moral authority would be idolatrous because it would recognize in it an authority and truth that we would not recognize in God.[44] An enduring temptation of anyone in leadership, whether national or ecclesiastical, is to encourage individuals to dispense with conscience in the name of loyalty or obedience. National leaders may call this patriotism; ecclesiastical leaders may call it faithfulness. But it is neither, because in each instance it is to usurp for themselves a loyalty that is owed only to God. As Livio Melina notes, "the Church can never bypass personal conscience, nor can it ever substitute for it." The church's role is not to tempt its members "to dispense with conscience in the name of obedience," but to provide them with a form of life that shapes them into persons who can truly be led by the Spirit of God.[45]

Prudence: The Virtue That Puts a Good Conscience to Work

We have described conscience as a wholehearted commitment to do what is right and good. But simply being committed to doing what is right and good is no guarantee that our acts will actually achieve it because, as we said at the outset, there is nothing simple about doing what the good requires. There is an art to goodness because bringing goodness to life demands a keen perception of circumstances and situations, an assessment of different possibilities, imagination and thoughtfulness, deliberation and reflection, and the ability to recognize the numerous ways an act can go wrong. Conscience is completed in action—its aim is to achieve excellence in goodness—but for this to occur we must become skilled in bringing goodness to life in the most fitting possible way, and this is the function of prudence, conscience's primary virtue.

The first of the four cardinal virtues that traditionally have been deemed essential for a good and successful life, prudence is the skill of making right judgments about things to be done.[46] It is wisdom about the good, but specifically *practical* wisdom, because prudence is geared to action; its aim is not to have us thinking about the good, but doing it skillfully and astutely. Josef Pieper captures the quintessential note of prudence when he describes it as the "perfected ability to make right decisions."[47] Pieper's description hints that making right decisions may not be nearly as easy as we sometimes think. Anyone who has ever been faced with caring for an elderly parent whose health is failing knows this. It is one thing to say we should always care for the sick and the dying, but quite another thing to know what exactly this means when dealing with particular persons in particular situations. Thus, when Aquinas summarizes prudence as the capacity "to deliberate well" about what needs to be done, we realize how difficult it can be to know precisely what that might mean.[48]

There is no "steps-to-be-followed" approach to moral decision making that can guarantee that our actions will always be right and good. There is no precise recipe for right decision making because there are so many variables in a situation that need to be attended to, any of which can shift the meaning of an act. Just as a doctor needs more than textbook knowledge of medicine to be skilled in diagnosis, living a good life requires more than textbook knowledge of morality. To achieve expertise in doing the good, we need experience, insight, good judgment, imagination, and keen analytical skills. We need what the philosopher John Casey calls "intelligent goodness," and this is what prudence provides.[49]

A person of prudence is wise about all that has to be considered to bring goodness to life *in the best way possible* amid the various situations and challenges of our lives. This is not easy because ultimately doing the good depends not only on a knowledge of general moral principles and rules, but also on being able to discern how they need to be applied in particular situations. Take the moral principle that love seeks the good of another. That seems straightforward enough until we start to apply it to all the people who make up our lives. What does it mean to seek the good of each of our friends? To work for what is best for them? This cannot mean exactly the same thing for each of them because they are all unique, people of different gifts, needs, talents, worries, and concerns. This is why prudence is indispensable for goodness. Prudence helps us discern not what *appears* to be good or *might* be good, but what in fact *actually* is good.[50] It is the ability to choose and act wisely based on an accurate perception of reality.[51] As Raymond Devettere puts it, "Prudence, correctly understood, never reduces ethics to the apparent good, to what I think is good; prudence seeks always what is truly good."[52]

Thus, prudence begins with deliberation, with assessing and evaluating a situation in order to figure out "what particular action in a particular situation will likely contribute to our doing well and living well."[53] A person of good conscience lives with the fundamental desire to do good, but that desire is not enough. The desire to do good has to work through prudence because there are many times when we aren't quite sure how the good can be done or needs to be done. If we are not to misfire in our desire to do good, we need to be able to tell the difference between the helpful and the harmful, between good intentions but clumsy (or even destructive) results. Should a concerned teacher inquire about the problems of a troubled student? When is it best to address a difficult situation and when is it best to be silent? If we are called by Christ to love our enemies, how should that love be expressed? What would it mean to love them as well as ourselves? How can we do this in a way that helps them but does not harm us? We can see why prudence makes an action good—why there is no goodness without it—and why prudence and goodness are substantially the same.[54] Every good act is born from prudence inasmuch as prudence helps us discern how to bring the good to life in the best possible way. Far from being rigid and inflexible, it is the kind of "on-the-spot reasoning" that assesses a situation and, as Devettere pithily puts it, "looks for a good move."[55]

Knowing a good move from a bad one is an important moral skill. As we make our way through life, we encounter all kinds of people, all kinds of situations and experiences. In each instance we are called to bring goodness to life, but the trick lies in knowing exactly how best to do this. Rules and principles can guide us, but they cannot always tell us precisely what needs to be done. They are helpful and need to be taken into account, but they are not always sufficiently illuminating. We have likely been in situations where we consulted the relevant moral teachings and principles, but realized that even though what they told us was important, they did not tell us enough. The reason is that moral principles and guidelines are necessarily general, designed to apply to a wide variety of circumstances; however, our task is to do the good not in some general, abstract way, but in light of the particular, often complex, and frequently changing scenarios of our lives. This is why Aquinas, in a famous passage, contended that the more we consider the particular details of a situation, the more we realize how often general rules admit of exceptions. They need to be hedged "with cautions and qualifications," Aquinas said, because the general rule or principle "all by itself" cannot tell us everything we need to know about what doing the good requires.[56]

He asks, for example, whether it is always right to return what belongs to another. The general principle says that if someone entrusts something of theirs to us (e.g., money, property), we are obliged to return it when they ask for it. But should we always? Suppose we suspect they might use it to do great harm—Aquinas gives the example of attacking one's country. Does the general rule still apply? Aquinas says no because the purpose of any moral rule is to achieve the good; however, as his example attests, there are times when strict adherence to a rule can result in something evil instead of good.[57] This is where prudence comes into play. Prudence helps us shape our acts to fit the situation before us so that they actually achieve the good. Prudence is more fundamental than principles and rules because prudence brings discernment, insight, and flexibility to our actions that a strict adherence to principles and rules lacks.[58] This explains why we may sometimes "keep the law" or "adhere strictly to the rule," but nonetheless miss doing what the good requires. In our quest for goodness we need more than laws and rules. We need prudence, the "ability to 'see' what is at stake where the application of rules may not be at all obvious, and to know how to respond."[59]

Components of Prudence

Prudence is necessary to lead a good life.[60] We cannot make progress in the moral life without it because deprived of prudence we remain inept at doing what is right and good. Besides, it is far easier to get things wrong than right, far easier to have our good intentions go awry than for them, thoughtfully and creatively, to bring goodness to life. Prudence brings ingenuity to our good intentions, it brings intelligence and thoughtfulness to our actions so that the good we wish to do is actually done. Any act that is right and good is a beautiful thing and like any beautiful creation involves more to bring to life than we might suspect. In his extended analysis of the virtue, Aquinas identified eight components of prudence, each of which plays a part in the production of goodness.

First, there is *memory*.[61] One way to determine what must be done in a situation is to consider our past experience to see if we have ever faced similar situations. Is there anything from our past that might guide us in determining what we ought to do now? Are there lessons from our experience that might be pertinent, memories that could be illuminating? Teachers do this when wrestling with how to make a frustrating class better or how to make disengaged students interested. They think back to similar incidents to see what might be helpful to them now. Parents return to lessons learned from raising a first child for insight about how to help their second child. When we are struggling with a relationship we often think back to previous relationships for insight and guidance. Prudence develops from experience, from a history of making good decisions and learning from them.[62] This is why memories of past experiences can be helpful to us when struggling to discern what to do now.

A second component of prudence is *insight*.[63] Insight is the capacity to evaluate correctly what is at stake in a situation. It is, as the word suggests, the ability to "see into" a situation, to probe it accurately and astutely so that we grasp as clearly as possible what the situation involves. Insight helps us determine the morally relevant features of a situation. With this second element of prudence, we are able to see both the advantages and the disadvantages of possible courses of action. We grasp what goods and values might be protected in a decision, but also what goods and values might be lost with that same decision. Too, with insight we know which general moral principles and rules are relevant to a situation and how best to apply them.

The third component of prudence is *docility*, which Aquinas defines as "being teachable."[64] A person of docility is not only open to being instructed by others, but also actively seeks whatever guidance and insight they can offer because he is wise enough to admit he doesn't know everything. An aspect of humility, docility is an essential attribute of prudence because, as Aquinas says, the situations we confront in life are "infinite in their variety" and "one person alone cannot consider them all sufficiently." That, he says, "would take ages," much more time than we can afford to spend pondering an action, especially when decisions have to be made quickly. And so the prudent person "carefully, frequently, and respectfully" seeks out the guidance of others, particularly those whose age and experience have given them greater wisdom into the complexity of human actions.[65] A person of docility knows he can learn something from others and will become more skilled in doing what is right and good if he is open to their counsel. In opposition to docility are pride and laziness. The proud person is unwilling to admit that he does not know everything and needs the guidance of others, and the lazy person is too indifferent to care.

A fourth component of prudence is the ability *to reason well* about what needs to be done.[66] To reason well about a situation is carefully to think through all that is morally relevant to that situation. It is to take everything pertinent into account so that we can make a thoughtful, judicious decision. But because it is almost impossible for any one of us to take into account everything that may be pertinent, Aquinas understood this fourth element of prudence to be a collegial activity, one that necessarily involves others. We ordinarily come to better, more reasonable decisions when we have taken time to confer with others because, as Aquinas suggests, what we might overlook another person may notice.[67] This is also true of groups and institutions. Well-founded policies and decisions most commonly result when the views, insights, and opinions of many are consulted.

Interestingly, Aquinas believed that if we are to reason well about an action or decision, we must also confer with God. This is why he said the virtue of prudence is completed by the gift of counsel, one of the seven infused gifts of the Holy Spirit. Sometimes the situations we face are so difficult or uncertain that even with the best of human guidance we are still unsure about what ought to be done. Human wisdom falls short and needs to be complemented with the wisdom of God who, Aquinas reminds us, "knows all things." With the gift of counsel we make eminently prudent decisions because "we are guided by the advice, as it were, of God." Our minds "are quickened and instructed by the Spirit about what to do," so that even amid great difficulty and uncertainty we do what is right and good in the most fitting possible way.[68]

Circumspection, which can be defined as "careful attention to circumstances," is a fifth element to prudence.[69] Prudence gives us the skill to find the best means for achieving good ends. But this can be difficult because what might work very well in one situation may, on account of different circumstances, be completely inappropriate in another situation. Doing the right and the good requires a keen eye for circumstances, the distinctive features of a situation whose presence can change the whole meaning of an act.[70] Circumstances are so important that sometimes an act that might be fitting in one situation may, despite our good intentions, be wrong and bring about harm in another situation.[71] Aquinas gives the example of showing love and affection to another person. Suppose, he says, we show affection at an inopportune time, perhaps when a person is in a bad mood or may be suspicious of our motives.[72] Ordinarily, showing affection to those we love is good; however, this is not always the case, and if we fail to notice what might account for the difference, our desire to do good can backfire. This sometimes happens in marriages or friendships when remarks we intend to be playful fall short or even hurt our spouse or our friends because we did not take time to apprise how things might be with them. These may seem to be trivial examples, but they illustrate why doing what is right and good requires that we be "sharp sighted," that is, that we be able to spot whatever might be exceptional about a situation and, therefore, impact its moral meaning.[73] We can appreciate the relevance of circumspection if we extend our examples to questions of sexuality, justice, war and peace, or medical ethics, areas where being "sharp sighted" is especially important if good is to be done and evil avoided. That circumstances have to be so carefully attended to can be dismaying, but it is the only way to ensure that the good we say we want to do is actually done.

Sixth, if an act is prudent, and therefore good, it has to include *foresight*, the ability to "look ahead" in order to see, as best as we can, its possible consequences.[74] When contemplating an act or decision, we want to be as certain as we reasonably can that it will actually achieve the good, and not do more harm than good. Will telling my wife that something she did upset me make things better or make her feel I'm always looking for faults in her? Will cramming all night for an exam improve my chances or leave me too tired to do well? More broadly, will this war bring about stability and peace or only plant the seeds for future destruction? Foresight is an "instinct for the future," the skill of being able to estimate the outcome of our actions before we do them.[75]

But foresight pertains not only to the consequences of an act on ourselves, but also on others. An act may seem to bring about very good consequences for me, but if it has unjust consequences on others, it cannot be called right and good. Similarly, prudence demands that we consider not only the immediate consequences of an act, but also the possible long-term consequences. Sometimes we can feel very confident about the immediate consequences of a proposed action but never consider its long-term effects. Both have to be taken into account before the act can be judged morally right and good. This is especially true today in light of the possible consequences of our actions on the environment. Prudence requires that we not only take human well-being into account, but the well-being of the earth and other species as well. What effect might a proposed housing development have on other species? Or in a world of quickly diminishing natural resources, is building bigger and bigger vehicles really prudent?

This is why *caution*, the seventh component of prudence, cannot be overlooked. Caution guards against deciding and acting too hastily. It counsels us to go slowly, to question our assumptions, to seek whatever counsel we might need from others, and to pay attention to all the factors of a situation. Often our actions do harm (both as individuals and as nations) not because our intentions were bad, but because we were impulsive and careless. Caution summons us to proceed carefully in order to be aware, as best as we can, of all the things that might hinder the good being done. It is an essential element of prudence because, as Aquinas observed, we face so many situations "in which bad may be mixed with good," situations in which "rights are often entangled with wrongs, and wrongs wear the air of good."[76] Any nation that has gone to war can surely verify Aquinas's point. Caution helps us separate the bad from the good in an action, the right from the wrong, in order to be sure that what we finally do is really good, not what only appears to be good.

Nonetheless, sometimes we have to make quick decisions. We do not have time to go slowly, to be cautious and circumspect, to seek the counsel of others or to think about similar situations from our past. We have to act and we have to act quickly. If you have ever been faced with a sudden emergency, you know this is true. At such moments we need *acumen*, an eighth and final element of prudence. Aquinas describes acumen as "the flair for finding the right course in sudden encounters," and the person who possesses this quality as "quick as lightning in coming to the right course of action."[77] There are moments when we do have to be "quick as lightning" in making the right decision because to delay would do harm. Snap decisions are called for, but snap decisions that "hit the mark" of what needs to be done. This is what makes prudence indispensable. The danger of snap decisions is that they can easily result in more harm than good because there is no time to consider all the decision might involve. But people who are truly skilled in the virtue of prudence display an uncanny ability to do what the good requires even in those highly pressured situations where there is little time to think about it. That it is so easy to miss the mark at such moments makes the goodness they achieve all the more impressive.

Prudence and the Christian Life—What Truly Good Acts Aim for and Accomplish

If prudence makes us astute about how to do what is right and good, what does it mean to live prudently when the good we are seeking is God? If happiness is inseparable from goodness, and the greatest possible happiness is found in the goodness of God, how must prudence inform our everyday acts and decisions so that they draw us more deeply into the goodness of God? The Christian moral life is a quest for happiness, and happiness depends on becoming adept at acts that further our participation in the love and goodness of God. Christian moral education has to include education in prudence because for Christians the purpose of prudence is not only to show us how to make good decisions today, but also how to make those everyday acts and decisions serve our overall goal of attaining union with God. Prudence connects the present with the hoped-for future. It links the ordinariness of the everyday with what we take to be the ultimate goal of our lives: rejoicing in perfect fellowship with God and the saints. The immediate purpose of prudence is to help us discover the right means for doing what is good now.[78]

How do I treat this person fairly? How do I be honest, but also thoughtful and respectful? How do I deal with this bitter disappointment? But the ultimate purpose of prudence is to show us how to live today in order to attain "the final good for the whole of human life."[79]

The horizon of prudence is vast. While attending to the concrete details of the present, prudence looks beyond the present to the final good in which our happiness consists. It focuses on the particular, but with our final goal always in mind. This is why, in the most proper sense, to be prudent requires more than deliberating well about present acts and decisions. The truly prudent persons are the man and woman who are able to "think things out" well, not just for today, but "for the whole of the good life."[80] They are truly prudent because they are able to judge wisely, in everything they do, about what helps or hinders their striving for God. As Aquinas noted, "Prudence is of good counsel about matters regarding a man's life in its entirety, and its last end." Only those "who are of good counsel about what concerns the whole of human life" are, in the most complete sense of the word, truly prudent.[81]

Furthermore, if Christians are called to carry on the story of God that comes to us in Jesus, a Christian account of prudence will connect wisdom about doing good with actions that make the reign of God visible and are consistent with the new way of life Jesus makes possible. How we finally determine what is prudent is informed by the narrative or story that most governs our lives. If my goal in life is to be as comfortable and secure as possible, what it means to live prudently will be quite different from one whose goal is to conform his life to Christ. For those trying to be faithful to the story of God, what might seem recklessly imprudent to others (e.g., a commitment to nonviolence, the practice of forgiveness) is eminently reasonable because it shares in and furthers God's ways in the world.

A Christian account of prudence is guided by the concern to make all of one's behavior fit the story of God. This is why it may seem odd, puzzling, or downright foolish to one with a decidedly different understanding of our purpose in the world. In fact, a Christian understanding of prudence is bound to be at least initially confounding because the norm for Christian prudence is found not in "the wisdom of the world," but in the Beatitudes. The special skill of prudence is to show us how to act in order to grow in the goodness constitutive of happiness, and for Christians the charter document on happiness is presented in the Beatitudes. There we learn that the paragon of prudence is the person who is poor in spirit, who hungers and thirsts for holiness, who shows mercy and is single-hearted about God, and who is a peacemaker and a truth teller, because each of these is a practice essential for happiness. In this respect, a Christian understanding of prudence may be captured best in the apostle Paul's postconversion claim that he completely reappraised what he once took to be true, good, and reasonable in light of the surpassing knowledge he had found in Christ (Phil. 3:7–8).

Conclusion

To live well is to act well. In this chapter we have explored the role of conscience and its accompanying virtue of prudence in the Christian moral life. We can neither live well nor act well unless we are people of good conscience, people whose love for the good results in a wholehearted commitment to the good. At the same time, we cannot live and act well without prudence because more than a wholehearted commitment to the good is needed for doing good. We need insight, imagination, and wisdom about how to bring the good to life amid all the diverse situations of our lives. We need ingenuity in goodness, and this is what prudence provides. Moreover, a well-formed conscience and prudence are both necessary for happiness because if happiness is excellence in goodness, we only achieve it through a history of making good decisions. For Christians, a well-formed conscience is one that attunes us to the goodness of God, and prudence is the virtue that guides all of our actions in imitating, sharing in, and furthering the goodness of God.

Nothing imitates, shares in, and furthers the goodness of God more than love because God is love. If the Christian moral life is training in happiness, it cannot overlook the central importance of love because it is love that makes us most like God. Love is the language of God. What it might mean to speak that language is the subject of chapter 9.

Some Questions for Reflection and Discussion

1. What role do you think the feelings and emotions should have in the work of conscience?
2. How can one's conscience grow stronger? How can it weaken and die? Have you ever met someone who seemed to have no conscience?
3. What role do you think the moral teaching of the church or a community should play in your decisions of conscience? What do you do if you disagree with a church's moral teaching?
4. Do you agree that freedom of conscience is more a privilege to be earned than a right to be presumed?
5. How would you describe the virtue of prudence and why it is important in the moral life? Why is it sometimes hard to make truly good decisions?
6. What might be different about a Christian understanding of prudence?

Notes

1. Thomas Aquinas, *Summa Theologiae* (New York: McGraw-Hill, 1966), I-II, 57,5.

2. Aquinas, *ST*, II-II, 110,3.

3. Josef Pieper, *The Four Cardinal Virtues* (Notre Dame, IN: University of Notre Dame Press, 1966), 11. Pieper notes "that the word 'conscience' is intimately related to and well-nigh interchangeable with the word 'prudence.'"

4. "Gaudium et Spes: The Church in the Modern World," in *Catholic Social Thought: The Documentary Heritage*, ed. David J. O'Brien and Thomas A. Shannon (Maryknoll, NY: Orbis Books, 1992), #16.

5. Vincent MacNamara, *Love, Law and Christian Life: Basic Attitudes of Christian Morality* (Wilmington, DE: Michael Glazier, 1988), 154.

6. MacNamara, *Love, Law and Christian Life*, 154.

7. Sidney Callahan, *In Good Conscience: Reason and Emotion in Moral Decision Making* (San Francisco: Harper, 1991), 31.

8. Callahan, *In Good Conscience*, 97.

9. Callahan, *In Good Conscience*, 132. Callahan writes: "The emotion of love is the great moral educator because it makes us pay attention to and value what we love. Love can be defined minimally as joyful interest with a predisposition to attend, approach, unite with, and care about the love object. . . . Love motivates fine and careful perception, which works against stereotypes, automatic dismissals, or habitual arguments made from inertia or carelessness."

10. Callahan, *In Good Conscience*, 132.

11. Callahan, *In Good Conscience*, 14.

12. G. Simon Harak, SJ, *Virtuous Passions: The Formation of Christian Character* (New York: Paulist Press, 1993), 71–98.

13. John Mahoney, *The Making of Moral Theology: A Study of the Roman Catholic Tradition* (Oxford: Clarendon Press, 1987), 290.

14. MacNamara, *Love, Law and Christian Life*, 156.

15. MacNamara, *Love, Law and Christian Life*, 114.

16. MacNamara, *Love, Law and Christian Life*, 114.

17. James F. Keenan, SJ, *Moral Wisdom: Lessons and Texts from the Catholic Tradition* (Lanham, MD: Rowman & Littlefield Publishers, Inc., 2004), 33.

18. Callahan, *In Good Conscience*, 198.

19. Richard M. Gula, "Conscience," in *Christian Ethics: An Introduction*, ed. Bernard Hoose (Collegeville, MN: Liturgical Press, 1998), 121.

20. Russell B. Connors Jr. and Patrick T. McCormick, *Character, Choices and Community: The Three Faces of Christian Ethics* (New York: Paulist Press, 1998), 145.

21. Callahan, *In Good Conscience*, 150.

22. Callahan, *In Good Conscience*, 146.

23. Sidney Callahan, "Conscience," in *Riding Time Like a River: The Catholic Moral Tradition Since Vatican II*, ed. William J. O'Brien (Washington, DC: Georgetown University Press, 1993), 102.

24. Callahan, *In Good Conscience*, 147.

25. MacNamara, *Love, Law and Christian Life*, 157.

26. Callahan, "Conscience," 102.

27. Callahan, *In Good Conscience*, 152. As Callahan explains, "Sometimes there are further moves to avoid the shame and guilt of self-judgment, and a morally debilitating dynamic can occur. Moral sensibility and moral reasoning become sources of pain and anxiety, therefore they are avoided. Just as with the muscles of the body, the unused capacities of conscience can begin to deteriorate and become blunted. An arm put in a cast withers away, and the moral sense may also atrophy."

28. Callahan, *In Good Conscience*, 152.

29. Richard M. Gula, SS, *Reason Informed by Faith: Foundations of Catholic Morality* (New York: Paulist Press, 1989), 124.

30. Callahan, *In Good Conscience*, 154.

31. Callahan, *In Good Conscience*, 159.

32. Gula, "Conscience," 115.

33. Allen Verhey, *Remembering Jesus: Christian Community, Scripture, and the Moral Life* (Grand Rapids, MI: William B. Eerdmans Publishing Co., 2002), 13.

34. Sean Fagan, SM, *Does Morality Change?* (Dublin: Gill & Macmillan Ltd., 1997), 91.

35. MacNamara, *Love, Law and Christian Life*, 157.

36. Gula, "Conscience," 118.

37. James T. Bretzke, *A Morally Complex World: Engaging Contemporary Moral Theology* (Collegeville, MN: Liturgical Press, 2004), 110.

38. Mahoney, *The Making of Moral Theology*, 291.

39. Keenan, *Moral Wisdom*, 34.

40. Cited in Keenan, *Moral Wisdom*, 35. Aquinas's statement can be found in *ST*, I-II, 19,5.

41. Donald Cozzens, *Faith That Dares to Speak* (Collegeville, MN: Liturgical Press, 2004), 70.

42. Cozzens, *Faith That Dares to Speak*, 70.

43. Cozzens, *Faith That Dares to Speak*, 89.

44. Bretzke, *A Morally Complex World*, 112. Bretzke observes, "Whatever authority one believes is absolute is, in effect, the voice of God for that person, and if we allow any outside authority—no matter how respected—to supplant the person's individual conscience, then we are, in effect, making this heteronomous moral authority into God for that person. Making into a 'god' that which is not truly God is idolatry, and it is possible to idolize even authority figures which are otherwise worthy and good in themselves. However, to relinquish one's obligation to follow one's conscience, which means seeking to follow what one honestly believes is God's voice, in favor of following the voice of an external authority, would be making that authority into a false God."

45. Livio Melina, *Sharing in Christ's Virtues: For a Renewal of Moral Theology in Light of Veritatis Splendor*, trans. William E. May (Washington, DC: The Catholic University of America Press, 2001), 191.

46. Aquinas, *ST*, I-II, 57,4. For a superb study of the virtue of prudence see Daniel Mark Nelson, *The Priority of Prudence: Virtue and Natural Law in Thomas Aquinas and the Implications for Modern Ethics* (University Park, PA: The Pennsylvania State University Press, 1992), esp. 27–104.
47. Pieper, *The Four Cardinal Virtues*, 6.
48. Aquinas, *ST*, II-II, 47,2.
49. John Casey, *Pagan Virtue: An Essay in Ethics* (Oxford: Clarendon Press, 1990), 160.
50. Raymond J. Devettere, *Introduction to Virtue Ethics: Insights of the Ancient Greeks* (Washington, DC: Georgetown University Press, 2002), 119.
51. Pieper, *The Four Cardinal Virtues*, 10.
52. Devettere, *Introduction to Virtue Ethics*, 119.
53. Devettere, *Introduction to Virtue Ethics*, 112.
54. Pieper, *The Four Cardinal Virtues*, 7. Pieper writes: "What is prudent and what is good are substantially one and the same; they differ only in their place in the logical succession of realization. For whatever is good must first have been prudent."
55. Devettere, *Introduction to Virtue Ethics*, 115.
56. Aquinas, *ST*, I-II, 94,4.
57. Aquinas, *ST*, II-II, 51,4.
58. Devettere, *Introduction to Virtue Ethics*, 85. "Principles (and moral laws, rules, and rights) are important but prudence does not follow principles; principles follow prudence."
59. Casey, *Pagan Virtue*, 146.
60. Aquinas, *ST*, I-II, 57,5.
61. Aquinas, *ST*, II-II, 49,1.
62. Aquinas, *ST*, II-II, 47,16.
63. Aquinas, *ST*, II-II, 49,2.
64. Aquinas, *ST*, II-II, 49,3.
65. Aquinas, *ST*, II-II, 49,3.
66. Aquinas, *ST*, II-II, 49,5.
67. Aquinas, *ST*, I-II, 14,3.
68. Aquinas, *ST*, II-II, 52,1.
69. Aquinas, *ST*, II-II, 49,7.
70. Aquinas, *ST*, I-II, 7,1.
71. Aquinas, *ST*, I-II, 7,2.
72. Aquinas, *ST*, II-II, 49,7.
73. Aquinas, *ST*, II-II, 51,4.
74. Aquinas, *ST*, II-II, 49,6.
75. Pieper, *The Four Cardinal Virtues*, 18.
76. Aquinas, *ST*, II-II, 49,8.
77. Aquinas, *ST*, II-II, 49,4.
78. Aquinas, *ST*, II-II, 47,6.
79. Aquinas, *ST*, II-II, 47,13.
80. Aquinas, *ST*, II-II, 47,2.
81. Aquinas, *ST*, I-II, 57,4.

CHAPTER NINE

~

The Gift That Makes All Gifts Possible

Learning the Language of Love

God is love. And we should be too.

That's Christianity in a nutshell, Christianity stripped down to its most elementary claims. We are loved and we are called to love. We are created from love; exist because we are loved; and find joy, depth, peace, and fulfillment in loving and being loved. To be a Christian is to take these truths and run with them for a lifetime because it is love that most makes us like God and, therefore, happy. Love is not one virtue among others for Christians; it is the animating principle for the entire Christian life. Take it away and Christians become chatty corpses, churches become suffocating tombs. Love is our lifeline to God, to our deepest selves, to the hearts and souls of others, and to the heart and soul of the world. Love is not only each of us at our best, it is what all of us have been brought into existence to do. We need to love if we are to live, and never to have loved—to have consistently chosen fear, selfishness, indifference, harshness, or hatred over love—is to have failed as a human being even if we might have achieved other standards for success. Love should be the legacy every person wants because love is good for everybody. It's good for the lover, good for the beloved, good for the world, and even good for the God in whom all love begins and through whom all love is possible.

In a way, the path to happiness is simple. We find happiness when we live who we already are, spiffy creatures fashioned in the image of a God who is the fullness and perfection of love, indeed the very definition of love. St. Paul says the God who is love has been "poured out into our hearts through the holy Spirit" (Rom. 5:5), infused into us in such a way that from first to last, now and always, we live from a love we could never have given ourselves. This is the love that got everything started and keeps everything alive—it really is our heartbeat—and since it is the gift that makes all other gifts possible, it is closer to us than we are to ourselves. We can spend a lifetime searching for happiness, never realizing that what we seek we already possess. The happiness that is our perfection is ours from the start, beating away in us and in everything that lives. To know happiness all we have to do is live according to the love by which we, as well as all other creatures, are made. Put differently, love is our destiny only because love is our starting point, and this means we reach happiness by growing more deeply into the grace that lives at the very center of our being. Jesus summarized everything he was about in the single commandment to love (Matt. 22:37–39; Mark 12:29–31; Luke 10:27). Jesus didn't ask that we would love or hope that we would love; rather, Jesus commanded us to love because our happiness and fulfillment depend on it.

Love is the language of God. It is the language in which each of us was spoken and it is the language we are called to learn. But it is easy to lose our way when it comes to the language of love because probably no word has been so frequently and flagrantly misspoken. A lot of harm is done in the name of love, particularly when the word love is used to name behavior that would more properly be described by language such as pride, selfishness, power, manipulation, infidelity, or even abuse. Most likely each of us has been careless with the language of love. But misuse the language of love and somebody always gets hurt, often very deeply and sometimes quite lastingly. For many people, the language of love has been so perverted by misuse that it is not only a word that no longer has any value for them, but also a word they hope never again to hear. For them, it is the four-letter word that is truly obscene because in their lives it has been more a curse than a blessing.

Still, no matter what one's history has been with love, it is not a word we can afford never to speak or hear. God gave the world hope when the divine word of love was spoken in Jesus and took flesh in our world. That word has to be heard, received, and taken to heart by each of us if the joy God wants for us is to be ours. Our task is to become eloquent in God's language of love, so articulate with the word we call Jesus that we bring that word to life in everything we do. Our training in happiness cannot be complete without gaining expertise in God's language of love. In this chapter we'll explore what this might mean by looking first at why the human vocation is indeed the vocation to love. Next, we'll consider what exactly it means to love. In a world where love wears so many faces, it will be important to be able to distinguish real love from the many impersonations of love.[1] Finally, following Jesus' command, we'll reflect on how we should go about loving God, ourselves, and our many neighbors.

Discovering Ourselves in the Call to Love

In 1981 Pope John Paul II wrote a letter on marriage and family life (*Familiaris Consortio*) built around the principle that human beings are made for love. Learning to give and receive love is not an option for us, John Paul II reasoned, but an unceasing need and an inescapable responsibility because it is what God brought us to life to do. Fashioned from love, we become ourselves in loving and being loved. We are, as biologists might put it, genetically wired to love. In more theological language, it is everyone's lifetime vocation; it is what every human being is called to do. "God inscribed in the humanity of man and woman," John Paul II wrote, "the vocation, and thus the capacity and responsibility, of love and communion. Love is therefore the fundamental and innate vocation of every human being."[2] Nobody escapes the call to love. I can run from it and spend my life contradicting it, but that will be a terribly expensive choice because I cannot erase the most persistent need of my nature. As Vincent Genovesi observes, "Because we are created for love, nothing else can fulfill us ultimately; lacking fulfillment, we cannot be truly happy. In light of our destiny our only chance for lasting happiness is our persistent willingness to love."[3] This does not deny that loving well is hard work, or that there are sometimes deep hurts and unbearable losses in love. But it is hard to give up on love, and awfully hard to stop wanting to be loved, because giving and receiving love is what we are born to do. "Love is not an option for human beings, it is a requirement. It is the most profound statement of who we are."[4]

We are fulfilled through love because as God's images there is an unbreakable connection between who God is and who we are called to be. We are perfected in the give-and-take of love because that is what makes us most like a God whose very being is a community of love. As we saw in chapter 4, Christians call this God "Trinity" and mean by that that God is not the loneliness of three utterly separated and disconnected persons, but a living community of three distinct persons united perfectly in love. God is a vibrant, intimate partnership of mutual, reciprocal love, a true and forever existing community in which each person's love gives life, identity, and joy to the other, and in which each one's love perfectly completes the other. Sometimes our thinking about God can be so ethereal and abstract (desiccated really) that even when we speak of God as a community of love we envision something lifeless and inert. Perhaps we believe that at one time God's love was vibrantly creative, totally alive, and passionately involved with everything, but that this is not the case any more. Now that the world is created and history underway, God's love has retreated into itself and become increasingly inaccessible to us. But for Christians to think this way is not only bad theology, it is heresy. As C. S. Lewis noted, when Christians say "God is love," they mean "that the living, dynamic activity of love has been going on in God forever and has created everything else,"[5] and continues to hold everything together in existence. Christianity teaches, Lewis insists, that "God is not a static thing—not even a person—but a dynamic, pulsating activity, a life, almost a kind of drama. Almost, if you will not think me irreverent, a kind of dance."[6]

As God's images, we are called to become part of the dance by living in partnership with "the living, dynamic activity of love" that is God. The God Christians worship is three persons intimately connected to one another in an unbreakable union of love, and if we are God's images the love that draws us to life and ultimately perfects us must be patterned on the love we see in God. God is a communion of persons joined together by generous, life-giving, mutual love, and as living, breathing expressions of God's creativity we grow and flourish only insofar as we practice such love in our lives. As André Guindon says, "The Christian God is not a lonesome figure,"[7] and as God's creatures we cannot afford to drift through life as lonesome figures either. We need to extend ourselves in love. We need to work at understanding intimacy. We need to nurture the friendships of our lives, be responsible in our marriages, and not give up on communities. We need to risk generosity, risk vulnerability, and risk forgiveness again and again because no matter how hard it can be to persevere in love, we touch life only when we do love. There is an intimate connection between who God is and who we are that explains why happiness cannot be had apart from love. As Elaine Storkey writes, "There is a community between the Father, Son and the Spirit. That community is love. But this same God has designed *us*, made us, shaped us, and loved us into being. We are to be called 'God's image.' So love too is part of our own identity."[8]

What do these initial reflections tell us about how Christians understand love? First and foremost, Christians believe love is a *gift*. We do not (and really cannot) earn God's love, because "the truth of Christianity begins with the fact that God already loves us and will love us forever."[9] This is why we can move through life without fear or anxiety, without skepticism or suspicion, and certainly without cynicism. It is why the most fitting human posture is not one of doubt and defiance, but of trust, openness, and receptivity.

We are always receiving God's love; it is the first gift that makes all other gifts possible. Consequently, our very capacity to love originates in God's unending love for us. In his first encyclical, *God Is Love* (*Deus Caritas Est*), Pope Benedict XVI echoed this fundamental Christian belief about love: "Since God has first loved us (cf. 1 John 4:10), love is now no longer a mere 'command'; it is the response to the gift of love with which God draws near to us."[10] God comes to us in love so that we can move toward God and others in love. This is the original grace, the truly original blessing. Love never really begins with us because any love we offer is always in response to having been loved first.

Second, in Christianity the most perfect expression of love is one characterized by mutuality leading to communion. Love's desire is for the lover to be united with the loved one. We want to be one with the people we love, not just close to them but intimately connected with them. This is not surprising because love does not create unity as much as it affirms and builds upon a unity that is already there. There is a preexisting unity among all creatures inasmuch as everything is created by God and cannot have life apart from God. This radical interconnectedness between God, every human being, and the whole of creation explains why mutuality, intimacy, and communion are the aim of love and the most perfect expression of love. In seeking union through love we are acting in harmony with what we already are, creatures that have life in God and with one another. To hunger for intimacy and communion with another human being, or indeed all of life, is to honor "a preexisting original oneness"[11] that it is the power of love to deepen or, sometimes, to repair and restore. As the philosopher Josef Pieper says, we could not love anyone or anything unless we lived in a world "in which all beings at bottom are related to one another and from their very origins exist in a relationship of real correspondence to one another." That this is so, Pieper adds, is "confirmed in our sensing that love not only yields and creates unity but also that its premise is unity."[12] It is no wonder that Jesus summarized the entire Jewish law in the threefold command to love God, our neighbors, and ourselves. Putting that command into practice sustains the nurturing relationships of intimacy, mutuality, and communion that are the highest expression of love and absolutely necessary for life.

Third, even though the fundamental Christian conviction is that all love originates in God and that God's love for us makes possible our loving at all, it is equally true that the love that begins in God is to continue through us. This is the purpose of the Christian community, to be a people through whom the love of God is brought more fully to life in the world. God loves the world not in some abstract, impersonal way, but through us, embodied, historical creatures placed in the world to bring God's love to life. God's love always takes flesh; it always comes to life in history. God's love took flesh in the people Israel, it took flesh in the prophets, and it was perfectly incarnated in Jesus. But Jesus did not see the history of God's love ending in him. He called disciples so that there would be a community who learned from him what it meant to be the living presence of God's love in the world and who were committed to carrying it forward. This is why Christians see themselves not primarily as individuals, but as members of a community. They are Christ's body in the world, and God's mission of love continues through them. This does not mean that it is exclusively revealed through the church, much less that the churches with all their sins, failures, and shortcomings ever embody God's love adequately. But it does mean that if God's love is truly to be visible and convincing, there must be a people who commit themselves to learning, embodying, and witnessing that love. Otherwise, how would the world know that God's love is real? As Karl Barth wrote, "Would the love of God then be revealed? Would I be able to perceive it and respond to it? Without the ministry of the people of God and its members, would I be loved by God at all, or free to love Him in return?"[13]

What Does It Mean to Love?

If God's love is to come into the world through us, what does it mean to love as God does? And is that even possible? At the Last Supper in his farewell address to his disciples, Jesus took the command to love one giant step further. He had said before that we must love God wholeheartedly and love our neighbors as we love ourselves, but on the night before he died Jesus told his disciples, "I give you a new commandment." The disciples were to love each other in the same way that Jesus had loved them (John 13:34). The decisive difference between this new articulation of the law of love and the previous one was that now Jesus presented himself as the rule or measure of love. In his teachings, in his attitudes and actions, in the shape of his entire life, Jesus was the perfect expression of divine love. To pattern our lives on the love of God, we must follow the way of love that we see in Jesus. Put differently, if it is not love that defines God, but God that defines love and Jesus who is God's love incarnate, then we rightly understand love when we follow the example of Jesus. "We now have a radically new norm for human loving," Vincent Genovesi explains. "No longer is our love for our neighbor to be measured by the love we have for ourselves. Rather, the measure of our love for others is to be the love we have first received from God. The norm for loving shifts from self-love to God's love for us as revealed in and by Christ."[14]

Thus, even though love is the deepest and most abiding need of our nature, we do not naturally know what love is. We learn the meaning of love in a life of discipleship with Jesus. Moreover, we are easily misled about love because so many conflicting ideas about it hit us every day. For instance, a philosophy of consumerism teaches us to love material things more than persons, to make the newest products rather than God our hearts' desire. Or we live in a culture that often reduces love to pleasure and pleasure to sex, and that sees sex as little more than gratification; consequently, casual, trouble-free sex is offered as the path to love. Or in a society saturated by the excesses of capitalism, love cashes out as greed, a lust for power, or intemperate ambition. We are daily bombarded with a variety of messages about love. Each grows out of certain narratives and traditions, and each is embedded within a particular way of life, such as consumerism and materialism. Consequently, even though we all use the word love, what we mean by it, and the way of life that is formed from it, can differ greatly from other accounts of love. Love is not an abstraction, it is not a theoretical concept or even an idea, but a specific way of life informed by particular narratives and traditions.

Thus, Christianity offers not so much different ideas about love, but a different way of life about love. What Christians think about love is derived from the narratives and traditions that guide and inform their lives. One learns the Christian way of love by becoming part of the community committed to being continually formed by that love. In short, one learns the love of God that comes to us in Jesus by being embedded in a community of Jesus' followers for a lifetime. For Christians, lessons in divine love begin at baptism and are sustained through the Eucharist. By becoming Jesus' disciples, Christians are schooled in the grammar of God's love. It is a love articulated through faithfulness, justice, mercy, truthfulness, patience, and forgiveness. This is why it is misleading to speak of Christian love primarily as a moral principle, for that tends to extricate love from the context, practices, and way of life that give it flesh and make it intelligible. For example, it is not a principle that leads Christians to connect love with forgiving enemies, but an encounter with their own sinfulness, an abiding spirit of contrition, and their unceasing gratitude for God's mercy, all of which are made possible by their participation in a community. Christian love will never be something upon which all reasonable people agree, any more than the accounts of love proffered by narratives of consumerism or hedonism will make sense to Christians.[15] The reasonableness of Christian love is derived from the narratives, traditions, and practices that teach us what it would mean to live such love and, most of all, from actually living it. As Stephen Post said so well, Christian love, or *agape*, has a particular and essential social location, namely the community of believers that is the church, and stripped of this context and particular way of life, it "wanders homeless."[16]

A First Rule of Love

What then do Christians learn about God's love that is meant to guide and inform their own love? Although there are many characteristics of God's love, three seem most essential. First, God's love is *creative and affirming.* In the most general sense, to love something is to find it good, which is what God declared about everything God created. To love someone or some thing is to approve of its existence; it is to say, as Josef Pieper puts it, "It's good that you exist; it's good that you are in this world!"[17] Love is the most basic affirmation we can give another person because it is to rejoice in the fact of their existence. This is why we are never neutral or indifferent about what we love, but always partisan. Love is a strong, passionate assertion that we want something to be and that we will do whatever we can to keep it in being. From a theological perspective we, along with everything else in the universe, exist because God wants us to be, because God not only approves of, but also delights in our existence. Christian love is shaped by the conviction that we have "to view all reality, again including ourselves, as something creatively willed and affirmed, whose existence depends solely on being so affirmed and loved."[18] And so a love modeled on God strives to continue what God's love began. If to be loved by God is to be creatively willed and affirmed into existence, to love another person is to devote our energy and attention to making her be. In this respect, love is more than affirmation because I can affirm someone and still remain uninvolved in her life. If we really rejoice in another's existence, we do what we can to bring her more fully to life.[19]

There is then a dazzling connection between God's love and human love. Our love for another has power, substance, and *reality* only because it is preceded by God's love.[20] But this also means that our love is real, quite creative, and can be powerfully effective precisely because it not only originates in God's love, but also actively participates in it and moves it along. Our love depends on God's love of us, but also works with God's love, shares in it, and furthers it. We are not passive channels of God's love, but active, insightful agents of that love. When husbands and wives love one another, when parents affirm and encourage their children, when friends support one another, and when any one of us reaches out to a stranger, we are not only imitating and continuing God's love, but also helping bring it to completion. Josef Pieper rightly says, "It is God who in the act of creation anticipated all conceivable human love and said: I will you to be; it is good, 'very good' (Gen. 1:31), that you exist." In this respect, Pieper argues, "Human love, therefore, is by its nature and must inevitably be always an imitation and a kind of repetition of this perfected and, in the exact sense of the word, *creative* love of God."[21]

Human love echoes God's love. At the same time, it has to be more than an echo—a weak, faint imitation of God's love. For human love to have both meaning and dignity, it must involve something more than miming God's love. This is not because God's love is deficient, but because God honors us in making us creative and responsible moral agents and true participants in the divine love. Our love is like God's love because anytime we affirm and uphold the goodness of another's existence we reenact God's primal declaration given at creation. All real love is a reenactment of God's originally creative love.[22] But it is also more. The great dignity and unsurpassable responsibility of human love is that it carries forward, and even creatively enriches, what God's love began. "If all goes happily as it should, then in human love something *more* takes place than mere echo, mere repetition and imitation," Pieper writes. "What takes place is a continuation and in a certain sense even a perfecting of what was begun in the course of creation."[23]

And so being created from the love of God and continually being loved by God are not enough for us. We not only want but also absolutely depend on the explicit confirmation by others of the life given us by God. We need God's love for us to be met, confirmed, and extended by the love and affirmation of others. God's love may give us life, but authentic human love continues to bring us to life. This is why the responsibility to love that God entrusts us with cannot be shirked. Each of us waits for another's love to delineate us, to prize our distinctiveness, to be singularly glad that we are. This is why when people feel unloved by others, it is little consolation for them to be told that they are loved by God. It is also why simply existing is not enough for us. If we do not experience love—if we do not experience ourselves as valuable to someone—we feel bereft and disconnected, empty, and without meaning or purpose; in fact, if we do not experience love, we feel invisible. "In other words, what we need over and above sheer existence is: to be loved by another person," Pieper explains. "That is an astonishing fact when we consider it closely. Being created by God actually does not suffice, it would seem; the fact of creation needs continuation and perfection by the creative power of human love."[24]

Existing is one thing, but meaningful existence, hopeful existence, depends on love. We see evidence of this all the time. All of us have witnessed the dramatic transformation that can happen when people experience being loved. They visibly come to life in ways they were not before. Sometimes we say that they even seem like totally different persons, so marked is the contrast between who they were before and who they are now that they are loved. There is a joy, spirit, and hope marking their lives in love that was so notably absent before that it is no exaggeration to say that they have been re-created. To see this happen is not only delightful to them and to those who love them, but it is also delightful to the God who gives us the exalted vocation to love.

A Second Rule of Love

A second quality of God's love is that it is *insightfully directed to the true well-being of others*. Love seeks the beloved's good. This is witnessed throughout the scriptures, as Yahweh sought the good of Israel, as Jesus sought the good of all who came to him in need, or as the apostle Paul sought the good of each of the communities he founded. At the least, to love is to wish that everything regarding a human being, or another creature or species, may truly be good.[25] Love is respect and reverence for another human being as a person, but also respect and reverence for other species as part of God's creation. It is to want beings to flourish and to prosper; it is to wish the greatest goodness and excellence that is possible for them. In its most fundamental and general expression, love is universal benevolence, it is wishing all things well. It is continuous appreciation and regard for another's good. This is why any kind of genuine love loosens the tentacles of self-centeredness and self-promotion.

But love must involve more than an attitude of general benevolence, especially when it regards those who most intimately inhabit our world. Universal benevolence is a necessary first element to love and it may be all we can offer those far removed from our everyday lives, but it is hardly sufficient for love. The people with whom we have forged strong commitments (spouses, children, friends, communities) certainly expect more from us than simply the desire that things go well for them. They want to see that desire enfleshed, they want to see it go to work in action on their behalf. Love has to be shown, demonstrated, and consistently brought to life if it is not to be little more than questionable rhetoric. It is easy enough to avow love, but much harder to show it in practical, insightful, and steady ways. That is why love is best understood not just as an attitude or disposition, but as a heartfelt commitment to seek, work for, and be involved in promoting what is best for another. For love fully to come to life, a disposition or attitude to favor the good of another has to mature into action.

In his well-respected study of love, Edward Vacek says to love someone is to devote our time and energy to helping that person grow toward "the fullness of value possible" for him or her.[26] It is to assist the loved one "in achieving higher goodness," recognizing that when we do so, we "cooperate with God's creative and transforming love."[27] And if the work of love is to help others achieve their greatest possible good, for Christians that means helping them fulfill their "inexhaustible destiny of being fully in relation to God."[28] Love works for the highest good of loved ones. It refuses to settle for lesser possibilities because it wants what is absolutely best for them, and for Christians this is life together in God. For Christians, love helps another person make his or her way in this life, but always sees that way as a path to God. The ultimate aim of Christian love is to help another grow in the love of God, believing that the most perfect happiness is found in the perfection of that love.[29]

Like Vacek, Vincent Genovesi also affirms that love has to be more than the general desire that all goes well for someone. For Genovesi, love is not something that happens by accident, it is not something we "fall into," but something we consciously and intentionally choose. It is, he writes, "my free response, my free decision to respond to and nurture the beauty and potential that I see in another human being."[30] Moreover, the life of Christ "suggests that the heart of true human love and Christian love is found in the desire and willingness to live creatively in the service of others' fulfillment."[31] Most of all, love moves us "to desire and seek on behalf of others simply what God wishes for them, namely, that they be friends of God and members of God's people, courageous and free enough not only to accept God's love for them but also to love God in return and to offer love for others."[32]

Three conclusions can be drawn from this second characteristic of love. First, it calls into question any accounts of love that would reduce love to mere sentimentality, as if love means always agreeing with another, supporting everything she might want to do, or being silent when she needs to be challenged. Love *labors*. It works with another to help her achieve what is truly best for her. But because we either are often confused about what is best for us or do our best to flee it, people who really love us are not afraid to challenge us, to speak truths we may not want to hear, and even to admonish us when we go wrong. Such acts are not failures in love, but indications of the depth of commitment and honesty that real love demands. Sentimental love flatters, but authentic love toils for what is really good for us, knowing that if any of us is to achieve our greatest possible good, which is companionship together with God and the saints, we must be willing to grow, to change, and to be challenged.

Second, love can only work for the true well-being of another if it is insightful and informed. Love is not an anonymous, undifferentiated regard for others; rather, love is the skill of being able to seek the good of another precisely because we have taken time to *discover* her as other and *discern* what respecting and responding to her "otherness" requires.[33] If I pledge myself to work for the good of another, I cannot do that well unless I understand what that would mean for her as a singular, unique human being.[34] Love requires perception, astuteness, and discriminating insight. Love requires sensitivity, sympathy, and imagination.[35] We cannot love persons graciously and thoughtfully unless we learn who they really are and have some knowledge of their distinctive desires, struggles, hopes, and fears. Love begins in a vision of the unique identity, dignity, gifts, needs, cares, and concerns of another. To love another as if she were anybody is not to love her well because such love fails to take into account what it is that makes her the special child of God she is. Good love requires attending to what makes someone "a unique expression of God's infinite creativity."[36] Who is this person called by God to be? What is the *imago Dei* in her that love works to make resplendent? This is what Christian love tries to bring to light as it seeks the good of another.

Third, love not only seeks the good of another, but also wants to share in it with them. If the highest expression of love is mutuality-in-communion, then we do not want to be detached from or uninvolved with those whose good we seek. We want to be one with them and we want to share life with them. And not only do we want to devote ourselves to their good, but we also want them to be just as actively devoted to our good. At its best, love is "a being together" in which two or more persons delight together in the good they share. If mutuality is lacking, if love is not a reciprocal participation in one another's well-being, it stands imperfect and incomplete. At love's best, we find joy in promoting another's good because they find joy in promoting our own. As Edward Vacek notes, "Put most formally, *love is an affective, affirming participation in the goodness of a being (or Being)*."[37] Whether we are talking about loving another person or loving God, we not only want to seek and promote their good, but we also want to share in it with them, just as we want them to seek, promote, and share in our own.

A Third Rule of Love

Finally, a third fundamental quality of God's love that should characterize Christian love is that God's love is *steadfast, patient, and faithful*. God's love never stops and God's love never fails, even if it means being so intimately involved in our lives that love brings suffering and loss to God, a fact the death of Jesus vividly attests. We can refuse to love God, but that does not keep God from loving us. We can be flagrantly unfaithful to God, but as Yahweh's love for Israel testifies, that does not weaken God's faithful, persevering love for us, a truth poignantly portrayed in the Book of Hosea where God is depicted as a spurned and humiliated husband who nonetheless forgives an adulterous Israel. In fact, nothing demonstrates the unwavering patience and faithfulness of the love of God more than God's limitless forgiveness, perhaps the most creative and liberating aspect of divine love. That God's love is steadfast, patient, faithful, and forgiving shows that even though God can be exasperated, disappointed, angry, and even hurt over our failures and refusals of love, God never gives up on us, God never stops loving.

These same qualities need to characterize human love if our love is to grow in depth, richness, resilience, and beauty. God's love lasts, and human love should too. But the only way love can last is if we are willing to be patient, steadfast, faithful, and forgiving with one another. God is tested in loving us, and we surely test one another in love. But real love works through the difficulties in order not to lose the gift and promise of love. God suffers in loving us and sometimes we suffer in loving one another because just like God with Israel or Jesus with his followers, we are not given perfect persons to love. Persons entrusted to our love are strikingly like ourselves, individuals hobbled by imperfections that a lifetime of love will never erase. In fact, sometimes loving another person is so difficult we do it only because we have *promised* to do so, only because we know we are *obliged* to or, as the gospels remind us, *commanded* to love the person. Spouses know moments like this, parents certainly do, and it is also part of the history of any real friendship. Every relationship is tested; every relationship feels the stresses and strains that come from dealing with one another's flaws, imperfections, and shortcomings. Moreover, the people we love can hurt us deeply precisely because of what we invest and hope for in love. There are breakdowns in every story of love, moments of failure, times of dark betrayal and deceit, periods of coldness, indifference, and even cruelty. Like God with faithless Israel, it is only through patience, fidelity, forgiveness, and reconciliation that we can move beyond the dark moments of love and reenvision love's original promise.

Love and Sexuality

Sadly, some of those dark moments of love can most painfully occur in the area of human sexuality. Sexual intimacy can bring some of the most enriching and powerful experiences of love, but it can also bring great pain, exploitation, and disillusionment. All of us are skilled in the art of self-deception, and this is especially true when it comes to our sexual needs, desires, and activity. But when we deceive ourselves about the real motives at work in a sexual relationship, we harm the persons we claim to love and, whether we admit it or not, we also harm ourselves. This is why Marie M. Fortune, building upon Paul's ethical mandate in Romans 13:10 ("Love does no evil to the neighbor; hence, love is the fulfillment of the law."), claims that all sexual behavior should be guided by the principle that "Love does no harm to another."[38] "'How do I avoid doing harm to myself and to another?' should be the first question we ask when we are considering our own actions,"[39] Fortunes writes. She defines harm as "that which inflicts physical pain, damage or injury and/or diminishes the other person's dignity and self-worth," and rightly suggests that too often today the "line between love and harm has become blurred."[40] We think the difference between love and harm is obvious, but it is easily blurred when sex is involved. Hopefully very few people would enter into a sexual relationship with the explicit intention of harming another person, but when it comes to sex it is easy not to consider the possible harmful effects of our behavior. Put differently, almost everyone assumes love is at work when they enter into a sexual relationship, but this assumption blinds us to other motives that might be driving our actions. This is why careful discernment of the motives and intentions behind our behavior, as well as the consequences that might result from it, is essential. At the very least, one must honestly discern whether a particular behavior or relationship is harming another person or whether it is, as it ought to be, building them up in love.

Like everything else in our lives, our sexuality should be at the service of love. We cannot follow Jesus' command to love our neighbor in every other area of our lives, then conveniently set it aside in our sexual relationships. In Christianity the law of love is the primary law that should illumine and guide every dimension of our lives. In this way sexual morality is integrated into the rest of Christian morality, all of which should be inspired by the primacy of love.[41] If this is so, certain questions regarding sexual behavior come to the forefront: Is love truly at work here or selfishness? Is this act a genuine expression of love between the partners or is it marred by the need to manipulate and control? Does it strengthen their love for each other or leave them feeling gloomy and estranged? Is it honest, or does it require deception of oneself and others? Will it deepen and increase each person's capacity to love, or will it weaken it? As Vincent Genovesi writes, "Sexual expression, whatever else it may involve, must be for the Christian an externalization of love; it must be love-in-action."[42] And it must be love-in-action not only for the other person we claim to love, but also for ourselves. Thus, the question that ought to guide all moral reflection on sexuality is this: How do we genuinely love God, ourselves, and our neighbor in this area of our lives?

Sexual relationships do not create love; rather, they build on a love that is already there.[43] They ought to express a care, concern, devotion, and commitment that the persons involved are confident exist. If this is not so, the relationships may be physically pleasurable, but they are not *personal* and, therefore, moral. There may be moments of physical unity in such relationships, but what is missing is the deeper personal, affective, psychological, and spiritual intimacy that is the gift of authentic love. This is why sex without commitment and love requires self-deception to be sustained, and why it often increases loneliness and isolation rather than lessening them. Sex without love separates more than it unites because what is missing is precisely the knowledge of another, and wholehearted commitment to his or her good, that is the mark of real love.[44] As we have suggested, to love another person is to validate his or her existence, to want him or her to flourish and prosper in every area of life. Love builds up, it strengthens and affirms, and it never loses sight of another person's dignity. This does not deny that we grow toward sexual integrity and, along the way, ordinarily struggle with much we may later regret. But it is to say that if any sexual relationship is to be an expression of Christian love, its effect must be to continue in both persons what God's creative, sustaining, healing, and redemptive love began and always aims to achieve. Each of us has been "loved into being," and we have been entrusted with the capacity and vocation to love so that we, continuing what God's love began, can love each other into fuller being. In this respect, sex is no different from any other area of our lives insofar as it ought to embody, express, and extend God's love for another person.[45] Any sex that does this is good sex.

If our sexuality is to be at the service of love, it must be disciplined, guided, and refined by the virtue of chastity. Unfortunately, many people associate chastity with sexual repression or even renunciation, as if chastity produces people who are uptight, prudish, and altogether uncomfortable with their sexuality. In this view, chastity is the opposite of a healthy sexuality. But that's silly. Chastity is a virtue (part of the virtue of temperance) and like any virtue it helps us achieve excellence in a particular area of our lives. As we saw in chapter 3, the virtues make both who we are and what we do good, they enable us to live and act in ways that are truly and fully human. Thus, far from denying, repressing, or warping our sexuality, chastity regulates and integrates it so that it can be truly and fully human for ourselves as well as others. Chastity does not eliminate sexual desire but, like any other virtue, orders it to the true good and happiness of a person, particularly in his or her relationships with others.[46] Chastity not only refuses to separate sex and love, but also helps to perfect our ability to love through our sexuality. People who are chaste do not fear their sexuality; rather, they respect its power and want to be sure that their sexual behavior reflects a healthy, genuine love of themselves and another. As John S. Grabowski writes, "Chastity . . . is the virtue that enables human beings to use their sexual powers wisely and well. In so doing they contribute not only to their own flourishing, but to a well-ordered society that reflects God's plan for human sexuality."[47]

Chastity is honesty in sex, and God knows we need more of that.[48] The virtue of chastity calls us to be honest about ourselves and some of the ways we can go wrong in our sexual lives. It draws our attention to some of our more wayward and destructive tendencies, tendencies we would prefer to overlook or pretend we do not have, and does so in order that we not be controlled or overpowered by them. Like all the virtues, chastity reflects an honest assessment about who we really are. We can be profoundly respecting of other persons in our sexual lives, but we can also be brazenly self-serving, egocentric, and manipulative. The desire to dominate can overpower the desire to love, just as the drive to put ourselves first can dim our appreciation of another. Without chastity, sexual relationships are no longer life-giving, but oppressive and destructive. Without chastity we lose freedom in relation to our sexuality and are drawn further away from what is right and good. Chastity ensures that our sexual behavior is humanizing, not demeaning, and it does so by not allowing us to lose sight of another's dignity and value, as well as our own. "No rational person wants to be used," Benedict Guevin observes. "Every rational person desires relationships that exhibit respect for his or her integrity and value as a person, that are vivified by love, and that are just. . . . Chastity is the virtue that brings this about."[49]

Loving God, Self, and Others—How Does It All Work Out?

How Our Loves Should Be Ordered

God is love and we should be too. But how do we go about it? Love is good for everybody, but we surely cannot love everyone in the same way. In fact, if we wait to love until we can love everybody, we'll never love anybody. We are embodied, finite, historical creatures, and this means there has to be a certain ordering of our loves. The only possible way for us to fulfill Jesus' love command is to give some loves priority in our lives. As Stephen G. Post notes, "due to human finitude we cannot actively love everyone equally, and therefore an ordering of love is essential to the moral life."[50] And so which loves ought to have priority? Jesus calls us to love God, our neighbors, and ourselves. Should some of those loves have precedence over others? Is it ever permissible to love a neighbor more than we love God? Or if we ought to love God most of all, does this mean it is acceptable to neglect our neighbor in order to favor God? And what about self-love? Must it always come last?

Christian theologians and ethicists have recently rediscovered Augustine's and Aquinas's accounts for why there must be priorities to the way we love, or what Aquinas called an "order in charity." For Aquinas, love is hierarchically ordered, with God necessarily being the supreme object of our love. In fact, both Augustine and Aquinas argued that if we fail to love God most of all, we cannot know what it rightly means to love ourselves or anyone else because we will be confused about love from the start. Our love begins with God because God is the source, center, and principle of all real love.[51] God is love and sets the tone for any subsequent love. Moreover, something is lovable in proportion to its goodness, and since God is supremely and perfectly good, God is more lovable than anything else. As Aquinas wrote, "goodness is the cause of loving, because whatever we love, we love precisely as good. . . . [W]ith God it is his own greater goodness that makes him more lovable."[52] And, finally, we should love God most of all because God is every creature's highest good, and fellowship with God is perfect and eternal happiness for everyone. "Accordingly, man is bound in charity to love God, who is the common good of all things, more than himself," Aquinas writes, "for eternal happiness is to be found in God as in the common principle and source of all things which are capable of sharing such happiness."[53]

In the order of love, it is not our neighbor but ourselves who come next. People are often uncomfortable talking about love of self, much less saying that it ought to come before love of others, because that goes against what we think love should be. If the work of love is to call us out of ourselves in order to attend to another's good, doesn't focusing on self-love contradict this? And if we put ourselves before our neighbors in the order of love, couldn't that foster the very self-concern that love works to weaken? Perhaps, but it all depends on what we take love to be. Besides, self-love is the unavoidable basis of all love; in fact, Aquinas called self-love the paradigm of our love for others.[54] We cannot help but love ourselves before we love our neighbors because we are made to seek our own fullness and completion. Self-love is wired into us. We have a natural inclination for our own good, and this desire not only cannot be eradicated, but also cannot be suppressed without great harm to ourselves. We cannot but will our own happiness, good, and fulfillment, which means we cannot help but love ourselves.[55] That we naturally love ourselves is not a sign of human weakness or sinfulness but, as Pieper says, a consequence of "the immutable fact that in the act of being created we were launched irresistibly toward our own fulfillment, toward our felicity too, toward the full realization of what was intended for us—or, as it is put in Christendom's sacred Book: 'For God created all things that they might be' (Ws 1:14)."[56]

But there is healthy and proper self-love and there is unhealthy and improper self-love. We rightly love ourselves when we seek our true good. We love ourselves rightly (and wisely) when we love God most of all because fellowship with God is our greatest possible good. In this way, to love ourselves first is not to turn inward but outward, it is to focus our lives on the absolute goodness of God and the happiness and love God offers us. To love is to wish our own good, and Christianity teaches that God is the consummate good for all creatures; therefore, human fulfillment depends on seeking and being with God. We love ourselves wisely and hopefully when we embrace a way of life that deepens the intimacy with God that is ours from the beginning. In this way, true self-love calls us out of ourselves and more deeply into God.

It also calls us more deeply into relationship with others. We may not be able to love our neighbors as much as we love ourselves because, as Aquinas noted, even our neighbors the saints who are closest to God are not, "for all that, as close to me as I am to myself."[57] But we can and should want for them the very good we want for ourselves: communion, intimacy, and fellowship with God. To love anyone is to want his or her greatest possible good, and for human beings, that is found in God. As Augustine put it, "what you do in your own behalf, you must do also for your neighbor, so that he, too, may love God with perfect love. But you do not love him as yourself unless you endeavor to lead him to the good which you yourself are pursuing."[58] Thus, to love our neighbors is to devote ourselves to helping them attain what we want for ourselves: perfect fellowship in the goodness and happiness of God. Even better, it is for us to help each other grow together in the ways of God's love so that we can be true companions in that love. As Aquinas said, the best way we can love our neighbors is to want them to be our partners in enjoying the perfect love and happiness of God.[59]

We may wish this for everybody, but we cannot be equally responsible for everybody. We are naturally more closely connected to some rather than to others, and consequently our love will be more intensely and permanently directed to them.[60] This is especially true with the relationships in which our lives are more deeply embedded. I may sincerely want what is best for peoples on the other side of the world, but I am not tied to them in the way I am to the primary relationships of my life: my wife, my family and friends, my colleagues and associates, my students. These relationships exert a stronger moral pull on my love and entail a deeper loyalty. This does not mean I have no responsibility to those far removed from my everyday life, but it does mean my responsibility to them is different—and ordinarily less—than what it is toward those more intimately connected to me. The natural ties and connections that constitute our lives are morally significant because they indicate where our priorities in love should ordinarily be. Love has to start somewhere if it is to come to life at all, and it should start in the settings where we customarily find ourselves: in our marriages, families, friendships, and closest communities.

We are called to love all our neighbors, but we are foremost summoned to love the neighbors who have been specially entrusted to us. Our lives are made up of "spheres of love" and the closest circle of love is composed of those relationships that carry special loyalties and obligations.[61] These relationships are at the center of our lives and are ordinarily the contexts where we learn what it means to love. Some theologians have disparaged the moral importance of love for one's spouse, family, and friends; in fact, they have claimed that such love falls short of genuine Christian love because it is neither partial nor universal.[62] But in reality love ordinarily cannot and should not be absolutely impartial, and it is difficult to envision how we could concretely make it universal. There are obviously times when the needs of those far removed from our lives must have precedence over the needs of those more closely connected to us but, all things considered, we learn our real capacities in love when we faithfully attend to those we are with every day. In fact, if we grow in our love for them, we are more likely to know how to extend the circle of love to others. As Post summarizes, "Universal love for humanity is a tremendously important moral ideal, but one that for most of us must be built up step by step from what is learned in committed special relations."[63]

Extending the Responsibilities of Love to the Whole of God's Creation

Today more and more theologians are rightly insisting that the circle of love needs to be extended to embrace the whole of creation. If we are called to love and to value everything God loves and values, then we are called to respect and care for everything that has been brought into being as an act of God's love. God did not create other species and the natural world simply to be a background for human beings, as if we alone mattered in the story of creation. At the end of the first creation narrative in Genesis 1, "God looked at everything he had made," not just the first human couple, and declared all of it not only good, but "very good" (1:31). The goodness of the rest of creation is established by God and exists apart from its value to us. This suggests that creation would have been good even if God had never created humans to enjoy it. All living things are intrinsically valuable and, therefore, have moral status, "simply because God made them" and loves them.[64] This does not mean they are equal in value to human beings, but it does mean God did not create them simply because we might find them useful. And since human beings are the only creatures who have the "rational, moral, and, therefore, creative capacities that enable us alone to serve as responsible representatives of God's interests and values,"[65] we are called to recognize, respect, and protect all the other species that God finds good. This is why when we ask, "Who is my neighbor?" the answer must include not only human beings, but "all God's beloved creatures" as well.[66]

Obviously, there is a difference between how we show love to other human beings and how we can and ought to love other species. And no amount of moral exhortation can erase the fact that we are predators for whom "killing is a biological necessity for existence."[67] We will always kill other forms of life in order to fulfill basic human needs. Extending the responsibilities of love to other species does not mean that they have equal moral standing with human beings or that the moral code we apply to our behavior with others applies to them in exactly the same way. But it does mean we are not the only creatures that matter. Other creatures count, and we have duties and responsibilities toward them.[68] Consequently, there are limits to what we can do to other creatures and their habitats. There are times when human interests and needs must yield for the sake of other species' well-being, especially those whose existence is most threatened. This is nothing more than extending the principle of self-sacrifice, which is part of all real love, to the love we owe other species.[69]

If love consists both in wishing another's good (benevolence) and doing what we can to achieve it (beneficence), then as God's "earth keepers" we are given the task to watch over the welfare of all creatures and to show unselfish concern for their good.[70] What would such ecological love of neighbor look like? What form might it take? At the very least, any practical expression of neighbor love to nonhuman creation would require renouncing the excesses of consumerism and embracing an ethic of frugality and restraint.[71] A frugal person is not someone who refuses to use and enjoy the goods of the earth, but one who uses "sparingly that which God has provided in order that others may live and flourish."[72] Frugality is born from the respect and regard that are due all God's creatures, not just the human ones. It is based in the realization that the resources and goods of the earth are limited and often nonrenewable. The opposite of unrestrained self-indulgence, the frugal person knows how to live without bankrupting the earth.

Similarly, ecological neighbor love would be characterized by humility. James Nash defines humility as "cautious love or careful caring."[73] Humility counsels us not to have "exaggerated confidence in human and technical reliability"[74] when it comes to our interventions in the natural world. When love is accompanied by humility, we admit that sometimes we are not sure what the consequences of our actions might be on the environment, and we confess that there have been times when arrogance regarding our technological powers blinded us to the environmental risks in our actions. "Given the manifest evidence of both unforeseen and unintended consequences, we ought not go too fast, cut corners, or ignore opposing points of view," Steven Bouma-Prediger writes. "We don't know everything (though we often think we do), and our fat, restless egos often get the best of us. Therefore, we should be careful, exercise caution, go slow."[75]

Conclusion

Love is the gift that makes all gifts possible, the gift that brings us to life, and the gift by which we are to bring others more fully to life. In this chapter we have investigated how Christians understand love by considering why human beings are given the vocation to love, what it means to live the love that is God, and how our love for God, ourselves, and others should be ordered. More than anything, we have confirmed that love is what we are brought into existence to do and ought to be what we learn to do best because love is what makes us most like God. God is love, and we enjoy the happiness that is God if we become love too.

That is the work of a lifetime and one that we can hardly accomplish alone. We grow in love together, in companionship with other human beings. But the companionship and community that are necessary for love are impossible if we do not learn how to live in right relationship with one another, to be fair to each other, to take one another's needs into account, and to give each other what is necessary for life. This is the work of justice, the virtue without which life together is not only grim, but also impossible. Love may inspire justice, but justice keeps love honest. Each informs and completes the other. In the final chapter we will explore what love's justice is all about because it, too, is part of the language of God.

Some Questions for Reflection and Discussion

1. Why is Jesus' command to love God, our neighbors, and ourselves eminently sensible? Why is it one commandment we cannot afford to break?
2. How can human love be said to live in partnership with God's love? What does it mean to carry God's love forward?

3. What would you consider the characteristics of "good" love?
4. Why do you think so many relationships that begin in love end badly?
5. Do you think Christianity, with its emphasis on chastity, takes sex too seriously? How would you explain the meaning of the virtue of chastity? Its importance?
6. Why do we have to rank and prioritize the different loves of our lives? How should our loves be ordered? Why is it sometimes hard to do this?
7. If we extend the responsibilities of love to other creatures and species, what might it demand of us?

Notes

1. Vincent J. Genovesi, *In Pursuit of Love: Catholic Morality and Human Sexuality* (Collegeville, MN: The Liturgical Press, 1996), 25.

2. John Paul II, *On the Family: Familiaris Consortio* (Washington, DC: U.S. Catholic Conference, 1981), #11.

3. Genovesi, *In Pursuit of Love*, 21.

4. Elaine Storkey, *The Search for Intimacy* (Grand Rapids, MI: William B. Eerdmans Publishing Co., 1995), 239.

5. C. S. Lewis, *Mere Christianity* (New York: Macmillan Publishing Co., 1952), 151.

6. Lewis, *Mere Christianity*, 152.

7. André Guindon, *The Sexual Language: An Essay in Moral Theology* (Ottawa: The University of Ottawa Press, 1976), 45.

8. Storkey, *The Search for Intimacy*, 239.

9. Genovesi, *In Pursuit of Love*, 36.

10. Benedict XVI, *God Is Love: Deus Caritas Est* (Washington, DC: United States Catholic Conference, 2006), #1.

11. Josef Pieper, *Faith, Hope, Love*, trans. Richard and Clara Winston, and Sr. Mary Frances McCarthy, SND (San Francisco: Ignatius Press, 1997), 160.

12. Pieper, *Faith, Hope, Love*, 159.

13. Karl Barth, *Church Dogmatics*, IV/2, trans. Rev. G. W. Bromiley (Edinburgh: T & T Clark, 1958), 813.

14. Genovesi, *In Pursuit of Love*, 24.

15. Stephen G. Post, *A Theory of Agape: On the Meaning of Christian Love* (Lewisburg, PA: Bucknell University Press, 1990), 80. "It is not from the abstract principles of the post-Enlightenment age that *agape* finds its motivating sources, so therefore why subject it to such abstraction? . . . Christian love is not an abstract concept anyway; it is rather a way of life among a people who form a storied tradition. To divert attention away from this center of gravity is to condemn *agape* to a slow decay. . . . *Agape* should never be considered a principle acceptable to 'all rational persons whatsoever,' that is, to all 'enlightened minds.' It is a peculiar people who carry on the life of *agape*."

16. Post, *A Theory of Agape*, 82.
17. Pieper, *Faith, Hope, Love*, 164.
18. Pieper, *Faith, Hope, Love*, 177.
19. Pieper, *Faith, Hope, Love*, 170.
20. Pieper, *Faith, Hope, Love*, 171.
21. Pieper, *Faith, Hope, Love*, 171.
22. Pieper, *Faith, Hope, Love*, 273–76.
23. Pieper, *Faith, Hope, Love*, 171–72.
24. Pieper, *Faith, Hope, Love*, 174.
25. Pieper, *Faith, Hope, Love*, 190.
26. Edward Collins Vacek, SJ, *Love, Human and Divine: The Heart of Christian Ethics* (Washington, DC: Georgetown University Press, 1994), 44.
27. Vacek, *Love, Human and Divine*, 57.
28. Vacek, *Love, Human and Divine*, 60.
29. Paul J. Wadell, *Becoming Friends: Worship, Justice, and the Practice of Christian Friendship* (Grand Rapids, MI: Brazos Press, 2002), 83–84.
30. Genovesi, *In Pursuit of Love*, 140.
31. Genovesi, *In Pursuit of Love*, 25–26.
32. Genovesi, *In Pursuit of Love*, 27.
33. Paul J. Wadell, "The Family as a Crucible of Grace: Finding God in the Mutuality of Love," in *Mutuality Matters: Family, Faith, and Just Love*, ed. Herbert Anderson, Edward Foley, Bonnie Miller-McLemore, and Robert Schreiter (Lanham, MD: Rowman & Littlefield Publishers, Inc., 2004), 16.
34. Vacek, *Love, Human and Divine*, 49.
35. Vincent MacNamara, *Love, Law and Christian Life: Basic Attitudes of Christian Morality* (Wilmington, DE: Michael Glazier, 1988), 69.
36. Wadell, "The Family as a Crucible of Grace," 16.
37. Vacek, *Love, Human and Divine*, 34.
38. Marie M. Fortune, *Love Does No Harm: Sexual Ethics for the Rest of Us* (New York: Continuum, 1998), 34.
39. Fortune, *Love Does No Harm*, 34.
40. Fortune, *Love Does No Harm*, 35.
41. Gareth Moore, "Sex, Sexuality and Relationships," in *Christian Ethics: An Introduction*, ed. Bernard Hoose (Collegeville, MN: The Liturgical Press, 1998), 229.
42. Genovesi, *In Pursuit of Love*, 115.
43. Storkey, *The Search for Intimacy*, 6.
44. Pieper, *Faith, Hope, Love*, 265. "The encounter that is sheer sex and nothing else has rightly been called deceptive in character. For the moment, an illusion of union arises; but without love this apparent union of two strangers leaves them more remote from one another than they were before. Thus it should cause little surprise that 'in a society that makes sexuality the prerequisite for love and not love the condition for the gift of physical union,' sex paradoxically 'rather separates than unites man and woman, leaving them alone and lonely precisely where they thought they would surely find each other.'"

45. Genovesi, *In Pursuit of Love*, 126.
46. John S. Grabowski, *Sex and Virtue: An Introduction to Sexual Ethics* (Washington, DC: The Catholic University of America Press, 2003), 79.
47. Grabowski, *Sex and Virtue*, 84.
48. Genovesi, *In Pursuit of Love*, 135.
49. Benedict M. Guevin, *Christian Anthropology and Sexual Ethics* (Lanham, MD: University Press of America, 2002), 70.
50. Stephen G. Post, *Spheres of Love: Toward a New Ethics of the Family* (Dallas, TX: Southern Methodist University Press, 1994), 133.
51. Thomas Aquinas, *Summa Theologiae* (New York: McGraw-Hill, 1966), II-II, 26,1.
52. Aquinas, *ST*, II-II, 26,2.
53. Aquinas, *ST*, II-II, 26,3.
54. Aquinas, *ST*, II-II, 26,4.
55. Pieper, *Faith, Hope, Love*, 234.
56. Pieper, *Faith, Hope, Love*, 237.
57. Aquinas, *ST*, II-II, 26,4.
58. Augustine, *The Way of Life of the Catholic Church*, trans. Donald A. Gallagher and Idella J. Gallagher (Washington, DC: The Catholic University of America Press, 1966), XXVI, xlix.
59. Aquinas, *ST*, II-II, 26,4.
60. Stephen J. Pope, *The Evolution of Altruism and the Ordering of Love* (Washington, DC: Georgetown University Press, 1994), 62.
61. Post, *Spheres of Love*, 6.
62. Anders Nygren, *Agape and Eros*, trans. Philip S. Watson (New York: Harper & Row, Publishers, 1969), 61–104.
63. Post, *Spheres of Love*, 12.
64. Steven Bouma-Prediger, *For the Beauty of the Earth: A Christian Vision for Creation Care* (Grand Rapids, MI: Baker Academic, 2001), 142.
65. James A. Nash, *Loving Nature: Ecological Integrity and Christian Responsibility* (Nashville: Abingdon Press, 1991), 149.
66. Nash, *Loving Nature*, 143.
67. Nash, *Loving Nature*, 147.
68. Bouma-Prediger, *For the Beauty of the Earth*, 142.
69. Nash, *Loving Nature*, 150.
70. Bouma-Prediger, *For the Beauty of the Earth*, 154–55.
71. Bouma-Prediger, *For the Beauty of the Earth*, 145.
72. Bouma-Prediger, *For the Beauty of the Earth*, 145.
73. Nash, *Loving Nature*, 156.
74. Nash, *Loving Nature*, 157.
75. Bouma-Prediger, *For the Beauty of the Earth*, 147.

CHAPTER TEN

Reimagining the World

Why the Happiness of One Demands Justice for All

"The world is sick."[1]

It's my favorite line from "Populorum Progressio" ("On the Development of Peoples"), Pope Paul VI's 1967 social encyclical on justice and human development, because it doesn't dance around the point. The world is sick, and the disease eating away at it is the cancer of injustice. It is not that things are only slightly amiss—a weak flu that just a little rest can overcome. No, the cancer of injustice runs deep, so much so that without radical personal and social transformation the survival of the world is in question. Injustice is a terminal disease because each day it brings destitution and diminishment to millions—and death to thousands of others. Too, left untreated it creates a world characterized by fear, instability, and violence. Alarm, urgency, desperation, and even anger are the tone of "Populorum Progressio" because Paul is convinced that we cannot wait to undo the webs of injustice in which so many lives are painfully trapped. "We must make haste: too many are suffering, and the distance is growing that separates the progress of some and the stagnation, not to say the regression, of others,"[2] the pope writes. When Paul looked around the world in 1967 he saw "situations whose injustice cries to heaven."[3] Is it really any different today? If justice is postponed, Paul warns, there is no hope for the future. The world is at a crisis point, and if individuals, communities, and nations do not work together on behalf of justice, the social order will crumble. As the Pope lamented in "Populorum Progressio," "Would that those in authority listened to our words before it is too late!"[4]

Injustice is a scandal, but one that we have learned to tolerate pretty well, especially if we profit from it. Justice means "we are all in this together," but the truth is we live as if we are not. As Patricia McAuliffe writes, "*Disorder, disharmony, and the already damaged humanum are not exceptions to the rule; they represent the rule*."[5] Take a look around the world, and it is not hard to conclude that what we see would more accurately be described as a "rule of injustice" rather than of justice.[6] The hundreds of thousands of persons who face starvation, the millions of people without adequate shelter or health care, the never-ending litany of victims of war and violence: This is the world we have grown so accustomed to that it is hard for us to imagine it any other way. Injustice is the air we breathe, and for the privileged of the world it may seem to be clean, healthy air even if for millions of others it is toxic. But the fact is that not only are its victims sickened by injustice, but those who perpetrate and profit from it are too because they have lost the moral vision needed to recognize that something is horribly wrong.

Injustice is a failure of moral imagination. In order to move from injustice to justice, we must be able to reimagine the world. The conversion to justice demands that we be able to see, think, and imagine differently. But for those who may be profiting from injustice, it equally demands radical and unsettling changes in our attitudes and values, and especially in the ways we live. Something like a conversion to justice occurred for Pope Paul VI when he was drawn into the world of the poor. Near the beginning of "Populorum Progressio" he mentions trips he took that changed his life. A few years before he was elected pope he traveled first to Latin America and then to Africa, and wrote that those journeys brought him "into direct contact with the acute problems pressing on continents full of life and hope."[7] After his election as pope in 1963, Paul "made further journeys, to the Holy Land and India," and in both places was "able to see and virtually touch the very serious difficulties besetting peoples with long-standing civilizations who are at grips with the problem of development."[8] There are certain memories we do not want to leave behind, memories we want to continue to shape and guide our lives, because they brought us to a very different way of looking at and understanding the world. Pope Paul VI's travels to Latin America, Africa, India, and the Holy Land left him with such memories and explain why when he wrote "Populorum Progressio" he was looking at the world through the eyes of the poor. This is the moral and spiritual challenge for those who have never known the ravages of injustice firsthand.

In many respects, a book on Christian ethics should begin, not conclude, with a chapter on justice because at its core the Christian moral life is about responding to persons in need. "If we ask ourselves, Why be ethical; why ought we, why must we, be ethical?" Patricia McAuliffe writes, "it seems our response must be because there is need. Ethics is a response to need. And the overwhelming need in our world is that massive excessive deprivation, suffering, and oppression be alleviated."[9] Justice is not an afterthought to Christian morality because none of us can claim to be moral if we ignore or remain indifferent to the marginal, forgotten persons of the world. As Jesus' famous parable of the Last Judgment (Matt. 25:31–46) indicates, the final assessment of our lives will be made in terms of the justice we either extended to or withheld from those most in need. It is through justice and compassion that we gain entry to the kingdom of God, while it is through greed, selfishness, and indifference that we are excluded. If the Christian moral life is an ongoing training in the nature of happiness, we must discover not only that no true happiness can be gained through injustice, but also that our happiness cannot be had apart from the well-being of others. For Christians, happiness is a communal enterprise; it is something we share in together. Thus, any one person's happiness is lessened in the measure that any other person is shunned, ignored, or excluded. In the Christian moral life, justice is the linchpin to happiness because it opens our eyes to the persons we need to recognize and respond to in order for all of us to be complete. Put bluntly, if there is any group we need to make connections with in order "to get ahead in life," it is the poor and the oppressed, not the wealthy, for the Bible suggests they are the ones with the inside track to God. In this chapter, then, we will look at this core virtue in the Christian life by first exploring the meaning and foundations of justice, as well as the different types of justice. We will then consider a more explicitly Christian theology of justice, and conclude with some considerations of how a conversion to justice might occur. That last step is crucial because it is only when our hearts are turned to the poor that we discover, oddly enough, what happiness really is.

What Justice Is and Where It Begins

The virtue of human togetherness, justice governs our relations with others by ensuring that we respect their dignity as persons and give them their due. But it is important to note that justice does not create a bond between ourselves and others, but recognizes and honors a bond that is already there.[10] It is precisely because of the deep connections that exist between us and everything else that lives—the web of relations we are born into—that we need to learn to live in a way that respects and strengthens those bonds instead of ignoring, denying, or violating them. A just person is the man or woman who knows how to live in right relationship with God, with friends and family, with coworkers or community members, with anyone he or she may come in contact with, and with the natural world. Such persons see the bonds that link all of life together and recognize the obligations and responsibilities those bonds create. They know we cannot be indifferent to the well-being of others who are connected to us and, therefore, family members. They know that every act of injustice is an attempt to deny what is irrefutably true: We are all members one of another. Justice is relevant to every relationship, to every situation and circumstance of life, because there is no setting in which we do not have to take into account our responsibilities to others. What justice requires will differ depending on the nature of those relationships, but it will always be pertinent and can never be dismissed without the fundamental fact of our moral existence being ignored. Viewed through the lens of justice, the principal moral question is always the same: What needs to be done here to honor a bond that always exists?

St. Thomas Aquinas defined justice as "the habit whereby a person with a lasting and constant will renders to each his due."[11] Aquinas's definition suggests that justice comes second—it is a response to something more fundamental—because we would be under no obligation to give anything to anybody if there did not already exist a relationship that created obligations and responsibilities.[12] "To be just means, then, to owe something and to pay the debt,"[13] Josef Pieper notes. But we owe something to others (and they owe something to us) because our lives are always enmeshed in relationships that carry inescapable moral demands. This is why, as Aquinas noted, our willingness to respond to the claims of justice must be "lasting and constant," not occasional or haphazard. A person of justice is *habitually* disposed to take the needs and well-being of others into account because he or she recognizes there is never a moment in which the claims of others, including God and other species, do not impinge on us. This does not mean that the needs and rights of others are absolute, but it does mean that they always matter and cannot be casually ignored. Thus, justice is both an abiding quality of character and a principle of action. It is, more precisely, a virtue because a person of justice is habitually attuned to the needs of others and characteristically attentive to their good. In this respect, justice can be described as "*fidelity to the demands of a relationship*,"[14] including those relationships we did not choose, but which nonetheless exert claims on us.

A just person lives with others in mind. But that so much of the world is not in "right relationship" reveals that many persons do not live with others in mind. Ideally, justice bolsters connections that are already there by ensuring that the rights of all persons are honored. Ideally, justice holds relationships, communities, and societies together by insisting that each person or group is given its due and that no person or group takes more than its share. That's the way it ought to be; but unfortunately injustice may be more common than not because we live in a world where greed, egotism, selfishness, and indifference bust the connections justice is meant to preserve. If God created a world that was "originally just," a world where all things lived in harmony and right relationship, it didn't take long for human beings to throw things out of balance and to invest a lot of their ingenuity to keeping it that way. Thus, because "injustice is the prevalent condition"[15] of the world, justice typically aims to restore or renew connections that should never have been broken. More pointedly, if justice means to give another person or group what is its due, justice commonly takes the form of *restitution* exactly because so many persons and groups are regularly denied what they rightly deserve.

Injustice is thievery because it is to take what belongs to others, whether basic human rights, economic resources, respect for their dignity, or truthfulness. As an act of restitution, justice works to return to others what was rightly theirs in the first place. It sets things right by correcting a wrong, by restoring balance and equity, by making amends. This is true whether we are talking about a lie that violates a person's right to the truth, gossip that destroys one's right to a good reputation, or economic policies that unduly favor the rich over the poor. In each case something is "stolen" from another and needs to be returned. In each case, the right relationships achieved by justice are undermined and demand to be addressed and remedied. This is why justice regularly takes the form of recompense and restoration.[16] It is why justice is so often about repairing what is broken, whether that be ruptures in a relationship, ruptures in a church, or the abiding rupture between the rich and the poor. As Karen Lebacqz notes, "Because the world is permeated with injustice, justice is corrective or reparative—it is dominated by the principle of redress or setting things right."[17]

Three Types of Justice

Justice is the virtue that orders the various relationships of our lives. In general, justice moves between three fundamental sets of relationships. It guides our relationships with other individuals, the relationship between societies and their individual members, and the relationships of individuals to the larger society or community.[18] The justice that regulates our relationships with other persons is *commutative justice*. Commutative justice oversees contracts, transactions, agreements, or promises between individuals to ensure that each person is treated fairly or to address transgressions when they are not. Theft would be a violation of commutative justice because to take what legitimately belongs to another upsets the order that ought to characterize relationships between persons in society. More broadly, lying violates commutative justice because it denies another person her right to know the truth and destroys the trust that is essential for good relationships. Anyone who has ever watched a friendship or marriage deteriorate because lying destroyed persons' trust in one another can testify to the importance of commutative justice. In the classroom, the dishonesty of plagiarism attacks commutative justice because it undermines the respect and honesty that ought to characterize students' relationships with their teachers, and with one another. To unfairly attack another person's reputation (the injustice of slander) is a clear transgression of commutative justice not only because it robs him of his right to a good reputation, but also because it negatively impacts how others will see him and relate to him.

The second type of justice, *distributive justice*, oversees the relationship between societies or communities and their individual members by ensuring that each person receives an equitable share of the common goods of a society. Distributive justice recognizes that all persons have a right to some share in the basic goods and services of a society, goods such as adequate food and housing, education, medical care, employment and a fair wage, and opportunities for advancement. And they have a right to these goods that are essential for human beings even if they are unable to directly contribute to them. For example, neither children nor the extremely infirm or elderly may be able to add anything to the economic goods of a society, but they nonetheless have a right to those goods because they are members of the community and share in the bond that connects all persons in a community and makes them responsible for one another.[19] More generally, distributive justice also maintains fairness and right order in society by ensuring that every person can participate in the political, cultural, religious, and social institutions of a society. The government is the primary agent of distributive justice because ordinarily it is best suited to guarantee a fair allocation of the goods, resources, and benefits of a society to all of its members.[20] As David Hollenbach summarizes, distributive justice "establishes the equal right of all to share in all those goods and opportunities that are necessary for genuine participation in the human community. It establishes a strict duty of society as a whole to guarantee these rights."[21]

But because not every member of society always has fair access to the fundamental goods that are necessary for life, the main task of distributive justice is often to *redistribute* those essential goods, benefits, and services so that the "disorder" wrought by their unjust allocation might be overcome. The purpose of distributive justice is to give every person his or her fair share of the common good. A fair share does not necessarily mean an equal share (although in some cases it might); but it does mean that it is unjust for certain persons or groups to have such disproportionate access to the goods and benefits of a society that others have little or none. When this is the case, distributive justice must work to protect the rights of those who are regularly shut out of the common good by limiting those who grab much more than their fair share of it. This is the corrective function of distributive justice. If any one person or group gains too much power and privilege at the expense of other persons and groups, distributive justice is violated. If this occurs, the policies and patterns that enable the unjust distribution of the community's goods must be changed. Practically, this means there are times when the needs and rights of the poor and powerless members of society have priority over the claims of the rich and privileged.[22] If patterns of privilege regularly deny persons and groups just access to the fundamental goods and opportunities of a society, then those patterns must be corrected. That the poor and the powerless are so regularly excluded from the common good is why David Hollenbach argues that distributive justice will be achieved only when societies adopt "three strategic moral priorities: (1) The needs of the poor take priority over the wants of the rich. (2) The freedom of the dominated takes priority over the liberty of the powerful. (3) The participation of marginalized groups takes priority over the preservation of an order that excludes them."[23]

Finally, the justice that guides the relationship between individuals and the larger society is *social justice*, sometimes called *contributive justice*, because it focuses on the obligation every member of society has to contribute to the common good of that society.[24] If distributive justice focuses on what we receive from the common good, the focus of social justice is on what we owe the common good; it is the debt we owe to society.[25] Creating and sustaining a just society depends on the commitment and investment of each of its members to the overall well-being of that society. Social justice is a "political virtue" because it underscores the obligation every citizen has to work for a social, political, and economic order in which the basic rights of every person are respected and the fundamental needs of every person are met.[26] We fulfill the obligations of social justice through paying taxes, by serving on juries, by being politically informed, and by voting. We fulfill them when we work on behalf of those regularly shut out of the common good, whether by protesting patterns of discrimination and exclusion, lobbying on behalf of more jobs, seeking better education and health care, or advocating fairer tax laws or more just economic policies.[27] Social justice reminds us that justice does not end when our personal rights are secured and our own good is honored, but only when the good of all persons is secured. And it especially reminds us that just societies depend on just persons, persons who see beyond their own needs, security, and comfort to the welfare of all citizens of the world.

This is why a fundamental work of social justice is to create the structures, institutions, and policies necessary for a truly just society, one that respects and serves the common good not only in our local communities, but also throughout the world. There is a close connection between distributive justice and social justice because social justice makes distributive justice possible. And it does so through a concerted effort to create institutions, structures, and policies that give every member of society (including global society) equitable access to the goods, benefits, and services of that society. It is through social justice that the demands of distributive justice are met.[28] By contrast, if the political and economic institutions of society create (rather than remove) barriers between those who are able to participate in the life of society and those who are not, then social justice is lacking and those institutions need to be transformed. There is no social justice in any community where people are homeless, hungry, chronically unemployed, or simply deemed expendable, because pushed to the sidelines of society they cannot share in its goods. Injustice denies the poor access to the common good by creating impermeable barriers between them and the privileged. We see these barriers today not only in our local communities, but across the world, barriers that divide the insiders from the outsiders, one ethnic group from another ethnic group, democracies from tyrannies, and the wealthy countries of the world from the destitute ones. Social justice works to remove these barriers wherever they exist, whether they are in our communities, between our country and other countries, or stretched across the world.[29]

The Foundation of Justice

There are two principal foundations for justice. The first is the *value and dignity of persons*, and indeed the value and dignity of all of God's creation. Justice calls us out of ourselves on behalf of others because every person and every creature has a dignity and a value that demands our respect, and to which we must fittingly attend. Justice begins in, and is sustained by, the discovery of the value of other persons (and species) because we will never feel we owe anything to someone we judge to be without value. The virtue of justice is born from a moral vision that apprises every person and every creature as valuable and, therefore, worthy of our attention. It is easy to be unjust if we convince ourselves that another person, group, race, or society lacks worth and dignity. It is easy to be unconcerned about the plight of any persons or creatures if we believe they are without value and, therefore, expendable. Injustice thrives when we persuade ourselves that some persons have value and others do not, that some racial groups are clearly superior to other racial groups, or that some nations ought to prosper even if that means other nations must be deprived. Inequities abound when we divide the world between people who matter and people who do not, between people who are clearly human and people we decide can never be. As Daniel Maguire writes in *A New American Justice*, "Justice is thus founded upon a perception of the worth of persons. We show what we think persons are worth by what we ultimately concede is due to them."[30]

For Christians, human beings have intrinsic value and dignity because they are created in the image and likeness of God. For Christians, justice hinges upon being able (and willing) to discern the presence of God in another human being, and on being able to see traces of God's goodness in other species, and indeed in all of nature. But such an essential moral skill cannot be assumed and can be easily lost. It is something we have to work at, something we must commit ourselves to deepening and refining every day. Injustice takes hold when our vision becomes overly selective, when it is skewed by self-interest or twisted by prejudice. Or injustice takes hold whenever we tire of trying to find God in the persons and groups we would rather dismiss. One reason it is easy to overlook the plight of the poor is that we are not able (or perhaps refuse) to see the beauty of God in them. The same is true with any person or group we are convinced cannot be God's presence in the world. In this respect, injustice "defaces and obscures" the image of God in others to the point that we may believe it is not really there.[31]

This is one way to explain the absolute indifference of the rich man to the beggar Lazarus, the two characters recounted in Jesus' parable in the sixteenth chapter of the gospel of Luke. The rich man "dressed in purple garments and fine linen and dined sumptuously each day" (16:19), while ignoring the beggar Lazarus, who sat outside his door and "who would gladly have eaten his fill of the scraps that fell from the rich man's table" (16:21). The rich man had taught himself not to see the poor man right outside his door because as long as he did not see him, he did not have to care for him. It is hard to see God's image in everyone; in fact, like the rich man, it is much easier to obscure and deface that image lest in seeing it we are budged from our complacency. As Enda McDonagh writes, recognizing the image of God in others "constitutes a way of life . . . and is constantly in danger of being obscured by the false beauties of gods created in our own image."[32] God's presence in Lazarus was obscured by the idols of wealth and possessions in the rich man's life; in fact, the rich man's way of life was the antithesis of justice because it prevented him from seeing the poor man at all. But it is also true that if the rich man had reached out to Lazarus, perhaps the poor beggar could have taught him to see. In the gospel story, Lazarus is not the only one in desperate straits. The rich man, who felt completely comfortable with himself, secure and unassailable in his wealth, was in a moral and spiritual crisis he could not recognize. He needed to be awakened from his blindness and his selfishness, but the person who could liberate him was the man he consistently ignored. That is why Jesus said the abyss the rich man had created between Lazarus and himself on Earth had become absolutely unbridgeable in the afterlife, the only difference being that then Lazarus is the one who is consoled and the rich man the one who is in desperate need (16:24–26). This is a disturbing parable because it suggests that the person most in peril is not Lazarus, the victim of injustice, but the rich man who thinks he has not a worry in the world.

The second foundation of justice is a *vision of interdependence and solidarity*. Solidarity means that all of humanity—and indeed the whole of creation—constitutes one body, a true fellowship of being. And interdependence suggests not only that we need and depend on one another, but also that the unity that exists between us is so penetrating and extensive that there is no way any one of us can exist apart from everyone else. In his 1961 encyclical on social justice, "Christianity and Social Progress" (*Mater et Magistra*), Pope John XXIII captured the essence of interdependence and solidarity when he wrote that we are all "members of one and the same household."[33] Instead of envisioning us as isolated and utterly disparate individuals who have little connection to each other besides the connections we choose or are willing to accept, John saw that human beings are morally and spiritually connected to one another and, therefore, responsible for one another. Solidarity makes justice both intelligible and imperative because it recognizes that human life, from first to last, is shared life; as Daniel Maguire wrote, "Everything about us is social."[34]

Solidarity was an even more prominent theme in the social encyclicals of Pope John Paul II, particularly his letter "On Social Concern" (*Sollicitudo Rei Socialis*). There John Paul described solidarity as "a *firm and persevering determination* to commit oneself to the *common good*; that is to say to the good of all and of each individual, because we are *all* really responsible *for all*."[35] The virtue of solidarity teaches us to think beyond our own individual good to the common good. It forms us into persons who commit themselves to watching after the good of others, particularly the poor. Moreover, as John Paul II realized, solidarity is a virtue that needs to be cultivated not only by individuals, but by communities and societies as well. The only way to create a just social order is for societies to embrace a vision of solidarity and interdependence. Otherwise, social life easily degenerates to the survival of the fittest or, perhaps more accurately, the luckiest. Regarding solidarity, David Hollenbach writes that it is "not only a virtue to be enacted by individual persons one at a time. It must also be expressed in the economic, cultural, political, and religious institutions that shape society."[36]

These two foundations of justice are continually eroded by the excesses of individualism. At its worst, individualism teaches that we are beholden to no one and can pursue our interests and desires with little consideration of their impact on others. Viewed through the lens of individualism, justice is reduced to protecting individual rights and liberties. Obviously, that is an important component to justice, but it is hardly all that justice involves. Overlooked in such an understanding of justice are the ties that bind us to others and the responsibilities that derive from them. When guaranteeing individual rights and liberties is seen as the almost singular business of justice, injustice always results because there is no way the poor and powerless can claim their rights and liberties to the degree that the wealthy and privileged can. Without a strong foundation in the value and dignity of persons and the interdependence and solidarity of peoples, justice is impotent because it cannot do what justice should always do, namely, seek the common good by attending to the needs of all persons. As Russell Connors and Patrick McCormick stress,

> [W]e have slipped into this corrupted vision of justice because the blinders of individualism screen out the social ties that bind us to our neighbors, to the social structures required to create and sustain a just community, and to the special duties we have toward the weakest in our societies. As long as we think that we are, first and foremost, individuals, and that our social obligations are weak, secondary ties, then the heart of justice will always be about defending our personal freedoms and punishing those who harm us. But such a stripped down view of either ourselves or the concept of justice lacks an adequate grasp of the common good, the need for social justice and the importance of compassion and love. Such skeletal justice can define the minimal standards of individual behavior in exchanges between persons, but it cannot construct truly good communities. It pays insufficient attention to the social systems and structures required for a good community and ignores the social obligations we have to all our neighbors, particularly the weakest and poorest in society.[37]

Similarly, solidarity vanishes and the rights of the poor of the world are trampled when greed is no longer viewed as a vice, but instead is esteemed and celebrated. This is not just a modern phenomenon. In their essay

"Patristic Social Consciousness—the Church and the Poor," William J. Walsh and John P. Langan show that a consistent theme of the earliest Christian writings was the dangers of greed because greed destroys the moral sensitivity necessary for justice. For example, the author of the *Didache* argues that greed makes the wealthy callous and ruthless. The greedy are "bent only on their own advantage, without pity for the poor or feeling for the distressed."[38] Another early Christian writing, *The Shepherd of Hermas*, warns that wealth weakens the sympathy and imagination necessary to understand the plight of the poor, and thus leaves the rich "untouched by the excruciating sufferings of the poor."[39] Both writings suggest that greed cultivates indifference and hardness of heart. Likewise, in the fourth century Basil of Caesarea described greed as an enslaving addiction that weakens compassion because the greedy are so completely absorbed by wealth that they see and care for little else, especially those most in need.[40]

These early Christian writers were astute. They railed against greed not only because it was utterly incompatible with the teaching and example of Jesus, but also because they recognized that greed produced a social order that was glaringly inhumane. Injustice excludes—it is designed to exclude—but for many of the world's citizens that exclusion is fatal. The most excluded members of our global society are denied throughout the whole of their brief lifetimes what anyone needs to survive. Each day their existence is threatened because what injustice allows and justice could alleviate is ignored.[41] To allow such injustice to continue is viciously inhumane. At its extreme, injustice so thoroughly violates the dignity of persons that it makes them nonpersons. At its extreme, injustice says to the poor and the oppressed: We would be better off without you. In her analysis of the dehumanizing effects of injustice, Karen Lebacqz stresses that the "net result of the web of injustice is the humiliated human being."[42] Injustice victimizes persons, but it also degrades them because it tells them they are expendable, that their survival is not important, and that their premature deaths are no loss. As the U.S. Catholic bishops wrote in their 1986 letter "Economic Justice for All," "The ultimate injustice is for a person or group to be treated actively or abandoned passively as if they were nonmembers of the human race. To treat people this way is effectively to say that they simply do not count as human beings."[43]

A Christian Theology of Justice

How then do we move from the "rule of injustice" to a "reign of justice"? If injustice is a failure of moral imagination, how do we need to reimagine the world? To begin to see, think, and act differently so that all persons can share in the world's goods?

A hopeful response to each of these questions may be found in a Christian theology of justice. What Christians think about justice comes not from theories about justice, but from a story. It is a story learned in a faith community called church.[44] Through the scriptures Christians not only hear, but are also formed in stories of a God who is passionate about justice, and especially passionate about justice to the poor and oppressed. The Bible abounds with passages about God's commitment to justice, about the importance of doing justice for those who claim to know God, and about the call to be instruments of God's compassionate justice in the world. The writer of Psalm 103 praises God, for "The LORD does righteous deeds, / brings justice to all the oppressed" (v. 6). The prophet Amos tells Israel that if they want to be pleasing to God they must "let justice surge like water, / and goodness like an unfailing stream" (5:24). Probably the most succinct summary of moral conduct given in the Old Testament is the oft quoted declaration of Micah 6:8: "You have been told, O man, what is good, / and what the LORD requires of you: / Only to do the right and to love goodness, / and to walk humbly with your God."

The Bible reveals God as a lover of justice and a doer of justice (Isa. 61:8), so much so that God is not only committed to justice, but defined by it.[45] In the Old Testament, justice is the chief attribute of God.[46] God is patient, God is faithful, God is compassionate, and God is merciful, but it is justice that most clearly expresses the very being of God, justice that most accurately *names* God.[47] The prominence of justice continues in the New Testament. Justice is the cornerstone of the reign of God, the central focus of Jesus' preaching. Jesus begins his Sermon on the Mount, the core of his moral teaching, with the memorable declaration that in the reign of God the prevailing order of the world will be turned upside down. In that new social order everything is reversed: The poor will be blessed, the lowly will inherit the land, the hungry will be filled, while those who laugh and prosper now "will grieve and weep" (Luke 6:25).

The paradigmatic event for confirming this understanding of God was God's deliverance of the Israelites while they were slaves in Egypt. Israel's decisive revelation about God came in God's response to the brutal suffering and affliction caused by the pharaoh's injustice. This was so pivotal for the Israelites that they interpreted their history, identity, and purpose in light of it, and certainly their thinking about God. The story begins in Exodus 3:7–8 where the oppression suffered by the Israelites rouses God to act on their behalf. Having "witnessed the affliction of my people in Egypt" and having "heard their cry of complaint against their slave drivers" (3:7), God enters into history to free them. What is striking about this story, Bernard Brady notes, is that God acts not because the Israelites were particularly religious and not because they had necessarily done anything praiseworthy to merit God's intervention; rather, God acts because God is moved by human suffering and angered by injustice.[48] For Israel, this is who God is, a God who does not remain silent or indifferent in the face of human suffering, but responds to it in an act of liberation and deliverance.

This story is the cornerstone in Israel's theology of God and indicates what set their God apart from other gods. A God who knows their suffering will not let pharaoh's tyranny prevail. Their God sides not with the rulers of the world, but with the oppressed and afflicted. Liberation from the bondage of injustice is what identifies Israel's God from other gods. Their knowledge of God began in the rescue of slaves, in the liberation of an oppressed and exploited people; that act, more than anything else, unlocked the mystery of God for them. As Karen Lebacqz writes, "The God known to the Israelites and the early Christians was a God who hears and responds to the suffering of the people. It was this that distinguished YHWH from other gods."[49]

From this key revelatory event in the history of Israel, certain conclusions can be made about a Christian theology of justice. First, like their Jewish ancestors, a Christian theology of justice is grounded in, shaped by, and depends on remembrance. What Christians believe about justice is rooted in a memory they cannot afford to forget or forsake, the memory not only of Israel's deliverance from slavery, but also of their own deliverance from sin by the death and resurrection of Jesus. Christians, like Jews, are a remembering people.[50] They know who they are and what they are called to do by continually remembering what God has done for them. It is by recalling God's saving deeds to them that Christians glean some understanding of the kind of people they are called to be and the mission entrusted to them. Like their Jewish sisters and brothers, Christians' justice in the world is done in memory of God's gracious justice toward them. It is justice shaped not through the lens of a philosophical theory, but from a memory that bequeaths gratitude. For Jews and Christians both, "Recollection is the root of justice."[51]

Second, if God sides with the poor and oppressed peoples of the world, Christians should "remember God" by doing the same. When trying to discern the demands of justice, Christians take a cue from the justice of God. If anything is demonstrably clear about God's justice, it is that God takes sides. God's justice is absolutely partial because God takes the side of the poor, God stands with the victims of the world, with the suffering and forgotten, and as followers of God Christians must do the same. As Daniel Maguire notes, if we popularly think of justice as blind and impartial, biblical justice is unabashedly "biased in favor of the poor and critical of the rich."[52] Therefore, if for Christians it is God's actions that determine the meaning and goal of justice, then "the poor become the litmus test of justice,"[53] not the powerful and the rich. Whether a community or society is just—as with any economic, political, or social order—must be measured by "the plight of the poor and oppressed."[54] As liberation theologians have rightly argued, a biblically informed understanding of justice will always privilege the poor because "they know better than the rich what justice requires, what it would take to have 'right relationship.'"[55] Practically, for Christians this means that conversations about justice and what justice requires must begin with the poor. To be faithful to the justice of God, they must be the first to speak.

Third, Israel was liberated from justice for the sake of justice. They who had known God's justice in their deliverance from slavery were to be agents of that justice to others. They were to show to others the same compassion and concern God had shown to them.[56] In other words, they understood who God called them to be and what God called them to do only by faithfully remembering their own rescue from slavery and oppression. Memory and vocation were intimately linked for Israel because it was their memory of God's intervention on their behalf that gave them the mission of being a people who sought liberation and justice for the oppressed in their midst. The same is true for Christians. Memory and vocation are intimately linked for them as well. The deliverance that gives Christians freedom and life in Christ also gives them a communal identity and an unmistakable responsibility. They are to be a sacrament of God's justice in the world, a people who vividly embody and practice God's special concern for the poor and forgotten. When churches fail to do so, when they turn in on themselves and become more concerned about their own status and security than they are about the needs of the poor, they betray the Christ who is their hope. For both Jews and Christians, faithfulness to God is measured in justice to the poor.

Fourth, if for Israel God was revealed through acts of justice on their behalf, then real knowledge of God comes only through lives spent doing justice for others.[57] Apart from doing justice, authentic knowledge of God is impossible. One knows God only when he or she lives justly and seeks justice for others (Jer. 22:16). It is not, then, that one first knows God and then does justice, but that one comes rightly to know God only in and through the practice of justice. As the prophets of the Old Testament declared, justice precedes knowledge of God and makes it possible; indeed, *justice is knowledge of God.* In this respect, justice is more important than worship if worship is not preceded by and followed by acts of justice on behalf of the poor. The Bible does not allow people to separate religion from their everyday lives, thus worshiping God one day a week and feeling comfortable with ignoring others the rest of the week. The prophets made it very clear that all sacrifices, prayers, and worship were not only worthless, but scandalously offensive to God if they were not accompanied by justice on behalf of the poor.[58] Worship without social responsibility is a sham, an arrogant affront to a God who cares much more about the well-being of the poor and oppressed than about the chants and burnt offerings of a people gathered for worship (Amos 5:21–24; Mic. 6:6-8, Isa. 1:10–17). This is why people who meet their liturgical obligations but neglect justice are religious failures, not religious exemplars.[59]

It is no different with Jesus' mission in the New Testament. The central element of Jesus' preaching and ministry is the "reign of God" or "kingdom of God," language that envisions a reordering of the world according to the justice and peace of God. In his inaugural sermon in the synagogue at Nazareth, Jesus identifies himself with the poor, imprisoned, and forgotten members of society and announces that his ministry will be especially directed to them. He will "bring glad tidings to the poor," "liberty to captives," "recovery of sight to the blind," and release to prisoners (Luke 4:18). And Jesus brings the reign of God to life through his table fellowship with those who have no place in the community. By taking his place at table with the misbegotten of society—the sinners and the sick, the lawbreakers and the poor, the wayward and the needy—Jesus shows that the reign of God begins when justice is shown to these neglected and forgotten ones. Those who are regularly last in the eyes of the world shall be first in the new social order that is the reign of God. And those who enter the reign of God are only those who have fed the hungry, given drink to the thirsty, clothed the naked, welcomed the stranger, visited the imprisoned, and comforted the ill (Matt. 25:31–46). Everyone else is excluded. As the metaphors of the "reign of God" and the "kingdom of God" attest, for Jesus, salvation entails deliverance from sin, but it is also inherently social and political because at its core salvation is the restoration of the justice and peace of God. As Daniel Maguire states, "Beyond any doubt *justice* is the primary distinguishing theme and hallmark of the new order envisioned by the reign."[60]

Furthermore, the gospels make clear that the reign of God is not a religious idea, a concept or a theory, but a new way of life and a new kind of community organized and guided by the justice of God. It is, as Stephen Charles Mott says, a "social reversal" that is meant to impact the institutions, structures, and practices of a community.[61] The temptation is to limit and reduce the reign of God either by identifying it exclusively with the eternal world of heaven or by restricting it to a purely private, interior, or spiritual state so that the kingdom of God lives within us, but nowhere else. But that is obviously not what Jesus had in mind. As Jesus' miracle of the multiplication of the loaves and fishes suggests, the reign of God is a new social and economic order characterized not by greed and hoarding, but by sharing and generosity. It is a new social and political order marked by radically different attitudes toward wealth and possessions, radically different attitudes about revenge and retaliation, about power, and especially about our obligations to those most in need. We pervert the kingdom of God when we interpret it in overly spiritual ways. We honor it when we answer its challenge to reenvision and reconstruct the world so that God's *shalom* can be experienced by all. Jesus never envisioned the reign of God as an unreachable social utopia. No, Jesus declared that the reign of God was a call to a new community and a new way of life that was to begin in him and be carried forward by his followers. As John Donahue summarizes, "Jesus as the eschatological proclaimer of God's Kingdom and God's justice shows that this Kingdom is to have effect in the everyday events of life. The Kingdom is the power of God active in the world, transforming it and confronting the powers of the world."[62]

We see one effect of this understanding of Jesus' preaching of the reign of God in the early church's attitude to wealth, property, and possessions. A prominent theme in the writings of the early church, and one that should guide a Christian understanding of justice, is that God intended the goods of creation to be for all persons, not just the rich. As Ambrose, bishop of Milan and mentor of Augustine wrote, "God has ordered all things to be produced so that there should be food in common for all, and that the earth should be the common possession of all."[63] If the goods of the earth belong by right to all, one should see himself not as an "owner" of his wealth and possessions, but as a "steward" who is entrusted by God to use what he has to serve those most in need.[64] Beginning with the *Didache*, patristic literature lightens one's hold on property by asserting that "sharing material goods is to replace possessing them as a value for Christians."[65] While not denying the right to private property, these early Christian theologians consistently proclaimed that the right to private property must always yield "to the demands of one's fellow human beings" because "rich and poor are all of the same stock," all members of the one family of God.[66]

A Christian should be concerned not with amassing wealth and possessions, but with how best to share them. And since the resources of the earth are meant for all persons, if the wealthy and powerful grab more than their share they are thieves who take what rightly belongs to the poor. Similarly, when from their excess wealth they give to those in need, they are not practicing charity but restitution, because they are returning to the poor what was rightly theirs in the first place. Far from consoling the rich, Ambrose bluntly tells them: "You are not making a gift of your possessions to the poor person.

You are handing over to him what is his."[67] John Chrysostom puts it even more strongly: "'The rich are in possession of the goods of the poor, even if they have acquired them honestly or inherited them legally.' If they do not share, 'the wealthy are a species of bandit.'"[68]

How a Conversion to Justice Might Begin

It might seem hopelessly utopian to suggest that a Christian theology of justice requires returning to such an unnerving understanding of wealth and possessions. Can we really afford to heed the teachings of Ambrose, John Chrysostom, and the other church fathers on justice? But if we cannot, what then would it mean to conform our lives to what the God of Israel and Jesus reveals justice to be? Can everything go on as it always does? The German theologian Johann Baptist Metz says if we take the gospel as a guide, the change of heart necessary for justice must go "through people like a shock, reaching deep down into the direction their lives are taking, into their established system of needs, and so finally into the situations in society they have helped to create." Such a conversion, Metz says, "damages and disrupts one's own self-interests and aims at a fundamental revision of one's habitual way of life."[69] For Christians who enjoy wealth, prosperity, and security, converting to the justice of God demands "struggle and resistance against ourselves, against the ingrained ideals of always having more, of always having to increase our affluence."[70] It demands that "the bourgeois of the first world" be freed "not from their poverty but from their wealth; not from what they lack but from their form of total consumerism; not from their sufferings but from their apathy."[71] And it demands this, Metz says, not because of some socialist vision of the "abstract progress of humanity," but because of the Eucharist.[72]

For Christians, a conversion to justice begins at the Eucharist because there they gather to listen to and be transformed by the stories of God that come to us through Israel, Jesus, and the apostles. To be a Christian is to be part of a community that places its life in the center of a story it wants to make its own. It is the story of the God of Israel and Jesus, and Christians are not voyeuristic tourists who listen to these stories idly and impassively, paying attention to them only when they are entertaining, but then moving on. No, at Eucharist Christians are participants who enter into the biblical narratives in order to appropriate them, in order to be formed in their vision and virtues, and especially in order to discern through them what their being in the world involves. The biblical narratives that liturgy and worship reenact reveal the basic truths by which Christians structure their lives.[73] It is there that they undergo the never-ending conversion to the justice and love of God, there that they enter again and again into the narratives that are normative for their lives. As George Lindbeck writes, the biblical narratives rehearsed at Eucharist supply "the interpretative framework within which believers seek to live their lives and understand reality."[74]

Most importantly, at worship Christians do not hear these stories as relics of a bygone past; rather, at worship these stories of God are released from the past and brought into the present precisely that Christians may become more fully part of them and carry them forward. "Every liturgical celebration recalls and re-presents the story of God's self-communication to humankind"[75] so that Christians can hear that story addressed to them now and choose to live by its light. Put more strongly, at Eucharist Christians not only remember the stories of a God of justice and love, but reenact those narratives in order to participate in them and re-present them to the world.[76] As Enda McDonagh notes, liturgical remembering "releases the past into the present"[77] so that the narratives outlining God's plan for the world and God's hope for all peoples can have practical relevance now.

What could this practically mean for how Christians understand and embody justice? For one, if the Eucharist commemorates and reenacts "the new covenant God established with all of humanity through the death and resurrection of Jesus," then celebrating it should deepen in Christians an awareness of the solidarity that exists among all persons.[78] Participating in the Eucharist should imbue Christians with a keen and penetrating vision of the interconnectedness of all humanity, but particularly of their solidarity with the poor and the obligations they have toward them. As the sacrament of unity, the Eucharist should form Christians in the moral imagination necessary for justice by continually challenging them to look beyond themselves so that they might see the poor and oppressed not as far-off strangers about whom they can be indifferent, but as sisters and brothers they cannot ignore.[79] Likewise, in contrast to the aggressive emphasis on wealth, property, and ownership that characterizes our consumerist economies today, the Eucharist reminds Christians that everything we have is a gift. The Eucharist is fundamentally about gift giving. Christians come to the altar with gifts, and the gifts they offer to God are met with God's gift of Jesus, who is present in the bread and wine. The "economy" of the Eucharist is not about earning and possessing and piling up wealth, but about receiving, giving, and sharing. The Eucharist is important for justice because it should form Christians in very different attitudes about property and possessions. As Timothy Gorringe writes, "If everything we have we have as gift from the Creator and Lover of all, we cannot hang on to it, fence it round, keep it from all others."[80]

In addition to the Eucharist, a conversion to justice can be aided by the experience of *conscientization*. A term rooted in the liberation theology of Latin America, "conscientization" occurs when social justice concerns "move from the edge to the center of our consciousness and our conscience."[81] "Conscientization" describes a fundamental change in awareness, and it is brought about by experiences that challenge the ways we customarily see the world. It can happen through experiences of "displacement and decentering" when we are drawn out of the comfortable security of our own world and into the world of the poor, the world of the victims and dispossessed, and challenged to see the world through their eyes. Such experiences not only call into question our ordinary attitudes and perspectives, but also reveal them as lacking. Perhaps we discover that a way of life we thought was harmless contributes to the impoverishment of others. Perhaps we learn that the comfort and security we take for granted are things most of the people of the world never enjoy.

And perhaps, too, the comfort and security deaden our moral sensitivity, making us less mindful of others and our obligations toward them. This is why we can often break through to a more morally sensitive and mature conscience only by first suffering a "bad" conscience. Our conversion of conscience and consciousness frequently begins when we feel the tug of a bad conscience, one that tells us all is not well with ourselves and our world. But such pricks of conscience are good because they signal growth in moral awareness and compassion. A bad conscience is a troubled and disturbed conscience, and this can be a very good thing to have because it signals that we are becoming increasingly attuned to the fact of injustice, our complicity in it, and what we can and must do to address it. To feel the tug of a bad conscience indicates that we are moving out of apathy and into compassion, away from denial and indifference and toward repentance and responsibility. Justice is possible only when we have the courage of a bad conscience, when instead of silencing the voice of a disturbed conscience, we listen to it, feel its sting, and allow it to lead us to a more just way of being in the world. As Metz says, when instead of being talked out of a bad conscience we listen to it, "many things begin to happen."[82]

This conversion of conscience can happen on service trips, in serving and working with the poor, through prayer and contemplation, or by reading the stories of the poor and oppressed and imagining what it must be like to be them. Sometimes it happens when we are confronted with our own complicity in injustice, even something as simple as trying to arrange things so that everything always works out to our own best advantage. No matter how it occurs, "conscientization" teaches us to see the world more truthfully—no longer so bent to our own interests and needs—and therefore to live more justly. Such a conversion of consciousness and conscience is a moment of enlightenment, a kind of waking up from our slumbers, because when it happens we are awakened to the injustice inflicted on people and commit ourselves to do what we can to change it.[83]

Finally, conversions to justice are more likely to occur when we are willing to hear the stories of the victims of the world, the stories of the poor, the destitute, and the seemingly disposable. They have much to teach us about the meaning of justice and what justice demands. But they can also vividly describe the expansive reality of injustice and the litany of suffering and diminishment that accompanies it. If the Lord hears the cries of the poor, we must too, because it is only when we allow those cries to penetrate our hearts that we will really begin to live differently. We need "counternarratives," narratives that not only challenge us to look at the world from the perspective of the poor, but that also help us imagine different possibilities. Too many of our dominant cultural narratives blind us to injustice because they teach us to put ourselves first, to be obsessively focused on our own comfort, pleasure, and security. Too many of our dominant cultural narratives teach us *not to see* lest our eyes be opened to the injustice around us. We need counternarratives, whether they come in the form of gospel parables, biographies, novels, music, poems, or other works of art. Any narrative that fosters the compassionate moral imagination necessary for justice should be heeded and embraced.

Conclusion

Even a letter can be a counternarrative, and it may be good to end with one. In August 1990 I had the privilege to travel to Africa. The trip took our group from Chicago to Rome, from Rome to Zimbabwe, and finally to South Africa. As we made our way, the first Gulf War broke out when Iraq invaded Kuwait, and with the United States's intervention not far behind. It was an unsettling and uncertain time in South Africa. Although Nelson Mandela had been released from prison, apartheid still reigned in South Africa, and the threat of violence was great. Tensions were so high that many of us who made the trip were convinced that change would not come to South Africa without violence and bloodshed. I remember thinking that if you were to strike a match, the whole country would go up in flames.

I spent my last weekend in South Africa as a guest of Mr. and Mrs. Zwane, a couple who lived in Soweto, the huge township outside Johannesburg that was home to several million black South Africans. They welcomed me, a stranger, into their home and introduced me to a world I had never known. They were good, gracious, generous people who did not hesitate to claim me as their brother even though thousands of miles separated us, and I, a white man, wore the face of the oppressor more than of a friend. But to Mr. and Mrs. Zwane what mattered was not the color of my skin, but the fact that the three of us were Christians. Our baptisms had joined us together in Christ and forged a connection between us that nothing could destroy.

After leaving South Africa I wrote to thank them for their hospitality, but also because I worried they might not be alive. Violence had erupted in South Africa, and people were being killed. Below is the letter I received from them in response, and it, better than anything, illustrates why we cannot separate our happiness from the happiness of others. Mr. and Mrs. Zwane remind us that we are all in this together and we grow in the goodness and happiness of God together. If the Christian moral life is training in happiness, then one indispensable lesson all of us must learn is that we cannot gain our own happiness by turning our backs on any of the beloved of God. If we are to make our way to the goodness and happiness of God, it can only be arm in arm with those, like the Zwanes, who know firsthand the suffering injustice brings. This was their gift to me, a letter that taught me to see the world differently and reminded me that our most powerful summons to justice can come from the people gratitude compels us to remember. Even more, perhaps justice is most likely, whether in our personal lives or across the world if, as Mr. and Mrs. Zwane said, whenever we pray, we do not forget one another. Regardless, this is the letter I turn to when I am trying to understand what happiness means.

Beloved Paul,

How are you, brother? We greet you in the name of our Savior Jesus Christ. We have been worried about you in the time of the Gulf War, but we are relieved as we got your letter. Things have gone from bad to worse in South Africa. Again in Soweto we live in fear. We don't sleep freely as people are being attacked every moment; especially at night there's shooting, hacking, we are in a big worry. Anywhere you are you are not safe. In the trains we are attacked, if you go to work in the morning you are not sure whether you'll be back to see all the family alive again. Please whenever you pray, do not forget us. Keep in touch with us always so you can know if we are still alive. God bless you,

Mr. & Mrs. Zwane

Some Questions for Reflection and Discussion

1. How do you experience the demands of justice in your everyday life? What are some common injustices you encounter or observe in your everyday life?
2. How would you explain the three types of justice? How is each related to the others?
3. Why is a vision of interdependence and solidarity important for sustaining justice? What today might weaken our sense of solidarity?
4. How does the early church's understanding of the "right" of private property challenge us today? Does it seem too extreme to you? Could it be liberating?
5. What does it mean to describe justice as a failure of moral imagination?
6. Have you ever had an experience of *conscientization*?

Notes

1. Pope Paul VI, "Populorum Progressio: On the Development of Peoples," in *Catholic Social Thought: The Documentary Heritage*, ed. David J. O'Brien and Thomas A. Shannon (Maryknoll, NY: Orbis Books, 1992), #66.

2. Paul VI, "Populorum Progressio," #29.

3. Paul VI, "Populorum Progressio," #30.

4. Paul VI, "Populorum Progressio," #53.

5. Patricia McAuliffe, *Fundamental Ethics: A Liberationist Approach* (Washington, DC: Georgetown University Press, 1993), 66.

6. Karen Lebacqz, *Justice in an Unjust World: Foundations for a Christian Approach to Justice* (Minneapolis: Augsburg Publishing House, 1987), 11.

7. Paul VI, "Populorum Progressio," #4.

8. Paul VI, "Populorum Progressio," #4.

9. McAuliffe, *Fundamental Ethics*, 2.

10. Bernard V. Brady, *The Moral Bond of Community: Justice and Discourse in Christian Morality* (Washington, DC: Georgetown University Press, 1998), 101.

11. Thomas Aquinas, *Summa Theologiae* (New York: McGraw-Hill, 1966), II-II, 58,1.

12. Josef Pieper, *The Four Cardinal Virtues* (Notre Dame, IN: University of Notre Dame Press, 1966), 45.

13. Pieper, *The Four Cardinal Virtues*, 57.

14. John R. Donahue, SJ, "Biblical Perspectives on Justice," in *The Faith That Does Justice: Examining the Christian Sources for Social Change*, ed. John C. Haughey (New York: Paulist Press, 1977), 69.

15. Pieper, *The Four Cardinal Virtues*, 79.

16. Pieper, *The Four Cardinal Virtues*, 78.

17. Karen Lebacqz, "Justice," in *Christian Ethics: An Introduction*, ed. Bernard Hoose (Collegeville, MN: The Liturgical Press, 1998), 167.

18. Daniel C. Maguire and A. Nicholas Fargnoli, *On Moral Grounds: The Art/Science of Ethics* (New York: The Crossroad Publishing Co., 1991), 31.

19. David Hollenbach, *Justice, Peace, and Human Rights: American Catholic Social Ethics in a Pluralistic Context* (New York: The Crossroad Publishing Co., 1988), 26.

20. Brady, *The Moral Bond of Community*, 114.

21. Hollenbach, *Justice, Peace, and Human Rights*, 27.

22. David Hollenbach, *Claims in Conflict: Retrieving and Renewing the Catholic Human Rights Tradition* (New York: Paulist Press, 1979), 151.

23. Hollenbach, *Claims in Conflict*, 204.

24. David Hollenbach, *The Common Good and Christian Ethics* (Cambridge: Cambridge University Press, 2002), 195.

25. Maguire and Fargnoli, *On Moral Grounds*, 30.

26. Hollenbach, *Justice, Peace, and Human Rights*, 27.

27. Hollenbach, *The Common Good and Christian Ethics*, 196.

28. Hollenbach, *Claims in Conflict*, 152. "Social justice is a measure or ordering principle which seeks to bring into existence those social relationships which will guarantee the possibility of realizing the demands of distributive justice. This means that it calls for the creation of those social, economic and political conditions which are necessary to assure that the minimum human needs of all will be met and which will make possible social and political participation for all."

29. Hollenbach, *The Common Good and Christian Ethics*, 202–3.

30. Daniel C. Maguire, *A New American Justice* (Minneapolis: Winston Press, 1980), 58.

31. Enda McDonagh, *The Making of Disciples: Tasks of Moral Theology* (Wilmington, DE: Michael Glazier, 1982), 128.

32. McDonagh, *The Making of Disciples*, 130.

33. John XXIII, "Mater et Magistra: Christianity and Social Progress," in *Catholic Social Thought: The Documentary Heritage*, ed. David J. O'Brien and Thomas A. Shannon (Maryknoll, NY: Orbis Books, 1992), #157.

34. Maguire, *A New American Justice*, 77.

35. John Paul II, "Sollicitudo Rei Socialis: On Social Concern," in *Catholic Social Thought: The Documentary Heritage*, ed. David J. O'Brien and Thomas A. Shannon (Maryknoll, NY: Orbis Books, 1992), #38.

36. Hollenbach, *The Common Good and Christian Ethics*, 189.

37. Russell B. Connors, Jr. and Patrick T. McCormick, *Character, Choices and Community: The Three Faces of Christian Ethics* (New York: Paulist Press, 1998), 67.

38. William J. Walsh, SJ, and John P. Langan, SJ, "Patristic Social Consciousness—the Church and the Poor," in *The Faith That Does Justice: Examining the Christian Sources for Social Change*, ed. John C. Haughey (New York: Paulist Press, 1977), 119.

39. Walsh and Langan, "Patristic Social Consciousness," 119.

40. Walsh and Langan, "Patristic Social Consciousness," 124. In a scathing passage, Basil of Caesarea says about the greedy: "The bright gleam of gold delights you.

. . . Everything is gold to your eyes and fancy; gold is your dream at night and your waking care. As a raving madman does not see things themselves but imagines things in his diseased fancy, so your greed-possessed soul sees gold and silver everywhere. Sight of gold is dearer to you than sight of the sun. Your prayer is that everything may be changed to gold, and your schemes are set on bringing it about" (Homily on Luke 12:18).

41. McAuliffe, *Fundamental Ethics*, 56.

42. Lebacqz, *Justice in an Unjust World*, 35.

43. U.S. Catholic Bishops, "Economic Justice for All," in *Catholic Social Thought: The Documentary Heritage*, ed. David J. O'Brien and Thomas A. Shannon (Maryknoll, NY: Orbis Books, 1992), #77.

44. Lebacqz, "Justice," 170.

45. Daniel C. Maguire, *The Moral Core of Judaism and Christianity: Reclaiming the Revolution* (Minneapolis: Fortress Press, 1993), 128.

46. Stephen Charles Mott, *Biblical Ethics and Social Change* (New York: Oxford University Press, 1982), 60.

47. Lebacqz, *Justice in an Unjust World*, 72.

48. Brady, *The Moral Bond of Community*, 25.

49. Lebacqz, *Justice in an Unjust World*, 71.

50. Charles R. Pinches, *A Gathering of Memories: Family, Nation, and Church in a Forgetful World* (Grand Rapids, MI: Brazos Press, 2006), 123–38.

51. Lebacqz, *Justice in an Unjust World*, 63.

52. Maguire, *The Moral Core of Judaism and Christianity*, 131.

53. Lebacqz, "Justice," 168.

54. Lebacqz, "Justice," 168.

55. Lebacqz, "Justice," 168.

56. Mott, *Biblical Ethics and Social Change*, 72.

57. Maguire, *The Moral Core of Judaism and Christianity*, 104.

58. Mott, *Biblical Justice and Social Change*, 75.

59. Brady, *The Moral Bond of Community*, 33.

60. Maguire, *The Moral Core of Judaism and Christianity*, 126.

61. Mott, *Biblical Ethics and Social Change*, 98.

62. Donahue, "Biblical Perspectives on Justice," 87.

63. Walsh and Langan, "Patristic Social Consciousness," 127.

64. Walsh and Langan, "Patristic Social Consciousness," 128.

65. Walsh and Langan, "Patristic Social Consciousness," 114.

66. Walsh and Langan, "Patristic Social Consciousness," 127.

67. Walsh and Langan, "Patristic Social Consciousness," 128.

68. Walsh and Langan, "Patristic Social Consciousness," 129.

69. Johann Baptist Metz, *The Emergent Church: The Future of Christianity in a Postbourgeois World*, trans. Peter Mann (New York: The Crossroad Publishing Co., 1981), 3.

70. Metz, *The Emergent Church*, 12.

71. Metz, *The Emergent Church*, 72.

72. Metz, *The Emergent Church*, 12.

73. McDonagh, *The Making of Disciples*, 51.

74. George Lindbeck, *The Nature of Doctrine: Religion and Theology in a Postliberal Age* (Philadelphia: Westminster Press, 1984), 117.

75. McDonagh, *The Making of Disciples*, 46.

76. McDonagh, *The Making of Disciples*, 47.

77. McDonagh, *The Making of Disciples*, 39.

78. Hollenbach, *Justice, Peace, and Human Rights*, 199.

79. Hollenbach, *Justice, Peace, and Human Rights*, 200.

80. Timothy J. Gorringe, "Property," in *Christian Ethics: An Introduction*, ed. Bernard Hoose (Collegeville, MN: The Liturgical Press, 1998), 182.

81. Connors and McCormick, *Character, Choices and Community*, 71.

82. Metz, *The Emergent Church*, 94.

83. Paul J. Wadell, *The Moral of the Story: Learning from Literature about Human and Divine Love* (New York: The Crossroad Publishing Co., 2002), 129–36.

~

Index

~

About the Author

Paul J. Wadell is professor of religious studies at St. Norbert College in De Pere, Wisconsin. He is the author of several books, including *Friendship and the Moral Life*; *The Primacy of Love: An Introduction to the Ethics of Thomas Aquinas*; *Becoming Friends: Worship, Justice, and the Practice of Christian Friendship*; and *The Moral of the Story: Learning from Literature about Human and Divine Love*. He has contributed chapters to several books on Christian theology and ethics and has written numerous articles for religious and theological journals. A native of Louisville, Kentucky, he received his PhD in theology from the University of Notre Dame.